APIL Guide to Tripping and Slipping Cases

APIL Guide to Tripping and Slipping Cases

Charles Foster

Ben Bradley

Outer Temple Chambers,
London WC2

JORDANS

Published by
Jordan Publishing Limited
21 St Thomas Street
Bristol BS1 6JS

© Jordan Publishing Limited 2010

British Library Cataloguing-in-Publication Data

A catalogue record for this book is available from the British Library.

ISBN 978 1 84661 205 3

Typeset by Letterpart Ltd, Reigate, Surrey

Printed and bound in Great Britain by CPI Antony Rowe, Chippenham, Wiltshire

FOREWORD

Injuries resulting from trips and slips are an important part of the work of most personal injury practitioners.

However, as the introduction to the book observes, the lawyer faces a number of challenges from identifying the appropriate defendant, through determining the applicable law to, of course, making an effective risk assessment on the merits of the claim.

This excellent book will be an invaluable aid to practitioners advising and acting in tripping and slipping claims, whether these occur on the highway, at work or on other premises.

Practitioners will also welcome the advice on how to effectively prepare a case for, and deal with, litigation in this type of claim.

The APIL guides are an increasingly comprehensive series written by practitioners for practitioners on key areas of personal injury practice. This latest guide is a very welcome addition to that series which I highly recommend to all lawyers dealing with any tripping or slipping claims.

John McQuater
APIL President (2009–2010)
February 2010

PREFACE

Tripping and slipping litigation is economically very significant. It pays the mortgages of many litigators, presents big bills to taxpayers and employers, and affects the policies of local and national government and private enterprise. It matters most, of course, to the victims: to the cliché little old lady with her Colles fracture; to the working mother with her ruptured cruciate.

You might think, unless you actually did it, that such commonplace, workaday litigation might be easy. It's not. You need to know quite a lot about quite a lot to be a competent tripping and slipping litigator. You need to know about the structure of local government, how highways spring or creep into legal existence, and how to read a mediaeval tithe map. You need to know when a highway starts, when it stops, and where to go to find out who is responsible for what. You need to be able to talk confidently about vaults, manhole covers, winter maintenance regimes, landlords' contractual liabilities to maintain, bollards, the direct effect of European legislation, delegation by highway authorities to independent contractors and statutory registers of road works. And so on and so on. The relevant law is often old, obscure and contained in inaccessible reports. Even if you can track it down, the principles are often cunningly concealed behind a mass of arcane fact.

As well as the law, there is a mass of guidance from various organisations that you will need at hand. You will need to cite it threateningly in correspondence, possibly plead it, and have it in your trial bundle if the case goes that far.

This book aims to be a one-stop shop for everyone who has to litigate in this area. It is brutally practical. It doesn't discuss the law for the law's sake, but hopefully has all the law necessary to give an answer to a judge who fancies him or herself as a lawyer. The key cases are distilled into case summaries. There is plenty of advice on case and trial preparation, and a big library of precedents – including checklists, letters and Statements of Case. The Appendices contain most of the relevant guidelines.

The first edition of this book's predecessor was published in 1994. One of us (CF) wrote in the Preface to that book that its main objective was to help hard pressed practitioners knock off earlier than they otherwise would. That's what we hope for this edition too.

The law in the book is, we hope, up to date to February 2010.

Charles Foster
Ben Bradley

Outer Temple Chambers,
London WC2

ASSOCIATION OF PERSONAL INJURY LAWYERS (APIL)

APIL is the UK's leading association of claimant personal injury lawyers, dedicated to protecting the rights of injured people.

Formed in 1990, APIL now represents around 5,000 solicitors, barristers, academics and students in the UK, Republic of Ireland and overseas.

APIL's objectives are:

- to promote full and just compensation for all types of personal injury;
- to promote and develop expertise in the practice of personal injury law;
- to promote wider redress for personal injury in the legal system;
- to campaign for improvements in personal injury law;
- to promote safety and alert the public to hazards;
- to provide a communication network for members.

APIL is a growing and influential forum pushing for law reform, and improvements, which will benefit injured people.

APIL has been running CPD training events, accredited by the Solicitors Regulation Authority and Bar Standards Board, for nearly twenty years and has a wealth of experience in developing the most practical up-to-date courses, delivered by eminent leading speakers, either publicly or in-house.

APIL training now runs almost 200 personal injury training events nationally each year, plus up to a further 100 meetings of our regional and special interest groups. Topics cover a wide range of subjects and are geared towards giving personal injury lawyers a thorough grounding in the core areas of personal injury law, whilst keeping lawyers thoroughly up-to-date in all subjects.

APIL is also an authoritative information source for personal injury lawyers, providing up-to-the-minute PI bulletins, regular newsletters and publications, information databases and online services.

For further information contact:

APIL
11 Castle Quay
Nottingham
NG7 1FW
DX 716208 Nottingham 42
Tel 0115 9580585
Email mail@apil.org.uk
Website www.apil.org.uk

CONTENTS

TABLE OF CASES

References are to paragraph numbers.

TABLE OF STATUTES

References are to paragraph numbers.

TABLE OF STATUTORY INSTRUMENTS

References are to paragraph numbers.

CHAPTER 1

SELECTING THE DEFENDANT

1.1 INTRODUCTION

When a victim of tripping limps into a solicitor's office, he is unlikely to say 'I would like you to issue proceedings for damages for personal injury against the local highway authority, who had a duty to maintain the road where I was injured', or 'Please sue the committee in charge of the racecourse where I tripped: it has sufficient control of the premises to make it liable under the Occupiers' Liability Act'. He is more likely to state the place where the trip occurred, and that he is hurt and outraged. One would hope that it is obvious that selecting the right defendant is important. This chapter offers guidance on how this should be done.

The starting point, obviously, is to discover where the accident occurred. This will lead to a number of questions which must be correctly answered. Is that place a highway? Was the accident caused by a failure to maintain; or by an act or omission of the maintaining authority wholly incidental to the performance of its duty to maintain; or by an act or omission of a party other than the maintaining authority? If it was caused by a failure to maintain, who was the maintaining authority? Will that authority be able to pass liability to anyone else?

If the accident occurred elsewhere than on a highway, and was caused by a failure to maintain, who had the duty to maintain? Are there a number of possible defendants in a case brought under the Occupiers' Liability Act? If so, which of them should be sued?

If the accident resulted from something other than a failure to maintain, who should be sued?

In this chapter, accidents are classified under the following headings:

(1) injuries on highways caused by a failure to maintain (**1.2** below), covering highways repairable at the public expense and by private individuals or corporate bodies, and which no one is liable to repair;

(2) injuries on highways caused otherwise than by a failure to maintain (**1.3** below); and

(3)   injuries other than on highways (**1.4** below) (breach of statutory duty; negligence; Occupiers' Liability Acts; private nuisance; and public nuisance).

Because the choice of defendant inevitably means choice of a cause of action, this chapter deals briefly with some of the substantive law relating to the relevant causes of action. Most of the causes of action are more fully discussed elsewhere.

1.2   INJURIES ON HIGHWAYS CAUSED BY FAILURE TO MAINTAIN

In tripping accidents on the highway which are caused by a defect in the highway resulting from failure to repair, the appropriate defendant is the body which is liable to repair the highway concerned. This raises the important preliminary question, what is a highway? This is so important and so complex a question that Chapter 2 is devoted entirely to it. That chapter also deals with the issue, important in selecting a defendant, of how to find out the legal category of the road in question.

1.2.1   Highways repairable at the public expense

By s 41(1) of the Highways Act 1980 (HA 1980), the authority, which is for the time being the highway authority for a highway maintainable at the public expense, is under a statutory duty to maintain the highway. For most practical purposes the appropriate defendant in a case of injury on a highway maintainable at the public expense is therefore the highway authority. Confusion sometimes arises from the fact that a county council is expressed to be the highway authority for all highways in its county, *whether or not maintainable at the public expense.* The apparent contradiction is a result of the complicated law which determines the circumstances in which a highway authority can be liable concurrently with another defendant who has liability for repairing the road concerned. Subject to this, it can be assumed that if the *locus in quo* is a road maintainable at the public expense, the highway authority concerned should feature in the Particulars of Claim. It is also important to note that by HA 1980, s 41(2), orders designating a particular road as a trunk road may contain special directions as to the duty to maintain both the trunk road and any part of a highway which crosses such a trunk road.

Occasionally, the local authority may dispute that the land is:

(a)   a highway; and/or

(b)   maintainable at the public expense.

Such arguments may well be rebuttable by calling evidence that the highway authority has adopted the highway (eg by undertaking maintenance works). Ultimately, the issue is a matter of fact for the Court to determine on a case-by-case basis (see *Sheila Lee v Devon County Council* (unreported) 28 February 2007).

Privately maintainable footpaths or bridleways may be highways maintainable at the public expense by the operation of HA 1980, s 36. This section keeps alive the rule in s 47(1) of the National Parks and Access to the Countryside Act 1949, which provides that all footpaths and bridleways which were in existence before 16 December 1949 are repairable by the inhabitants at large of the relevant area, but without prejudice to the responsibility of any person under an obligation to repair a footpath or bridleway under any enactment, or by reason of tenure, enclosure or prescription.

If a road is not shown on a tithe map and there is no evidence that it has at any time been repaired at the public expense, the court will infer that it is a private street (*Kent County Council v Loughlin* [1975] JPL 348).

Highway authorities are not liable under the Occupiers' Liability Acts for injuries which occur on highways.

1.2.1.1 Who is the highway authority?

The highway authority is the body which has a statutory liability for repair and maintenance. It is deemed to own the top two spits of the land comprising the highway (see *Tithe Redemption Commission v Runcorn Urban District Council* [1954] 2 WLR 518).

In tripping cases involving allegations against the highway authority there are a number of possible candidates for the post of defendant. They are:

(1)   The county council or the metropolitan district council

In most tripping actions outside London, the defendant is the county or metropolitan district council. These authorities are the local highways authorities for all highways in their areas, except highways in respect of which the Minister (see below) is the highway authority (see HA 1980, s 1(2) as amended by the Local Government Act 1985). The Minister can delegate to these authorities responsibility for the improvement and maintenance of trunk roads (HA 1980, s 6(1)), and they can be the Minister's agent for the construction of trunk roads (HA 1980, s 6(5)). They can, in turn, and with the agreement of the Minister, delegate their own delegated functions to a district council.

(2)   The Secretary of State for Transport or, in Wales, the Secretary of State for Wales

The relevant Secretary of State ('the Minister') is the highway authority for:

(a)   any trunk road (HA 1980, s 1);

(b)   any road in respect of which he is appointed highway authority by statutory instrument;

(c)   any other highway constructed by him, except where the local highway authority is designated as the highway authority for the road (eg by order under HA 1980, s 6(1)).

The Minister's powers to delegate are outlined in (1) above.

(3)   Highway authorities in London

The council of a London borough or, in the case of the City of London, the Common Council, is the highway authority unless, for one of the reasons set out above, the Minister is responsible (HA 1980, s 1(2)). The exercise of local government functions, including the functions of a highway authority, by and in the Inner Temple and the Middle Temple may be permitted by an Order in Council made under s 94 of the Local Government Act 1985. No such Order in Council has yet been made.

(4)   Non-metropolitan district councils

By s 50(2) and Pt 1 of Sch 7 to HA 1980, non-metropolitan district councils may, on giving notice to the county council, undertake the maintenance of certain highways within the district which are maintainable at the public expense. These are footpaths, bridleways and urban roads which are neither trunk or classified roads. Non-metropolitan district councils intending to exercise these powers must inform the county council of the highways in respect of which they intend to exercise them. If the county council disagrees, it can serve a counter-notice. The Minister will resolve a dispute between the parties. If the non-metropolitan district council opts to exercise its powers of maintenance, it is obliged to indemnify the county council in respect of any claim arising out of failure to maintain.

(5)   Parish and community councils

These bodies can make representations to the highway authority (see HA 1980, s 130) concerning the protection of public rights of way, and may undertake the maintenance of footpaths and bridleways. Importantly, if a parish or community council does undertake this maintenance, it does so without prejudice to the duty of any highway authority or person to maintain them (see HA 1980, ss 43 and 50).

1.2.1.2   Liability for the torts of independent contractors

This section considers the general rules governing liability for the torts of independent contractors. It is not restricted to the liability of highway authorities for negligent performance of statutory works by their independent contractors. Generally, employers are not liable for the torts of their independent contractors. There are a number of important caveats to this which are considered below (see also Chapter 4 for a discussion of the relevance of HA 1980, s 58 to the liability for a contractor's torts).

Statutory duties are in general non-delegable. Where a highway authority delegates part or all of the performance of its statutory duty to repair and maintain under s 41 of HA 1980, it cannot delegate away legal responsibility for repair and maintenance: a claimant who sustains personal injury as a result of the failure by the sub-contractor to do the works necessary to discharge the s 41 duty need not sue the sub-contractor (see *Hardaker v Idle District Council* [1896] 1 QB 335 (Appendix B, Case Summary 26); *Penny v Wimbledon Urban District Council* [1898] 2 QB 212 (Appendix B, Case Summary 41); *Black v Christchurch Finance Co* [1894] AC 48). That is a consequence of a breach of s 41 of the 1980 Act being actionable in damages and non-delegable. If there is no breach of statutory duty, the issue of delegability never arises.

Where a contractor is engaged to perform works on a highway which are authorised by statute but which would, unless so authorised, be a nuisance, the highway authority is under a duty to ensure that due care is taken by the contractor (see *Salsbury v Woodland* [1970] 1 QB 324 at 338 (Appendix B, Case Summary 40). Writers on the subject always state this principle as distinct from and additional to the requirement under HA 1980, s 41(1), but it is difficult to see why. It follows that the default of another statutory undertaker, for example in failing to reinstate a pavement after performing statutory works, is no defence to an action against the highway authority: (see *McNair v Dunfermline Corporation* (1954) 104 LJ 66 (Appendix B, Case Summary 27).

Subject to the operation of the defence under HA 1980, s 58, the highway authority will be liable to a claimant injured by a dangerous characteristic of a highway, however that dangerous characteristic arose. The highway authority will often be able to share responsibility with, or shift it to, a statutory undertaker by way of proceedings under CPR Part 20, but this need not worry the claimant. Claimants need to sue the statutory undertaker direct if the s 58 defence does or might apply. Beware, though, of the potential costs consequences of suing unnecessary defendants.

1.2.1.3   *Authorisation of torts affecting highway*

The highway authority is also liable for the torts of its independent contractors if the tortious act is specifically authorised by the authority, or if the authority has prescribed the manner in which the works will be carried out (see *McLaughlin v Pryor* (1842) 4 M & G 48). It may also be liable for failing to prescribe or failing to ensure that precautions are taken. In *Penny v Wimbledon UDC* (above), Bruce J said:

> 'When a person employs a contractor to do work in a place where the public are in the habit of passing, which work will, unless precautions are taken, cause danger to the public, an obligation is thrown upon the person who orders the work to be done to see that the necessary precautions are taken, and, if the necessary precautions are not taken, he cannot escape liability by seeking to throw the blame on the contractor.'

The principle is not restricted to the highway: It applies to places other than the highway where the public may lawfully pass (see *Pickard v Smith* (1861) 10 CB 470).

The rule does not, however, extend to work done near the highway. Thus in *Salsbury v Woodland* [1970] 1 QB 324, (Appendix B, Case Summary 34), when the negligence of a contractor caused a tree standing 28 feet from the highway to fall onto some telephone wires which, in turn, fell onto the highway, the Court of Appeal refused to hold the defendant liable for the negligence of his contractor.

1.2.1.4   *Withdrawal of support from land*

This is a particular instance of a nuisance being created. Most of the cases in the area are 'neighbour cases'" (see *Hughes v Percival* (1882–83) LR 8 App Cas 443: *Alcock v Wraith* [1991] EGCS 137; but the courts have shown themselves ready to stretch the neighbour analogy. If a statutory undertaker's or a highway authority's independent contractors undermine or otherwise withdraw support from a claimant's land and personal injury results, the principal contractor is likely to be primarily liable.

1.2.1.5   *Particularly hazardous acts*

If injury is caused by particularly hazardous acts, and the work contracted for involves such acts, principal contractors cannot escape liability by asserting that only the sub-contractor is liable (see *Honeywill and Stein Ltd v Loukin Brothers Ltd* [1934] 1 KB 191).

1.2.1.6   *Collateral negligence*

There is no liability, even in the case of work on highways, for damage caused by the negligence of an independent contractor which is collateral to the main sub-contract work being performed. If, for instance, a sub-contractor leaves a hammer lying on a pavement, and a pedestrian trips over the hammer and is injured, the pedestrian will not succeed in an action for damages against the main contractor: the sub-contractor's negligence was not in acting or failing to act in a way which was closely or necessarily occasioned by the performance of the contract works themselves (see *Penny v Wimbledon Urban District Council* above).

Note the important caveat considered below, to select competent contractors. If reasonable care was not taken in selecting sub-contractors, it is possible that a main contractor might be found liable even for the collateral torts of the incompetent contractors.

1.2.1.7   Negligent selection of contractor/insufficient men

Main contractors are under a duty to take reasonable care to select competent contractors. They are also under a duty to employ reasonable numbers of men to perform a task safely, and to give to the contractors adequate instructions. Thus if for example, an insufficient number of highly competent men are engaged, and injury results from the inadequacy of the number, the main contractor will be liable.

1.2.1.8   Liability of occupiers for their independent contractors

Section 2(4)(b) of the Occupiers' Liability Act 1957 provides that:

> 'Where damage is caused to a visitor by a danger due to the faulty execution of any work of construction, maintenance or repair by an independent contractor employed by the occupier, the occupier is not to be treated without more as answerable for the danger if in all the circumstances he had acted reasonably in entrusting the work to an independent contractor and had taken such steps (if any) as he reasonably ought in order to satisfy himself that the contractor was competent and that the work had been properly done.'

1.2.1.9   Predecessors in title

Highway authorities are not generally liable for the acts of their predecessors in title (see *Nash v Rochford Rural District Council* [1917] 1 KB 384; *Baxter v Stockton-on-Tees Corporation* [1959] 1 QB 441 (Appendix B, Case Summary 38)).

1.2.1.10   Agreements between local highway authorities

Agreements between local highway authorities under which one authority discharges the liabilities of another are common. They are examined in Chapter 4. If an agency agreement for highway maintenance is in place, the highway authority originally liable to maintain remains liable; the responsibility cannot be delegated. Obviously the agency agreement will form a basis for Pt 20 claims by the liable authority against the authority which agreed to deal with the maintenance.

1.2.1.11   Toll roads and concession agreements under the New Roads and Street Works Act 1991

Section 1 of the New Roads and Street Works Act 1991, enables highway authorities to enter into agreements ('concession agreements') with third parties ('concessionaires') by which the concessionaire agrees to undertake obligations specified in the agreement relating to 'the design, construction, maintenance, operation or improvement' of a 'special road'. The concessionaire, by shouldering those obligations, becomes entitled to charge tolls in respect of the use of that road.

By s 2, a concession agreement may authorise the concessionaire to exercise, in place of the highway authority, the functions of the highway authority specified in the agreement. Most of the highway authority's functions can be delegated in this way to a concessionaire: certainly all of the functions relevant in tripping cases can be delegated.

A highway function which, by a concession agreement, is exercisable by a concessionaire, can (by s 2(3)) be exercised by the highway authority only:

–   in an emergency;

–   if it appears to the authority that such exercise is necessary or expedient in the interests of road safety;

–   if it appears to the authority that the concessionaire has failed or is unable properly to discharge the delegated functions in any respect.

The highway authority is not liable for anything done or omitted to be done by the concessionaire in the exercise or purported exercise of a highway function.

The vast majority of concession agreements will cast the burden for maintenance and repair onto the shoulders of the concessionaire. Under these circumstances, the appropriate defendant will be the concessionaire. It is conceivable that a failure by a highway authority to intervene if one or more of the conditions listed above which results in personal injury could give rise to judicial review with the possibility of an award of damages.

1.2.1.12   The highway authority for a road ceases to be a trunk road

Section 10(2) of HA 1980 empowers the Minister by order to direct that a trunk road shall cease to be a trunk road. When this happens HA 1980, s 2(1) provides that the highway authority for the road is the county or metropolitan district council if the road is outside Greater London, or the London borough council if the road is in London.

1.2.1.13   The highway authority for roads on bridges spanning different counties

Assuming that the Minister is not the highway authority responsible, responsibility for the highway on a bridge, one part of which is in one county and one part in another, will have been determined by agreement between the possible highway authorities or, in default of agreement, by the Minister (see HA 1980, s 3(1) and (2); Boundary Bridges (Appointed Day) Order 1973 (SI 1973/2147)).

Where part of one or more approaches to a bridge lies in a county different from that in which the bridge is situated, the highway authority for the whole of that approach or approaches is the council of the county in which the bridge is situated. An approach is defined as the highway situated within 100 yards of either end of the bridge (see HA 1980, s 3(3) and (4)).

1.2.1.14   Extinction of liability to repair

Liability to repair, whether of the highway authority or anyone else, is extinguished when:

(1)   a highway is physically destroyed; or

(2)   a highway is declared unnecessary by the magistrates' court after an application by the highway authority under HA 1980, s 47(1), for an order that the highway should cease to be maintained at the public expense; or

(3)   a highway is lawfully stopped up (eg under the general power in HA 1980, s 116 or under one of the many specific provisions in statutes as various as the Defence Acts, the Civil Aviation Act 1949 and the Countryside Act 1968).

An owner's liability to repair is extinguished when:

(1)   a highway is completely altered in character; or

(2)   a highway comprising a bridge becomes a trunk road or a special
      road.

1.2.2   Highways repairable by private individuals or corporate bodies

Individuals, bodies corporate and bodies politic cannot, by definition,
become highway authorities liable to repair highways, but they can under
certain circumstances (by tenure, inclosure, prescription, or under statute)
become responsible for repair. The existence of liability to repair does not,
however, necessarily mean that an action for personal injuries caused by a
breach of this duty can be brought.

1.2.2.1   How can non-highway authorities become liable to repair highways?

There are three ways in which an individual or body corporate other than
a highway authority can become liable to repair a highway – by tenure,
prescription or statute.

First, if a potential defendant and his predecessors or their tenants have,
for time immemorial, repaired a highway, an action arising out of failure
to repair it may lie against that defendant. 'Immemorial' really does mean
immemorial. If either the road or its usage originated within legal
memory the action will fail. There are some arguable exceptions to this
rule (such as the presumed existence of a lost grant, or the case where,
under a grant, licence or statute, a liability to repair has arisen as
consideration for holding land), but detailed consideration of these
possibilities is outside the scope of this book.

The appropriate defendant in a case where liability by tenure is being
pleaded is the occupier (see *Daventry Rural District Council v Parker*
[1900] 1 QB 1; *Cuckfield Rural District Council v Goring* [1898] 1 QB 865).
If the occupier is sued he may well be entitled to an indemnity from the
owner (*Baker v Greenhill* (1842) 3 QB 148). Complex arguments about
joint and/or several liability can arise when the land is divided between
two or more owners. The normal rules relating to contribution and
indemnity apply.

Secondly, liability may arise by prescription, which is closely related to
tenure. Immemorial usage must again be established, and, again, proof
that the usage or the road itself originated within legal memory will
absolve the potential defendant from liability. Individuals (but not bodies
corporate and politic) are only liable by prescription to repair the highway
if there is proof that there was some consideration given for the repair. As
with the doctrine of tenure, a presumption of lost grant may aid a
claimant.

Note, however, that acts of maintenance performed by any body will be relevant in deciding whether that body has a duty to maintain only if the history of the road concerned is unclear. They cannot in themselves alter the status of a highway. Thus in *Doncaster Rural District Council v Freeman* (1973) 229 EG 263, although a council had already surfaced a road and installed lighting and services at the public expense and had caused the pavements to be swept regularly, they had not become the highway authority. The acts of the council had not changed the status of the road; it remained a private road.

Finally, liability may be imposed by statute. But even where this happens, highway authorities may, if the relevant highway came into existence before 1836, be concurrently liable with the individual (see *R v Brightside Bierlow Inhabitants* (1849) 13 QB 933).

1.2.2.2 Concurrent liability of the highway authority

Even if a private individual or body other than a highway authority is liable for repairs, the highway authority for the area may still be concurrently liable, or ultimately liable, for repair. Interesting Pt 20 proceedings involving delicate questions of land law can arise in this way (see *R v Brightside Bierlow Inhabitants* (1849) 13 QB 933; *Sandgate Urban District Council v Kent County Council* (1898) 79 LT 425).

1.2.2.3 Does liability to repair provide grounds for an action for personal injuries?

Whether or not liability to repair provides a ground for a personal injury action is undecided. There are a number of conflicting authorities. In *M'Kinnon v Penson* 8 Ex 319, at 327, Pollock CB said:

> 'There is no doubt of the truth of the general rule that where an indictment can be maintained against an individual or corporation for something done to the general damage of the public, an action on the case can be maintained for a special damage thereby done to an individual, as in the case of a nuisance in the highway by a stranger digging a trench across it, or of the default of a person bound to repair *rationae tenurae*.'

The House of Lords expressly approved this judgment in *Borough of Bathurst v Macpherson* (1878–79) LR 4 App Cas. 256. This view would probably prevail over the dissenting voice of Martin B in *Young v Davis* (1862) 7 H & N 760.

It will hardly ever be necessary to moot these very difficult points. Nuisance, negligence, and the Occupiers' Liability Act are much simpler ways of extracting compensation.

1.2.2.4   Liability under charter

A corporate body which is liable under charter to repair a highway will be liable in damages for personal injuries (see *Lyme Regis Corporation v Henley* (1834) 1 Bing NC 222, HL).

1.2.2.5   Independent contractors and extinction of liability to repair

The comments in **1.2.1.1–1.2.1.7** and **1.2.1.14** above about the liability of independent contractors and the extinction of liability to repair apply equally to privately maintained highways.

1.2.2.6   Approaches to bridges

By HA 1980, s 49, where a person is liable to maintain the approaches to a bridge because, by tenure or prescription, he is liable to maintain the bridge, his liability to maintain the approaches extends to 100 yards from each end of the bridge.

1.2.3   Highways which no one is liable to repair

The Highways Act 1959 (HA 1959) greatly simplified the question of liability for repair by saying, in effect, that unless there were special and well defined local claims for the duty and privilege of highway repair, the local highway authority would shoulder the burden. The Act swept away some tortuous common law and some incomprehensible statute law. After the 1959 Act there was light. But, generally, if a highway dedicated between the commencement of the Highways Act 1835 and the commencement of the 1959 Act was not, under the old law, repairable by the inhabitants at large, no one is now liable to repair it. Advisers to would-be claimants injured on such roads should turn to the chapters on negligence, nuisance and occupiers' liability.

1.3   INJURIES ON HIGHWAYS CAUSED OTHERWISE THAN BY FAILURE TO MAINTAIN

Injuries caused by the collateral negligence of contractors engaged by the highway authority for the performance of the authority's statutory duty to maintain have been discussed under *Independent contractors* in **1.2.1.1** and **1.2.1.6** above.

1.3.1 Injuries resulting from statutory works other than maintenance

A number of statutory undertakers interfere with highways. They include the gas, electricity, telephone and water authorities. The exercise of the powers of statutory undertakers is now regulated by The New Roads and Street Works Act 1991. It was previously regulated by the Public Utilities Street Works Act 1950.

1.3.1.1 The New Roads and Street Works Act 1991

Part III of the 1991 Act is headed 'Street Works in England and Wales', and sets out a comprehensive code regulating street works and the relationship between statutory undertakers and highway authorities. The structure of this part of the Act is outlined below.

1.3.1.2 'Street'

A "street" for the purpose of this part of the Act (s 48(1)(a)–(c)) is the whole or part of any of the following, irrespective of whether it is a thoroughfare:

(a) any highway, road, lane, footway, alley or passage;

(b) any square or court; and

(c) any land laid out as a way, whether it is for the time being formed as a way or not.

A street which is not a highway maintainable at the public expense is, generally, covered by this part of the Act (s 48(2)).

1.3.1.3 'Street works'

When the Act refers to 'street works' it means works (other than works for road purposes) executed in a street pursuant to a statutory right or a street works licence which involve the placement, inspection, maintenance, adjustment, repair, alteration, renewal, removal or change of position of apparatus, or works required for or incidental to any such works (s 48(3)).

1.3.1.4 'Street authority'

For the purposes of the Part, 'street authority' is, for a maintainable highway, the highway authority, and for a street which is not a maintainable highway, the street managers (ie the authority, body or person liable to the public to maintain and repair the street (s 49(1)).

1.3.1.5   Street Works Licences

Section 50 deals with the issue of Street Works licences, which are issued by the street authority and permit street works (as defined in s 48(3) above). It is, unsurprisingly, an offence (see s 51) to perform street works otherwise than pursuant to a Street Works licence or a statutory right.

1.3.1.6   The Street Works Register

Section 53 is a section important to personal injury practitioners. Section 53(1) requires street authorities to keep a register (known as the Street Works register) which shows, with respect to each street for which they are responsible, information as to the identity of the contractors and the location and type of the works involved. Section 53(3) requires the authority to make the register available for inspection, at all reasonable hours and free of charge, to any person (so long as the information is not 'restricted information', which information relating to personal injury cases is unlikely to be). The register should often be the first port of call for solicitors trying to identify the appropriate defendant in cases involving injury resulting from street works.

1.3.1.7   Notice of Works

Also in this Part of the Act are provisions requiring undertakers to give advance notice of certain works (s 54) and to give notice of the starting date of works (s 55). Street authorities have a general duty to coordinate works (s 59), and can give directions as to the timing of street works (s 56). Undertakers have a general duty to co-operate with the street authority and with other undertakers (s 60).

1.3.1.8   General obligation: the conduct of works

Section 65 imposes on undertakers a duty to guard and light street works and provide adequate traffic signs (which include directions to pedestrians). Section 66 specifically provides:

> 'An undertaker executing street works which involve –
> (a)   breaking up or opening the street, or any sewer, drain or tunnel under it, or
> (b)   tunnelling or boring under the street,
> shall carry on and complete the works with all such dispatch as is reasonably practicable.'

Works must be supervised by an appropriately qualified person (s 67).

1.3.1.9 Reinstatement

Undertakers have a duty to reinstate the street they have interfered with (s 70). This must be done as 'soon after the completion of any part of the street works as is reasonably practicable and shall carry on and complete the reinstatement with all such dispatch as is reasonably practicable' (s 70(2)). Before the end of the next working day after the day on which the reinstatement is completed, the undertaker must inform the street authority that he has completed the reinstatement of the street, stating whether the reinstatement is permanent or interim (s 70(3)). Section 71 enables the Secretary of State to prescribe materials, workmanship and standards of reinstatement, and requires undertakers to reinstate accordingly.

The street authority retains a power to force undertakers to discharge their statutory duty to reinstate. Section 72 empowers a street authority to investigate whether there has been adequate reinstatement, and enables the authority to serve notices on undertakers requiring them to discharge their obligations. If the notice is not complied with, the authority can do the works itself and recover the costs of the reinstatement from the undertaker.

It is important to note that the street authority, as highway authority, will itself be liable under s 41 of HA 1980 for failure to reinstate if it knows (or should have known) that the reinstatement was not done adequately by the undertaker and did not perform the works itself. Under such circumstances the highway authority would have no difficulty recovering an indemnity from the undertaker, but the availability of this indemnity is irrelevant to the issue of liability as between an injured claimant and the highway authority.

The statutory predecessor of the New Roads and Street Works Act 1991 was the Public Utilities Street Works Act 1950. Schedule 9 of the 1991 Act repealed the whole of the 1950 Act. The relevant part of Sch 9 was brought into effect and the 1950 Act consequently repealed on 1 January 1993 (see New Roads and Street Works Act 1991 (Commencement No 5 and Transitional Provisions and Savings) Order 1992 (SI 1992/2984). Although the 1950 Act is unlikely to be directly relevant in new or ongoing cases, lots of the cases deal with it and so it is important to understand a bit about how it worked.

1.3.1.10 The statutory codes under the Public Utilities Street Works Act 1950

The 1950 Act established three codes. The first is the Street Works Code, found in Pt I of the 1950 Act and in Schs 1–3. The code regulated the exercise by statutory undertakers of their powers to break up or open highways. Part II and Sch 4 governed the relationship between statutory undertakers and highway authorities, and Pt III controlled the relationships between statutory undertakers. Section 8(1) of the Act imposed obligations on undertakers to ensure that safety requirements were met during and in connection with the execution of works. There were also obligations to reinstate and to make good.

1.3.1.11   *Does breach of the statutory obligations sound in damages?*

Pleaders should note, that failure to meet the obligations imposed by the 1991 Act or to satisfy the criteria under s 8 of the 1950 Act will not give rise to an action in damages for a breach of statutory duty by a person injured as a result of that failure (*Keating v Elvan Reinforced Concrete Co Ltd* [1968] 1 WLR 722 (Appendix B, Case Summary 42)). *Keating* concerned s 8 of the 1950 Act. It will almost certainly be held to apply at least to ss 65–67 and 70 of the 1991 Act. This does not mean that the claimant has no remedy. Where a statutory undertaker interferes with a highway, and is negligent in the execution of its power under the enabling statute, or in the performance of the works, and such negligence causes personal injury, the statutory undertaker is liable in damages. The statutory undertaker may also be liable if the statutory power has been exceeded or has been exercised in bad faith. Statutory powers must be exercised with reasonable care (*Howard Flanders v Maldon Corporation* (1926) 90 JP 97). This duty applies to the original construction, the choice of the method and the site for the execution of the power, and subsequent maintenance of whatever has been constructed.

1.3.1.12   *Study the enabling statute and consider other causes of action*

In all cases where statutory undertakers are involved, the enabling statute should be examined to see if it creates a helpful statutory duty which sounds in damages. More general statutory duties, such as those created by the Workplace (Health, Safety and Welfare) Regulations 1992 (SI 1992/3004) should also be considered. Nuisance will generally feature in the Particulars of Claim, and common law negligence will almost always be pleaded too.

1.3.1.13   *Consider all possible defendants*

Where statutory undertakers are involved, the choice of defendant can sometimes be difficult. If, for example, a sewer authority lays a defective sewer pipe which causes a defect in the road over which a claimant trips, the sewer authority is liable for the injury which results (see *Nash v Rochford Rural District Council* [1917] 1 KB 384). If the highway authority took over the defective drain from the sewer authority, and the highway authority, with the exercise of reasonable diligence, should have realised that the drain posed a potential risk to members of the public, it is arguable that the highway authority will be concurrently liable with the sewer authority. If reasonable diligence on the part of the highway authority would not have revealed the potential danger, a cause of action will lie against the sewer authority only.

1.3.1.14 Can undertakers rely on the highway authority's inspections?

Statutory undertakers are not negligent in relying on the (reasonably frequent) inspections of a highway authority to determine whether something in the highway which belongs to the undertaker is dangerous. But if an undertaker does rely on the highway authority, the undertaker will be taken to have the same knowledge that it would or should have had if it had carried out its own inspection of the relevant site at the time that the highway authority carried out its inspection (see *Reid v British Telecommunications*, (1987) *The Times*, 27 June (Appendix B, Case Summary 46)).

1.3.1.15 Responsibility to maintain things created

If works are done under statute the thing created must, usually, be maintained by its creator and, in the event of injury caused by a failure to maintain, the creating authority is the appropriate defendant (see, eg, *Skilton v Epsom and Ewell Urban District Council* [1937] 1 KB 112; *Bathurst Borough v Macpherson* (1878–79) LR 4 App Cas. 256). Some instances of liability may at first sight seem to be exceptions to this rule, but closer examination will reveal that they are not. If a sewer authority has placed a manhole cover flush with the highway, and the highway then wears away to leave the manhole cover protruding dangerously, the tripper whose Colles' fracture evidences the difference in levels must sue the highway authority (see *Thompson v Brighton Corporation* [1894] 1 QB 332).

1.3.1.16 Drains and manhole covers

Openings generally belong to the body which owns the thing opened onto. Manhole covers leading to drains which drain the highway are part of the highway and are maintainable by the highway authority, and manholes leading to public sewers are vested in and maintainable by the sewerage authority (see *Winslow v Bushey Urban District Council* (1908) 72 JP 259). The general question to ask about drains is 'why, and at whose behest, did they come into existence?' Thus a drain which is provided by the highway authority for the purpose of draining the highway is deemed to be part of the highway although it may carry water which did not come from the highway (see *Rickarby v New Forest Rural District Council* (1910) 26 TLR 586). If the purpose of the sewer is the draining away of effluent from houses by the side of the highway, the sewer will be vested in the sewer authority, even though the domestic sewage is joined by water from the highway by way of street gullies (see *Wilkinson v Llandaff and Dinan Powis Rural District Council* [1903] 2 Ch 695).

1.3.1.17   Negligence

The creators of statutory works are liable for injury caused by their negligent use. See Chapter 6.

1.3.1.18   Failure to provide adequate street lighting

Section 97(1) of HA 1980 empowers the Minister and every local highway authority to provide lighting on any highway or proposed highway for which they are the highway authority. It also empowers them to contract with third parties for the purpose of providing that lighting. Section 98 of the 1980 Act enables a highway authority to delegate any of its lighting functions to the lighting authority.

Section 3 of the Parish Councils Act 1957 gives power to parish and community councils or, in the case of a parish for which there is no parish council, the parish meeting, to light roads and other places in the parish or community and to contract with third parties for that purpose.

By s 161 of the Public Health Act 1875, any urban sanitary authority may contract with any person for the supply of gas or other means of lighting the streets, markets and public buildings in their district, and may provide such lamps, lamp posts and other material and apparatus as they may think necessary for lighting those places.

Section 180(1) of the Local Government Act 1972 provides that the local authority or sanitary authority for the purposes of the 1875 Act is, for a district, the district council; for a London borough, the borough council; for the City of London, the Common Council; for the Inner Temple, the Sub-Treasurer; and for the Middle Temple, the Under Treasurer.

All those provisions are permissive. They do not require the authority concerned to provide street lighting in ordinary circumstances. Thus where an authority decided to provide street lighting but to turn it off at 9 pm, and the claimant wandered about the street at 11.30 pm and was injured, the authority was not liable; it was not bound to continue to light the street, having done nothing to make the street dangerous (see *Sheppard v Glossop Corporation* [1921] 3 KB 132 (Appendix B, Case Summary 48); *Burton v West Suffolk County Council* [1960] 2 QB 72). A policy decision not to exercise statutory powers will, in practice, be very hard to challenge. (For a discussion of this topic, see **5.3.4.1**.)

If the authority or anyone else has done something to make the road dangerous, the creator of the danger will be liable in negligence and nuisance for injuries caused by that danger if he has not taken reasonable steps to eliminate it. Warnings of the danger are important, and adequate warnings of highway dangers often involve lighting the danger. For examples of what constitutes reasonable steps, see *Murray v Southwark Borough Council* (1966) 65 LGR 145 (QBD) (Appendix B, Case Summary 52); *Lilley v British Insulated Callenders Construction Co Ltd* (1968) 67 LGR 224 (Appendix B, Case Summary 51); *Whiting v Middlesex County Council and Harrow Urban District Council* [1948] 1 KB 162, QBD (Appendix B, Case Summary 50); and *Fisher v Ruislip-Northwood Urban District Council and Middlesex County Council* [1945] KB 584, CA (Appendix B, Case Summary 49).

1.3.2 Injuries resulting from the default of private individuals or non-statutory bodies

If anyone interferes with a highway, in so doing he accepts the responsibility for the consequences of that interference until the highway can again be used safely by the public (*Shoreditch Corporation v Bull* (1904) 68 JP 415). The comments above about the duty to warn (for example by lighting) of any danger on the highway apply equally to persons who are not a highway authority or other kind of authority.

1.3.2.1 Cellars and vaults

There is a statutory duty to repair vaults, arches and cellars opening onto a highway (HA 1980, s 180(6)). This sometimes features, wrongly, in tripper pleadings. The section cannot give rise to a civil action against the relevant owner or occupier. It does, however, give the relevant occupier sufficient control of the grating or cellar cover concerned to enable him to effect repairs of it. He is accordingly under a duty to ' . . . use reasonable care to see that it is safe, and if he fails in his duty, he is liable in nuisance or negligence as the case may be' (see *Scott v Green & Sons* [1969] 1 WLR 301 at 302, per Lord Denning MR).

Where a highway is dedicated subject to the existence of a cellar, the owner or occupier has no liability to repair the cellar roof or fixed gratings if they are worn out by the passage of the public (see *Hamilton v St George, Hanover Square* (1873) LR 9 QB 42). The qualification '*fixed* gratings' is important. Owners or occupiers will be liable for wear and tear caused by the use of movable cellar flaps and appendages and for any personal injury which results from such wear and tear (*Robbins v Jones* (1863) 15 CBNS 221).

An owner of a building may be liable for a grating, ventilator or opening adjacent to the building even if the grating, ventilator or opening forms part of a dedicated highway (see *Macfarlane v Gwalter* [1959] 2 QB 332, CA).

1.3.2.2   Injuries on highways adjoining the property of a tort-feasor

Where a claimant slips or trips on a highway outside the premises of an occupier, as a result of the default of that occupier, the occupier will be liable. Thus where a claimant slipped on a piece of fat outside a butcher's shop, the butcher was liable for the injury because it was found as a fact that the fat came from the shop and that it either flew from the shop when meat was being cut up or was carried out on the shoe of a customer (*Dollman v A & S Hillman Ltd* [1941] 1 All ER 355). The butcher here was held to be liable in both nuisance and negligence. In such a situation it is submitted that the highway authority owed a duty to remove the fat. On the facts, of course, it would have been ridiculous for the claimant to suggest that the highway authority was in breach of that duty. But the position would be different if there was evidence that, over several months or years, the highway outside the butcher's shop had been contaminated with fat, that it was reasonably foreseeable that the fat would present a danger to users of the highway, and that the highway authority could and should have discovered and removed the danger. Here the butcher and the highway would both be liable. The injured claimant could join both as defendants. If the highway authority were sued, it could join the butcher as a Pt 20 defendant, and would be likely to be successful getting a contribution in those Pt 20 proceedings.

1.3.2.3   Ice

In *Lambie v Western Scottish Motor Traction Co* [1944] SC 415, the claimant slipped on ice which had formed on a pavement as a result of water escaping from the defendant's nearby garage where buses were washed. The defendant was liable. If there had been evidence that ice regularly formed on the highway as a result of the defendant's negligence, and the highway authority should have known about it and could and should have done something about it, it is submitted that the authority would have been concurrently liable with the bus owners.

1.3.2.4   Tree roots

If tree roots emanating from the land of a defendant adjoining the highway disrupt the highway and make it dangerous, the highway authority will be liable for breach of statutory duty and probably also in nuisance. The landowner could be liable in nuisance also. The highway authority might be able to invoke the defence in s 58 (see **4.1** and **4.1.1** below), but this would depend on, for instance, how obvious and how long-standing the danger was.

1.3.2.5 Fencing of dangers adjoining highways

Unless the danger can be stepped into inadvertently from the highway, there will generally be no duty on the owner of adjoining land to fence it (see *Caseley v Bristol Corporation* [1944] 1 All ER 14 (Appendix B, Case Summary 53)).

1.3.2.6 Damage to the highway by excavation of adjoining land

If the owner of land adjoining a highway excavates his land and so causes the highway to be damaged, he has committed the tort of public nuisance (see *Barnes v Ward* (1850) 9 CB 392; *Att-Gen v Roe* [1915] 1 Ch 235 and *Lodge Holes Colliery Co Ltd v Wednesbury Corporation* [1908] AC 323).

1.3.2.7 Animals

This possibility is not as far-fetched as it sounds. Many people are injured by falling over dogs. A classic example is *Carroll v Crawford*, (1968) *The Times*, 22 November. Here, the claimant tripped over a dog in a pub. She sued the owner and the landlord. Her claim failed, Paull J holding that there was no duty on a pub landlord to forbid customers from bringing in their dogs, or to insist that dogs be kept on leads (although it might be different if the dog was making a nuisance of itself), and that the owner was under no duty to keep an eye constantly on it. As to whether fear generated by a dog can amount to an actionable obstruction, see **6.5.6** below. The difficulty about alleging that a dog is an obstruction and/or a nuisance will be the transience of its presence at the material place. Negligence will generally be the best cause of action. If the dog is roaming free at the time it causes the claimant's injury the claimant is likely to fail to prove negligence. *Ellis v Johnstone* [1963] 2 QB 8 establishes that in the absence of special circumstances a dog owner is under no duty to prevent his dog from straying onto the highway. Just what the special circumstances would be is not clear. The case involved a dog running in front of a car. Donovan LJ solemnly opined that special circumstances would include the dog often bounding ' . . . out of a gate more like a missile than a dog', and Ormerod LJ said that the topographical circumstances would be relevant. Foreseeability of danger was the test, said Pearson LJ, in perhaps the only really enduring remark in the case. For an audacious and unsuccessful attempt to fix a highway authority with liability for dogs which ran out into the road causing a road traffic accident, see *Allison v Corby District Council* (1979) 78 LGR 197, QBD.

A claimant who slips in dog faeces may well have an action against the owner in nuisance. The difficulty, obviously, will be linking the owner with the faeces concerned. If the presence of dog faeces on the relevant street is a persistent and obvious problem an action in nuisance against the highway authority should be considered.

1.4   INJURIES OTHER THAN ON HIGHWAYS

Tripping accidents occurring elsewhere than on highways are treated in the same way as any other personal injury case, and the choice of defendant will usually follow the choice of cause of action. The principles are discussed in detail when the individual causes of action are dealt with. Briefly, the principles when selecting the defendants to go with the possible causes of action are as follows:

(1)   In a case of breach of statutory duty, the defendant is identified in the statute concerned.

(2)   In negligence, the defendant is the person who owes the particular duty of care which has been breached.

(3)   Under the Occupiers' Liability Acts, the defendant is the occupier. An occupier is a person who has a sufficient degree of control over premises to put him under a duty of care towards those who come onto the premises. The circularity of this definition is explored in **7.2** below. There can be more than one 'occupier' of one part of land or one structure or part of a structure.

(4)   Where an accident occurs on a public right of way, the occupier of the land over which the right of way passes and upon which the accident occurs is not liable as an occupier (see *McGeown v Northern Ireland Housing Executive* [1994] 3 WLR 187 (considered further at **7.4.1**)).

(5)   In private nuisance, it is choosing the claimant which is crucial. To succeed in private nuisance, a claimant must have an interest in land. A non-occupier cannot, therefore, recover damages for personal injuries in private nuisance (see *Malone v Laskey* [1907] 2 KB 141; *Cunard v Antifyre* [1953] 1 KB 551; *Halsey v Esso Petroleum Co Ltd* [1961] 1 WLR 683).
Generally, the person who, by an act of misfeasance (as distinct from nonfeasance), creates the nuisance can be sued. The occupier of the land where the nuisance occurred is generally liable. An occupier will be liable for a nuisance created by a trespasser or an act of nature if he adopts or continues the nuisance.
An occupier will be liable for a nuisance for which a predecessor in title was responsible if the occupier knew, or ought reasonably to have known, of the existence of the nuisance. Non-occupying landlords are generally not liable for a nuisance on the premises, and the appropriate person to sue in nuisance will usually be the tenant. A landlord may be liable if he has expressly or impliedly authorised the nuisance, or if he knew or ought to have known of the nuisance before letting, or where he reserves a right of entry and repair or has an implied right to do so, or where there is a covenant to repair.

Where the landlord is under a duty to repair and injury to a third party has resulted from a breach of the duty, the tenant is also liable (see *St Anne's Well Brewery Co v Roberts* (1929) 140 LT 1).

(6)   When choosing a defendant in a public nuisance case, the principles are the same as for private nuisance. Any person who has suffered special damage may sue in public nuisance, and this is a cause of action which has real value in tripping cases.

1.5   GENERAL POINTS

There is clearly no point in suing a defendant who has no funds, or does not have a valid insurance policy.

The possibility of suing more than one defendant should always be considered, but if a court concludes that a defendant has been unreasonably joined, it may order that the costs of that defendant be paid by the claimant. These orders are not readily made, but the possibility has to be balanced against the risk of failing to join the right defendant and the consequent loss to the client, with all that that entails.

CHAPTER 2

THE DEFINITION, CLASSIFICATION AND CREATION OF HIGHWAYS

2.1 INTRODUCTION

In Chapter 1, accidents were classified according to the places where they happen. The word 'highways' was used freely. In practice, it is not always clear that the place in question is in fact a highway. Readers are advised to read this chapter if they are uncertain that they are dealing with an accident on a highway; it is a crucial appendix to Chapter 1.

There is obviously no point in suing the highway authority if the accident did not occur on a highway at all or cannot be otherwise attributed to the state of the highway. This chapter deals with the various types of highway, and their boundaries. It answers questions such as 'Does a cellar grating form part of a highway?' and 'Is the grass at the side of a lane part of the highway?'

2.1.1 The statutory definition

Section 328 of HA 1980 states, unhelpfully:

'(1) In this Act, except where the context otherwise requires, "highway" means the whole or part of a highway other than a ferry or waterway.

(2) Where a highway passes over a bridge or through a tunnel, that bridge or tunnel is to be taken for the purposes of this Act to be a part of the highway.

(3) In this Act, "highway maintainable at the public expense" and any other expression defined by reference to a highway is to be construed in accordance with the foregoing provisions of this section.'

The problems caused by the deficiency of this definition are discussed in **2.4.1–2.4.2** below.

2.2 CLASSIFICATION

For personal injury lawyers highways are most significantly classified by reference to responsibility for repair. Every highway (since HA 1959) falls into one of three classes. These are:

(1)   highways repairable at the public expense;

(2)   highways repairable by private individuals or corporate bodies;

(3)   highways which no one is liable for repair.

This is the categorisation used in Chapter 1. It is not, though, always possible to fit a particular road immediately into the right class. Another and more detailed system of classification is needed. The broadest division in this other system is between carriageway highways and non-carriageway highways. There are many important sub-divisions.

2.2.1   Carriageway highways

By HA 1980, s 329(1), a carriageway is:

> 'a way constituting or comprised in a highway, being a way (other than a cycle track) over which the public have a right of way for the passage of vehicles.'

Pavements by the side of roads are 'footways' (s 329(1)). Paths for pedestrians running by the sides of roads and forming part of them (as most pavements do) are repairable by the body or person liable to repair the road (see *Derby County Council v Matlock, Bath and Scarthin Nick Urban District* [1896] AC 315). Whether or not a particular pedestrian path by the side of a carriageway is part of the carriageway highway and therefore liable to be maintained by the highway authority liable to maintain the carriageway is a question of fact. Pedestrians have a right to use the whole of a carriageway, and not just the footway.

There are general carriageway highways and other special types created by statute.

2.2.1.1   *General carriageway highways*

Most carriageway highways upon which tripping accidents occur fall into the general class.

2.2.1.2   *Trunk roads*

Trunk roads are carriageway highways which form part of the national system of routes for through traffic. The Minister of Transport is the highway authority for such roads.

2.2.1.3 *Special roads*

Special roads are carriageway highways which are created under a scheme under s 16 of HA 1980 or its statutory predecessors. The relevant highway authority will be specified in the scheme.

2.2.1.4 *Principal roads*

Principal roads are roads which are essential routes for traffic and are sufficiently important in the national highway network to justify the interest of central government in their planning and improvement. Either the Minister of Transport or the relevant local highway authority may be responsible for such roads.

2.2.1.5 *Classified, county, main and metropolitan roads*

These categories are now almost redundant. They are no longer of significance to the personal injury lawyer, but they are mentioned here because their names still appear in a number of texts.

2.2.2 Non-carriageway highways

Non-carriageway highways, again, fall into a number of sub-groups.

2.2.2.1 *Footpaths*

By HA 1980, s 329(1), footpaths are highways which carry only a public right of way on foot and are not footways. For all tripping purposes, they are normal highways.

2.2.2.2 *Public paths*

By s 66(1) of the Wildlife and Countryside Act 1981 a public path is a highway, being either a footpath or a bridleway, and so is a normal highway so far as tripping accidents are concerned.

2.2.2.3 *Bridleways*

By HA 1980, s 329(1), a bridleway is a highway over which the public have a right of way on foot and on horseback and leading a horse, with or without a right to drive animals. No other rights attach to a bridleway. It is a highway for all purposes relevant here.

2.2.2.4 *Roads used as public paths*

This classification is now almost redundant. The Wildlife and Countryside Act 1981 required all roads used as public paths to be reclassified. However, because reclassification is not yet complete, such roads may appear on the definitive map kept at the relevant county council's offices (see **2.3** below). Roads used as public paths are deemed to carry footpath and bridleway rights. It follows that they are treated as normal highways for present purposes.

2.2.2.5   Byways open to all traffic

These are exactly what their name suggests. They are creatures of s 66(1) of the Wildlife and Countryside Act 1981. Again, they are normal highways for present purposes.

2.2.2.6   Cycle tracks

By HA 1980, s 329(1), a cycle track is a way constituting or comprised in a highway over which there is a public right of way on pedal cycles, with or without a right of way on foot, and over which there is no other right of way.

Whether or not the cycle track in question is part of a highway, the highway authority for the associated highway will be responsible for maintaining the cycle track.

2.2.2.7   Walkways

Personal injury lawyers have to be particularly careful in dealing with accidents on walkways. Walkways are footpaths which pass through, over or under a building and are legally as well as physically attached to the building. Indoor shopping centres often incorporate walkways. They are created by specific agreements made pursuant to HA 1980, s 35. No useful general comments can be made about liability for maintenance. It is necessary in each case to see what provision was made in the parent agreement.

2.2.2.8   Urban pedestrianised areas

Pedestrianised areas, where many tripping accidents occur, also cause problems. Often they are merely footpaths, but they may be s 35 walkways, or walkways created by local Acts of Parliament. If they are s 35 walkways, the agreement must be examined. If they are local Act walkways, the Act itself must be consulted.

2.3   IDENTIFYING THE CATEGORY OF ROAD

Most tripping accidents occur on highways maintainable at the public expense. By HA 1980, s 36(6), the council of every county and London borough, and the Common Council of the City of London, must keep an up-to-date list of all the streets in their areas which are so maintainable. By s 36(7) the list has to be deposited at the offices of the council and can be inspected at all reasonable hours, free of charge, by any person.

Where a list is made by a county council, the county council has to supply to each district council in the county an up-to-date list of all such highways in the relevant district. Again this list has to be kept at the district council's office and may be inspected free of charge by any person at all reasonable hours.

The Wildlife and Countryside Act 1981 requires county councils to maintain definitive maps which display all the public paths in their areas.

These lists should be the first port of call for the claimant's lawyer. If the road where the injury occurred is on the list, the correct defendant is probably the highway authority.

If the place where the accident happened is not mentioned on the list and does not appear on the map, it is not a highway maintainable at the public expense. Walkway agreements or local Acts establishing walkways may be in place. The local highway authority should be able to help. If there is nothing to establish a walkway, the road may be a privately maintainable highway, or one which no one is liable to maintain. Although it has no obligation to keep records of roads which are not maintainable at public expense, again a competent highway authority should have information about them.

If the highway authority cannot help, the accident may not have occurred on a highway at all, and local enquiries, Land Registry searches or both will be necessary to identify the owner and/or occupier of the land concerned.

2.4 PROBLEMS OF DEFINITION

There is clearly no point in suing the highway authority if the accident occurred in a place which is not legally a highway.

2.4.1 The circular argument

The definition of a highway in HA 1980, s 328 (see **2.1.1** above) is not comprehensive or particularly useful. For this reason, arguments about liability tend to be circular, and are typically as follows: the accident occurred on a stretch of road which the highway authority has in the past been known to maintain; therefore the accident occurred on a highway; therefore the highway authority is responsible. Sometimes (and particularly early in the life of a tripping action) this argument has to do but the following points may help to break out of the circularity.

The materials and scrapings from a highway vest in the highway authority, which is therefore responsible for them (HA 1980, s 263(1)).

For the purposes of defining a highway authority's interest in, and therefore its responsibility for, a highway, the courts have said that the highway authority has title in and control of the thickness necessary to do what its statutory duty demands it do (*Coverdale v Charlton* (1878) 4 QBD 104). How much of the subsoil is dedicated to the highway authority for its statutory purposes is a matter of evidence in each case (see *Schweder v Worthing Gas Light and Coke Co (No 2)* [1913] 1 Ch 118).

The general principles about what constitutes a highway emerge reluctantly from a number of contradictory decisions about retaining walls, stiles and culverts. It is submitted that in law the ruling decision is, and in common sense should be, *Sandgate Urban District Council v Kent County Council* (1898) 79 LT 425. This case lays down two principles which apply when deciding whether any place or structure forms part of the highway. First, whether anything is part of a highway is a question of fact. The purpose for which that thing was constructed and the time it was constructed will be relevant in answering this question. Secondly:

> ' . . . assuming a thing to be necessary for the preservation of the road, and assuming that the local authority is under obligation to keep up the road, the law of England is that you shall keep up that road by whatever means are appropriate and necessary to do it' (per Lord Halsbury at 427).

Section 130 of HA 1980 provides that a highway authority has a duty to assert and protect the rights of the public to the use and enjoyment of any highway for which it is the highway authority.

This obligation specifically extends to any roadside waste which forms part of the highway. This clearly implies that roadside waste can be part of the highway. The obligation of the authority therefore extends to ensuring that these wastes are not dangerous. Of course the standard of maintenance and inspection applying to these wastes will be much lower than that applying to the metalled surface. Strips of grass bordering the metalled road can qualify as roadside wastes (*Curtis v Kesteven County Council* (1890) 45 Ch D 504).

Where there are strips of land between the metalled carriageway and fences or walls which mask the boundary of the highway, it is presumed that the public have a right to use the whole space between the carriageway and the fence or wall (*Friern Barnet Urban District Council v Richardson* (1898) 62 JP 547; *Att-Gen v Lindsay-Hogg* (1912) 76 JP 450). The presumption is rebuttable. In *Bishop v Green* (1971) 69 LGR 579, (see Appendix B, Case Summary 30), a grass verge was held not to constitute part of the footway. Section 130 would seem to imply that the highway authority's obligations extend as far as the public's rights.

The circular argument – that if the need for maintenance results from use as a highway, then a highway exists and the highway authority is responsible – has been applied widely by the courts in difficult cases. Thus when the flagstones of a pavement which formed the roof of a private cellar deteriorated, liability to repair the flagstones was decided by asking the question, 'Is it use of the flagstones as part of the highway or use of the flagstones as part of the cellar which has resulted in the need for the repair?' The answer (see *Hamilton v St George, Hanover Square* (1873) LR 9 QB 42) was that use as a highway had caused the deterioration. Therefore, went the reasoning, the flagstones were part of the pavement. As common sense and equity the decision is flawless, but as the articulation of a legal principle it is dubious. It is submitted that the only coherent basis for such a decision is unprecedented extrapolation from the doctrines of adoption and dedication or acceptance (see **2.4.3.2** and **2.5** below). It would make sense to say that the public's feet in passing over the flagstones, impliedly dedicated the deeper layers of the flagstones to the public, and that title to those deeper layers therefore passed to the highway authority.

A claimant injured on a defective gate or stile which exists or is used because a highway is used may be able to sue the highway authority. If, on the other hand, the gate or stile exists because it was reserved by the landowner when the highway was dedicated to the public, the highway authority will not be responsible and the landowner must be pursued.

The question of liability for drains and sewers which run under or in or by the highway is discussed in Chapter 1.

By s 90E of HA 1980, a road hump constructed pursuant to regulations made under s 90D is treated as forming part of the highway, so that the s 41 duty will extend to its maintenance and repair.

Where a highway passes across land in private ownership, the owner of that land is not liable to highway users for the safety of the highway or for dangers on it. It is irrelevant that any such dangers were present at the time of dedication or came into existence only later. Thus in *Gautret v Egerton* (1867) LR 2 CP 371, Willes J said 'If I dedicate a way to the public which is full of ruts and holes, the public must take it as it is'.

2.4.2   The common law

If the statutory definitions do not help, common law definitions may help to establish the status of the place where an accident occurs.

In *Ex p Lewis* (1888) 21 QBD 191, it was held that a highway is a way over which there exists a public right of passage, that is, a right for all Her Majesty's subjects at all seasons of the year freely and at their will to pass and repass without let or hindrance (per Wills J at 197).

Footpaths and bridleways which are open to the public generally are highways. The fact that a particular road may be limited to a certain class of traffic, or is subject to certain obstructions or restrictions, does not mean that it is not a highway.

Cul-de-sacs may be highways, but mere use by the public is unlikely to lead a court to the conclusion that a cul-de-sac has been dedicated as a highway (see **2.4.3.2** below for the meaning of 'dedication'). If the cul-de-sac has an attraction (such as the sea, a river or noted vantage point) at one end of it, so that the public may want to use the cul-de-sac as a route to the attraction, dedication may be inferred (see *Williams-Ellis v Cobb* [1935] 1 KB 310; *Att-Gen v Antrobus* [1905] 2 Ch 188).

2.4.3   How highways are created

The way in which highways come into being in the first place may shed light on the status of the *locus in quo*.

Highways can be created either by statute or by the operation of the common law doctrines of dedication and acceptance. The doctrine of prescription could, theoretically, create a highway, but if the right originated after 1188, a claim based on prescription will fail.

2.4.3.1   By statute

Highways can be created by agreement under a statutory power (see HA 1980, s 30). Where this occurs, creation is complete without any user. Walkways can be created in the same way (HA 1980, s 35).

Pubic path creation orders made under s 26 of HA 1980 can be made to establish both footpaths and bridleways.

A declaration made by a street works authority under s 34 of HA 1980 can transform into a highway a street which is not a highway, or land which has been treated as a private street.

Some statutes simply authorise the creation of roads. Until the road is complete, no highways will exist unless dedication and acceptance in accordance with the common law rules can be inferred. Thus if a road so authorised has been left partly finished but is regularly used by the public, there may be a fully constituted highway.

The Minister of Transport and the Secretary of State for Wales may construct new highways with the approval of the Treasury (HA 1980, s 24(1)). Importantly for practitioners, the relevant Minister is generally the highway authority for highways which he has created (HA 1980, s 1(1)(d)). The significance of this is discussed under *Who is the highway authority?* at **1.2.1.1** above.

2.4.3.2   *By common law*

Two elements – dedication and acceptance – are needed to constitute a highway at common law. For a highway to be created at common law the owner of the land over which a potential highway passes must dedicate that land to the public, and the public must accept the offer. Whether or not there has been valid dedication is a question of fact. It will involve asking whether there has been a sufficiently definite expression of intent to dedicate; whether it is sufficiently clear just what is being dedicated; and whether the would-be dedicator has the right and capacity to give away what he is dedicating. This is often simpler than is sometimes suggested.

There is a rebuttable presumption under HA 1980, s 31 that dedication is to be inferred after an uninterrupted period of 20 years of public use. See *Garside v Bradford and Northern Housing Association Ltd* (2001) CL 1 November; *National Trust for Places of Historic Interest or Natural Beauty v Secretary of State for the Environment* [1999] JPL 679; *Secretary of State for the Environment v Beresford Trustees* [1996] NPC 128; *Jaques v Secretary of State for the Environment*, (1994) *Independent*, 18 June 18.

The presumption under s 31 is rebutted where the landowner can show 'sufficient evidence that there was no intention during that period to dedicate it'. The ambit of the rebuttable principle was considered by the House of Lords in *R (on the application of Godmanchester Town Council) v Secretary of State for Environment, Food and Rural Affairs* [2007] UKHL 28.

When considering whether there was 'sufficient evidence' of the 'intention', their Lordships held that it was insufficient to rely on the witness evidence of the landowners alone in support of such a contention. Whether or not the necessary intention was present was to be determined by an objective test, to be considered in the context of what the relevant audience, namely the users of the way, would have reasonably understood the landowner's intention to be.

It is surprising how often s 31 needs to be invoked. Tripping accidents quite commonly occur on land which appears to belong to nobody. Collecting the evidence to support a claim that this statutory dedication has occurred is often difficult. There are sometimes legally exotic suggestions that the principle of *bona vacantia* (under which unclaimed land reverts to the Crown), might operate to make the Crown liable for accidents on unclaimed land. But the principle is unlikely to help. Probably more than title is required to establish liability: see, by way of analogy, *Toff v McDowell* (1993) 25 HLR 650.

2.5   THE ADOPTION OF HIGHWAYS

This is governed by HA 1980, ss 36–40. Sections 37 and 38 lay down the procedure whereby a person or a body (other than a highway authority) who is responsible, by tenure, inclosure or prescription or under a special enactment, for the repair and maintenance of a highway can extinguish his or its responsibility to repair and maintain. This is achieved by agreeing with a highway authority (the Minister in the case of a trunk road; the local highway authority in other cases) that, from a date specified in the agreement, the highway will become maintainable at the public expense. A highway so transferred to the care of a highway authority is said to be adopted by it.

By HA 1980, s 38, a local highway authority can agree with any person to undertake the maintenance of a private carriage or occupation road which the person is willing and legally able to dedicate as a highway. An 'occupation road' is a road the use of which is limited to the occupiers of the land or premises served by the road. The highway authority can similarly, under s 38(3)(b), enter into an agreement with a person in respect of a way which that person intends to construct, or which the highway authority intends to construct on his behalf, and which the person proposes to dedicate as a highway.

A highway authority can also, pursuant to HA 1980, s 38(4), enter into adoption agreements with railway, canal or tramway undertakers. Under such agreements, the highway authority maintains, as part of a highway maintainable at the public expense, bridges or viaducts which carry or are intended to carry the undertaker's railway, canal or tramway over the highway, and which are constructed by the undertaker or by the highway authority on the undertaker's behalf.

Where there is an adoption agreement, the date on which the highway becomes a highway maintainable at the public expense is the date specified in the agreement. Adoption agreements are often complex, but personal injury lawyers need look to them only for confirmation that the relevant highway is maintainable at the public expense, and for the date at which it became so maintainable.

By the Walkways Regulation 1973 (SI 1973/686), reg 3(2), the adoption provisions set out above do not apply to walkways or proposed walkways, unless the particular walkway agreement expressly so provides. As has already been pointed out, when dealing with a walkway, it is vital to consult the agreement.

Section 40 of HA 1980 enables a county or London borough or the Common Council of the City of London, to adopt private streets. After such adoption, they become highways maintainable at the public expense.

CHAPTER 3

THE STRUCTURE OF LOCAL GOVERNMENT

3.1 INTRODUCTION

Claimants' legal advisers need to know something about the organisation of local government so that they can:

(a) check the list of documents produced on disclosure to see that everything which is likely to have been generated during the policy-making and policy-execution stages of the authority's activities has been disclosed;

(b) make intelligent applications for specific disclosure;

(c) draft meaningful requests for further information/clarification;

(d) properly investigate, where necessary, the reasonableness or otherwise of the highway authority's decision-making;

(e) invoke remedies in addition to, or instead of, the remedies which the court can give. A demand by a Residents' Association that their road is repaired properly may be best dealt with in the first place by contacting the responsible council officer rather than immediately commencing proceedings in the magistrates' court or the county court.

The local authority's legal advisers also need to know about its structure, so that when dealing with the local government they can talk intelligently or at least in its own language.

The Local Government Act 1972 established in England six metropolitan counties divided into 36 metropolitan districts, and 39 non-metropolitan counties divided into 296 districts. It established in Wales eight non-metropolitan counties divided into 37 districts. The metropolitan counties (Greater Manchester, Merseyside, West Midlands, West Yorkshire, South Yorkshire and Tyne & Wear) were abolished in 1986. By s 1(6) of the 1972 Act, the old English rural parishes continue to exist as parishes. Part V of Sch 1 to the 1972 Act gives the Secretary of State power to create parishes out of former urban districts or boroughs. Wales does not have parishes, but a system of 'communities'. A one-tier system of local government was imposed on London by the Local Government Act 1985.

The councils of counties, districts and London Boroughs are called principal councils. Personal injury lawyers in tripping cases will deal mainly with these principal councils.

The provisions for the constitution of councils, joint authorities and committees are contained in the Local Government Act 1972, ss 2–5, 13–15, and 33–34. Principal councils are composed of a chairman, who is elected annually by the council from among its members, and the councillors, who are elected at local elections.

An authority can generally discharge its functions through a committee, a sub-committee another authority or through officers. In some circumstances a committee *must* be established.

3.2   RESPONSIBILITY FOR HIGHWAYS

Local government functions are allocated by a number of provisions of the 1972 Act. A full catalogue is in the Department of Environment Circular 121/72, annex A (see (1972) 70(2) LGR 1348). Generally, in non-metropolitan areas, county councils are responsible for most roads, highways generally, and traffic. They share responsibility for recreation with district councils. Both county and district councils may provide off-street car parks – an example of a power of a district council exercisable with the consent of the county council. District councils are responsible for minor urban roads, housing, coast protection and public health and sanitary services. Parish or community councils or meetings are responsible for footpaths, bus shelters, recreation grounds and parking places for motor cycles and bicycles.

Under ss 101 and 102 of the Local Government Act 1972 authorities may appoint committees as they think fit. In some cases, statute requires the appointment of a committee; here the authority may not act other than on a recommendation or a report from the committee, unless the matter in question is urgent.

The membership of committees and sub-committees is fixed by the appointing authority, authorities or committee. Section 102(3) provides that committees (with the exception of those which control finance) may include persons who are not members of the authority. Generally such co-opted members cannot vote (s 13 of the Local Government Act 1989), but highway authority committees are an exception to this rule. Members co-opted onto highway committees can vote.

Section 101 of the Local Government Act 1972 enables an authority to discharge any of its functions by agency arrangements with other authorities. But if there is such an agency agreement, responsibility for the performance of the statutory obligation remains with the authority upon which statute specifically imposed it.

As noted in Chapter 1, agency arrangements for highway maintenance are common. Section 8 of HA 1980 provides that local highway authorities may enter into agreements with each other for, inter alia, the maintenance of highways in respect of which any party to the agreement is the highway authority. This is a specific statutory example of the general provision in s 101 of the 1972 Act. A county council may not, however, enter into such an agreement with another county council unless the counties adjoin one another (see HA 1980, s 8(4)).

The Local Authorities (Goods and Services) Act 1970 provides that, subject to HA 1980, s 8(4), works of maintenance, but not construction, can be carried out for other authorities.

3.3 ACCESS TO INFORMATION ABOUT ACTIVITIES

The Local Government (Access to Information) Act 1985 gives greater public access to local authority meetings, reports and documents. It applies, inter alia, to all principal councils. Meetings of such councils must normally be open to the public. There are various provisions for the mandatory exclusion of the public from meetings if it is likely that confidential information will be disclosed, and that that disclosure would, if the public were present, be a breach of confidence.

Public notice of the time and place of the meeting of the council body must be published at the offices of that body 3 clear days before the meeting or, if the meeting is called at shorter notice, when the meeting is convened.

Copies of the agenda and reports for the meeting must be open to public inspection at least three clear days before the meeting or, if the meeting is convened at shorter notice, at the meeting.

After a meeting, various documents must be open to public inspection at the council's offices for 6 years. These documents include the minutes of the meeting, a summary of the proceedings, the agenda and any report compiled *for* the meeting if it relates to a part of the meeting open to the public. Copies of lists of background papers relating to such reports for a meeting must be open to public inspection for 4 years after the meeting.

Sections 2–4 of the Local Government, Planning and Land Act 1980 impose on local authorities a duty to publish information about the discharge of their functions.

CHAPTER 4

THE STATUTORY DUTY OF HIGHWAY AUTHORITIES TO MAINTAIN

4.1 INTRODUCTION

The following words from s 41(1) of HA 1980 are the most important words in this book:

> 'The authority who are for the time being the highway authority for a highway maintainable at the public expense are under a duty . . . to maintain the highway.'

Most tripping actions are brought for breach of this duty and the appropriate defendant is the highway authority. Where the highway authority primarily liable had entered into an agency agreement with another authority for the performance of some of its highway functions, the highway authority, which is primarily liable, can safely be sued although in practice it is sometimes agreed between the potential defendants that one or other, rather than both, is sued. The authorities then argue between themselves as to who should pay out.

Section 58 of the Act provides the highway authority with a possible defence. If a breach is found, the highway authority will not be liable for the consequences if it can establish that it took such care as in all the circumstances was reasonably required to secure that the part of the highway to which the action relates is not dangerous for traffic.

4.1.1 The interplay between HA 1980 s 41 and s 58

It is perhaps tempting to consider the issues arising from the application of ss 41 and 58 together. Practitioners should not fall into that trap. When bringing or defending highway claims, the effect of each individual section needs to be considered separately. In *Jones v Rhondda Cynon Taff County Council* [2008] EWCA Civ 1497, Laws LJ said this, at para 16 (see Appendix B Case Summary 4):

> 'I do not consider that a finding here that there was no breach of s 41 in some way conflates the test or tests for s 41 and those for the s 58 defence. There is, on the authorities . . . no breach of s 41 if the highway is reasonably passable for ordinary traffic without danger. If that test is not

met, then there will be a breach; but the local authority may show that they have taken reasonable care to avoid the danger, albeit on the particular facts they have not succeeded in doing so. The two sections both require regard to be had to the circumstances of the case but there is no need for conflation between the two. For s 41 the circumstances of the case are relevant to the ascertainment of a standard of repair that is required for s 58. They are relevant to an assessment of what a reasonable highway authority should put into effect by way of maintenance and repair.'

Section 41 and s 58 raise distinct issues which will need to be considered individually. Where a claimant cannot satisfy the court that there has been a breach of s 41, the defendant will not be under any obligation to satisfy the court of its s 58 defence.

In *West Sussex County Council v Sarah Caroline Russell* [2010] EWCA Civ 71, the first instance trial judge gave swift consideration to the s 41 issue, before focusing his attention upon s 58. As in *Jones* (cited above), the Court of Appeal felt it necessary to address the s 41 issue and s 58 separately, and in some detail. Practitioners must take the same course of action when assessing the merits of their cases. It is understandable why the trial judge gave swift consideration to the s 41 issue. The expert evidence plainly suggested that the highway was hazardous (by reason of the fact that the highway's grass verge was not level with the carriageway itself). As is noted in *Jones,* the extent of the s 41 breach will have a direct effect on the standard of repair that is required for the purposes of s 58. Thus, the council was held to be liable in failing to ensure that the verge was level with the carriageway.

Nevertheless, both *Jones* and *Russell* confirm the importance of considering the application of s 41 and s 58 separately. Therefore, the scope of the s 41 duty and the s 58 defence are now considered below in some detail.

4.2 NATURE OF THE DUTY

4.2.1 Which highways are covered by the duty?

The duty to maintain extends to highways which are maintainable at the public expense only. See Chapter 2 for a detailed consideration of what constitutes a highway maintainable at the public expense. Note especially that pedestrian ways in urban areas may be 'walkways' and therefore not subject to the statutory duty to maintain under s 41.

4.2.2 To whom is the duty owed?

The duty is owed to members of the public using the highway for the purposes of passage. 'Passage' includes almost all conceivable pedestrian activities. But if, for example, a very heavy man were to jump repeatedly up and down on a paving stone, causing subsidence which resulted in injury to him, this activity would be unlikely to be regarded as normal pedestrian passage, and he would be unlikely to succeed in a claim.

Rider v Rider [1973] QB 505 (see Appendix B, Case Summary 11) was a case which concerned the duty under s 41 owed to drivers. It was contended that the duty was owed to reasonably careful drivers only. The contention was rejected by the Court of Appeal. Sachs LJ, at p 514, said:

> '... the corporation's statutory duty ... is reasonably to maintain and repair the highway so that it is free from danger to all users who use that highway in the way normally to be expected of them – taking account, of course, of the traffic reasonably to be expected on the particular highway ... The highway authority must provide not merely for model drivers, but for the normal run of drivers to be found on their highways ...'

But reckless and drunken drivers, said Sachs LJ, were not using the highway in a way normally to be expected. Accordingly no duty was owed to them.

It is unclear if this restriction of the ambit of the duty has any relevance to pedestrians. No court would say that a highway authority did not owe a duty to a drunken pedestrian, who is still 'in the normal run' of highway users. But drunken and reckless pedestrians who have accidents and make claims may find their damages reduced under the principle of contributory negligence. It is arguable that roller-skates and skateboarders (particularly drunk ones) using pavements may be outside the scope of the duty.

If a robber rushes out of a bank, is tripped over by a member of the public and in that trip breaks his nose, he cannot sue the tripper for personal injuries. The tripper is helping to effect an arrest. However, if the same trip, with the same effect, is caused by a paving stone which is defective because of a breach of the highway authority's statutory duty, the robber can sue that authority.

The duty is owed to pedestrians walking in the carriageway of a road as well as on the pavement (*Bird v Tower Hamlets London Borough Council* (1969) 67 LGR 682). However, generally speaking, less stringent standards apply when considering the state of a carriageway, as opposed to the state of a pavement (see *Cenet v Wirral MBC* [2008] EWHC 1407 (QB), discussed in more detail at **4.3.2** below).

Donoghue v Stevenson applies. The duty is owed to all persons who it is reasonably foreseeable might be affected by the breach of duty. This includes blind people (see *Haley v London Electricity Board* [1964] 3 All ER 185 (Appendix B, Case Summary 5)).

4.2.3   The meaning of 'maintenance'

Maintenance includes repair (HA 1980, s 329(1)), but is wider than repair. In *Haydon v Kent County Council* [1978] QB 343 Shaw LJ (at p 364) said:

> "' . . . the ordinary meaning of "to maintain" is to keep something in existence in a state which enables it to serve the purpose for which it exists. In the case of a highway that purpose is to provide a means of passage for pedestrians or vehicles or both (according to the character of the highway). To keep that purpose intact involves more than repairing or keeping in repair . . .
>
> . . . there may be extreme cases in special circumstances where a liability for failure to maintain not related to want of repair may arise. Such cases are not readily brought to mind although I would not wish to exclude them by confining the scope of maintenance to matters of repair and keeping in repair.'

But it is not as simple as that, said the House of Lords in *Goodes v East Sussex County Council* [2000] 1 WLR 1356 (see Appendix B, Case Summary 1). Classically, a highway is out of repair when its surface is defective or disturbed. The mere presence of an obstruction does not render it out of repair (see *Hereford and Worcester County Council v Newman* (CA), *Worcestershire County Council v Newman* [1974] 1 WLR 938 (Appendix B, Case Summary 29)). Snow and ice obviously do not render a highway out of repair, and until *Goodes* it was as settled law that failures to remove snow and ice could constitute breach of the duty to maintain. In *Goodes* the House of Lords decided that one could not simply construe 'maintain' in the 1980 Act as if the Act had no legal ancestors. The duty to maintain, said the House, was the same as that which common law had imposed on the inhabitants of parishes before statute enshrined the duty. Looking at all the old cases, it was clear that the highway authority had no duty under s 41 to take measures either to prevent the accumulation of snow or ice or to remove them once they had accumulated. The duty extended only to the maintenance of the fabric of the highway.

This is a much criticised decision. It amounts to saying that a highway authority (the purpose of whose existence is to facilitate safe and expeditious travel over highways) has no duty under s 41 to facilitate this when what is getting in the way of such travel is eminently removable or preventable snow or ice.

Whether *Goodes* still represents the law remains a matter of debate almost a decade after judgement was given. The Railways and Transport Safety Act 2003 inserted a new s 41(1A) into HA 1980. It states:

'In particular, a highway authority are under a duty to ensure, so far as is reasonably practicable, that safe passage along a highway is not endangered by snow or ice.'

This section came into effect on 31 October 2003: see the Railways and Transport Safety Act 2003 (Commencement No 1) Order 2003 (SI 2003/2681).

It is uncertain whether this reverses *Goodes*, or even, in practice, mitigates it significantly. The s 41 duty is an absolute one, subject to the defence in s 58. But s 41(1A) is not at all absolute. It allows the highway authority to escape through a 'reasonably practicable' clause which might prove to be very wide. The subsection seems to invite a lot of litigation about (for example) resource allocation, which might make it possible for claimants to rely on s 41(1A) only if the highway authority has been unreasonable in a public law sense in its decisions about whether and if so where and how to grit.

There is some authority for the proposition that we are now back in a pre-*Goodes* world. In *Sandhar v Department of Transport, Environment and the Regions* [2004] EWCA Civ 1440 (Appendix B, Case Summary 36), May LJ said, at para 11: 'The effect of Goodes has been reversed by a statutory amendment to section 41 of the 1980 Act . . .', and implied that the result of that appeal (which would have resulted in a finding for the claimant before Goodes) would have been different if s 41(1A) had been in force. But this was not a case which required detailed consideration of s 41(1A).

Similarly in *Thompson v Hampshire County Council* [2004] EWCA Civ 1016 (see Appendix B, Case Summary 13), the Court of Appeal referred to s 41(1A) and said, at para 11: 'Parliament thereby effectively reversed the decision of the House of Lords in [Goodes]'. But this was obiter. It remains to be seen whether a court considering the issue directly agrees. Clarification is urgently needed, but s 41(1A) is still yet to receive detailed consideration by the courts.

Goodes has forced practitioners to consider ways of recovering damages for claimants injured by failures in winter maintenance regimes. Section 150 of the 1980 Act might help: this possibility is considered at **4.3.4** below. Where winter maintenance is undertaken, but done badly, liability in negligence is a possibility. If highway authorities opt to exercise their statutory powers, they must do so competently and may be liable in the law of negligence if they fail to do so and that failure can be characterised as misfeasance rather than non-feasance. It should not be difficult to express many such failures as misfeasance. The issue is considered further in Chapter 5. Highway authorities also retain an obligation to abate highway nuisance, and it may be possible to say that snow or ice constitute such a nuisance: see Chapter 6.

Another possible route of redress is via the line of authority which deals with liability for water on roads. The duty to maintain the highway does not include a duty to maintain anything other than the highway itself (eg it does not require the highway authority to create structures which stop water reaching the road in the first place), but if the authority opts to allow water to reach the road, it has been said in the past that it owes a s 41 'maintenance' duty to provide an adequate drainage system: see *Thorburn v Northumberland CC* (1999) 1 LGLR 819. But this authority arguably does not survive *Goodes*. The issue needs to be litigated.

Maintenance and improvement are distinct. Highway authorities are under no duty to improve highways. This principle sometimes arises in personal injury cases involving road traffic. If a pedestrian asserts that he tripped solely because he was forced to walk on the carriageway of a road which has no pavement, and had to move quickly to avoid an oncoming vehicle, he could not assert that the highway authority had a duty to improve the road by providing a pavement.

In *Thompson v Hampshire County Council*, above, the claimant was walking along an earth path which went along the verge of a highway. She strayed a little from the path and fell into a ditch beside the track. The judge found that the path was safe. The claimant submitted that the highway authority was liable because of the unsafe juxtaposition of the path and the ditch. This was wrong, said the Court of Appeal. The duty to maintain was the limited duty described in *Goodes*. It did not extend to a duty to alter layout. The ditch was not out of repair, and nor was the path. Accordingly there was no breach of the s 41 duty.

The distinction between maintenance and improvement is important if it is necessary to decide the standard of maintenance required of a highway authority in respect of a particular highway. The traditional rule has been that when a highway is dedicated to public use, the public must take it in the state in which they find it. The courts have therefore said that, unless a highway authority improves a highway, the authority will not be required to exercise a higher standard of maintenance than was appropriate when the highway first became maintainable at the public expense (see *Owen v De Winston* (1894) 58 JP 833).

It is submitted that *Owen* is correct. But in the more recent case of *Sharpness New Docks and Gloucester and Birmingham Navigation Co v Att-Gen* [1915] AC 654 (see Appendix B, Case Summary 3) Lord Atkinson said (at p 665):

> 'it is the duty of road authorities to keep their public highways in a state fit to accommodate the ordinary traffic which passes or may be expected to pass along them. As the ordinary traffic expands or changes in character, so must the nature of the maintenance and repair of the highway alter to suit the change.'

It is respectfully submitted that Lord Atkinson reached the right conclusion by the wrong route. *Owen* and *Sharpness New Docks* can be reconciled without violence to either. Since the highway authority has a power to improve, it can be liable in damages if it fails to exercise that power by reason of negligence (see *Anns v Merton London Borough Council* [1978] AC 728). *Owen* is correct: there is no duty to maintain to a standard higher than that originally appropriate. But it may be negligent not to exercise the power to improve. Of course if a highway authority decides to exercise its power to improve, it also takes on the duty to maintain the improved road to the appropriately higher standard. And so the conclusion in *Sharpness New Docks* is correct also.

Actions (especially actions relating to road traffic accidents) are sometimes brought on the *Anns v Merton London Borough Council* principle, claiming damages for loss caused by the negligent failure to exercise the power to improve a highway. This is a potential cause of action in highway tripping cases too.

4.2.4 Is fault required?

There has been a lot of very tedious academic discussion about this, but *Goodes* makes the position clear. Fault is not required. The highway authority's duty is an absolute one, subject only to the statutory defence.

4.2.5 The 'fabric' of the highway and the extent of the s 41 duty

Many practitioners think that *Goodes* laid down principles relating to winter maintenance only. For the reasons given above, the effect of *Goodes on winter maintenance cases is now doubtful* given the introduction of HA 1980, s 41(1A).

The courts continue to rely on *Goodes* in support of the general proposition that s 41 only imposes a duty to maintain the 'fabric' of the highway. However, what constitutes the 'fabric' of the highway remains a matter of debate. Maintenance of materials or objects which are not to do with the 'fabric' of the highway (such as street furniture) do not fall within the scope of the s 41 duty. By contrast, recent case law suggests that s 41 does impose a positive duty to maintain drainage, so that any accidents arising out of standing water on the carriageway have the potential to trigger a breach of s 41. Each category is addressed in turn below.

4.2.6 Street furniture

In *Shine v Tower Hamlets LBC* [2006] EWCA Civ 852 (see Appendix B, Case Summary 37), the Court of Appeal held that the s 41 duty did not apply in respect of the maintenance of street furniture. Section 41 seems to be construed narrowly by the courts: it and applies solely to the fabric of the highway itself.

Note, though, that the claimant in *Shine* succeeded on the basis of an alternative cause of action in negligence. Of course, each case will turn on its own facts, to which the ordinary common law principles of negligence will be applied. It seems though, that negligence is likely to be the correct cause of action in most cases involving injury caused by poorly maintained street furniture. Such claims are outside the scope of s 41.

4.2.7   Water on the highway

Where a highway authority has breached its s 41 duty to maintain drains to a road, with a resulting dangerous accumulation of water on the road, an injured claimant can recover damages under s 41: (see *Burnside v Emerson* [1968] 1 WLR 1490). In order to obtain a finding of liability, the claimant must establish that:

(a)   the road was in a condition such that it was dangerous to traffic;

(b)   the danger was caused by the authority's failure to maintain. A distinction is to be drawn between a permanent danger due to the want of repair, and a transient danger due to the elements. Where there is a transient danger due to the elements, the existence of a danger for a short period is not evidence of a failure to maintain;

Prima facie liability results if these elements are established. *Burnside* predates HA 1980. Probably if these elements are proved, the defendant will fail unless it makes out a s 58 defence.

In *Department of Transport, Environment and the Regions v Mott MacDonald Ltd and others* [2006] EWCA Civ 1089 (see Appendix B, Case Summary 25), the defendants argued that *Burnside* was no longer good law in the light of *Goodes*. This submission was expressly rejected by the Court of Appeal. *Burnside* remains good law; s 41 dictates that the 'structure and fabric of the roadway' should be maintained as a whole (*Mott MacDonald*, at para 40).

It may seem odd that the courts draw a distinction between surface water which causes a danger to traffic by reason of a failure to maintain the highway, and ice/snow which causes a danger to traffic by reason of a failure to maintain the highway. The extent to which *Goodes* remains good law continues to be unclear. The above cases and s 41(1A) suggest that the core principles of *Goodes* are slowly eroding away.

4.3 WHAT THE CLAIMANT HAS TO PROVE

A claimant has to prove, on the balance of probabilities, that the part of the highway where his accident occurred was not reasonably safe, and that the accident was caused by the dangerous condition of the highway.

If the claimant surmounts these two hurdles, the defendant can then raise the statutory defence afforded by HA 1980, s 58. The burden of establishing the defence is on the defendant; the claimant does not have to prove the negative.

4.3.1 When is a highway not reasonably safe?

The principles used to decide whether or not a highway is reasonably safe may be summarised as follows:

(1) The test is reasonable foreseeability of danger.

(2) Minor irregularities do not render highways legally unsafe.

(3) The courts have consistently said that the question of whether a particular highway is unsafe is one for the trial judge to decide. They have declined to give binding declarations, in terms of specified size of irregularity, as to what constitutes an unsafe highway. They have consistently disapproved of this tariff approach.

(4) Nevertheless, differences in level of one inch or more are likely to be found to be unsafe.

(5) It is unclear whether the carriageway of roads must be as safe for pedestrians as the pavement.

(6) A trivial defect may give rise to liability if it is suddenly and unexpectedly created.

Griffiths v Liverpool Corporation [1967] 1 QB 374 (CA) (see Appendix B, Case Summary 6) involved a trip on a flagstone which stood half an inch proud and rocked. The county court judge found that this made the pavement dangerous. There was no appeal from that finding, but in the Court of Appeal Sellers LJ, at p 382, obviously thought it was wrong:

' . . . We are all of us accustomed to walk on uneven and irregular surfaces and we can all of us trip on cobblestones, cat's-eyes, studs marking pedestrian crossings, as well as other projections.

If the finding that the half-inch projection of a solitary flagstone in a wide pavement has to be accepted as a danger because of the technicalities of this case, as my brethren think, I have perhaps said enough to indicate that it is a standard which in my view should not become a precedent or guide in ordinary circumstances.'

In *Meggs v Liverpool Corporation* [1968] 1 WLR 689 at p 692 (see Appendix B, Case Summary 7), Lord Denning MR, upholding a judge's finding that a quarter inch discrepancy in a pavement did not make the pavement dangerous, said:

> 'It seems to me, using ordinary knowledge of pavements, that everyone must take account of the fact that there may be unevenness here and there. There may be a ridge of half an inch or three-quarters of an inch occasionally, but that is not the sort of thing which makes it dangerous or not reasonably safe.'

A passage from the judgment of Cumming-Bruce J in *Littler v Liverpool Corporation* [1968] 2 All ER 343, (see Appendix B, Case Summary 8) summarises the law very well, but is generally thought to be rather generous to highway authorities in, apparently, excusing one inch trips. The case concerned a discrepancy of half an inch. He said, at p 345:

> 'The test in relation to a length of pavement is reasonable foreseeability of danger. A length of pavement is only dangerous if, in the ordinary course of human affairs, danger may reasonably be anticipated from its continued use by the public who usually pass over it. It is a mistake to isolate and emphasise a particular difference in levels between flagstones unless that difference is such that a reasonable person who noticed and considered it would regard it as presenting a real source of danger. Uneven surfaces and differences in level between flagstones of about an inch may cause a pedestrian temporarily off balance to trip and stumble, but such characteristics have to be accepted. A highway is not to be criticised by the standards of a bowling green.'

In *Mills v Barnsley Metropolitan Borough Council* [1992] PIQR 291, the Court of Appeal again emphasised that the test of dangerousness is the test of reasonable foresight of harm to highway users, and that accordingly each case must turn on its own facts. Steyn LJ said, at p 293, that in inferring that the defect in question (which was less than one inch) was dangerous, the trial judge:

> ' . . . impliedly set a standard which, if generally used in the thousands of tripping cases which come before the courts every year, would impose an unreasonable burden upon highway authorities in respect of minor depressions and holes in streets which in a less than perfect world the public must simply regard as a fact of life. It is important that our tort law should not impose unreasonably high standards, otherwise scarce resources should be diverted from situations where maintenance and repair of the highways is more urgently needed. This branch of the law of tort ought to represent a sensible balance of compromise between private and public interest. The judge's ruling in this case, if allowed to stand, would tilt the balance too far

in favour of [the plaintiff]. The risk was of low order and the cost of remedying such minor defects all over the country would be enormous . . .'

This passage was cited with approval by the Court of Appeal in *James v Preseli Pembrokeshire District Council* [1992] PIQR 114. In *Lloyd v Redbridge LBC* [1996] CL 4480 a clump of grass with a spread of five inches and a height of four inches at the edge of a footway close to the wall of a property was held not to be dangerous. The notion of a foreseeable risk of injury can give problems to non-lawyers. Lots of things are foreseeable without strenuous stretches of the imagination. Eady J pointed out in *Galloway v London Borough of Richmond upon Thames* (unreported) 20 February 2003, that in this context a foreseeable risk of harm means that the relevant defect gives rise to a 'real source of danger'. Even a trifling defect, which in the normal course of events would not give rise to liability, might constitute or evidence a breach of duty if it has been suddenly and unexpectedly introduced into a highway (see *Pitman v Southern Electricity Board* [1978] 3 All ER 901, (Appendix B, Case Summary 9)).

It is not always necessary to identify a particular defect. If a pavement is generally scruffy to the point of dangerousness then that will be enough. See, e g *Hartley v Burnley BC* [1996] CL 5670. Conviction will often be a problem in such cases, however.

4.3.2   Safety of the carriageway for pedestrians

There are conflicting decisions on the question of whether the carriageway of a road must be as safe for pedestrians as the pavement.

Applying the test of foreseeability of danger, the obvious answer is that the carriageway does have to be as safe for pedestrians as the pavement. This was the conclusion reached by Nield J in *Bird v Tower Hamlets London Borough Council* (1969) 67 LGR 682. The claimant's ankle was injured when he stepped out of his van into a depression in the carriageway which was not so deep as to be a danger to vehicular traffic. It was contended that, so far as pedestrians were concerned, the standard of 'reasonable safety' applying to carriageways was lower than that applying to pavements. This contention was rejected, Nield J saying that (at p 685):

> 'The highway authority must foresee that pedestrians will cross the carriageway as they, indeed, are entitled to do, to pass and repass, and must, therefore, keep that part of the highway, as much as any other, safe for pedestrians.'

However, *Bird* appears to be the lone voice in support of such a proposition. Subsequent authorities accept that less stringent standards apply to the carriageway than the pavement.

In *Ford v Liverpool Corporation* (1972) 117 SJ 167, (see Appendix B, Case Summary 10), however, Watkins J held that the public must expect some obstructions to appear in the roadway, and held the highway authority not liable for an injury caused by a metal grid in a carriageway which created a step of over an inch. It is inconceivable that such a defect would not have attracted liability had it been on a footway.

In *McLoughlin v Strathclyde Regional Council* [1992] SLT 959, a local authority was found not liable to a claimant who, while crossing a road, had tripped over a defect caused by the subsidence of paving stones around a drainage gully. The kerbstones had subsided 1.5 inches and the surrounding tarmac was 1–1.25 inches below the surrounding roadway. Apparently the road had been in this state for years. Again, such a defect would unquestionably have made the authority liable if it had been present on a pavement.

More recently, in *Cenet v Wirral MBC* [2008] EWHC 1407 (QB) (see Appendix B, Case Summary 12), Swift J, hearing an appeal from the county court, held that the trial judge had erred in law when he held that the location of the accident had been 'more akin to the pavement that the carriageway'. Where the defective area is part of the carriageway, standards appropriate to a pavement should not be applied. The correct standards to apply are those applicable to the carriageway.

Ford, McLoughlin, Cenet and common sense all suggest that *Bird* is simply wrong. It is difficult to think of a situation where 'pavement standards' would be applied to the carriageway.

4.3.3   Country roads

The difficulties encountered in *Bird* and *Ford* are also met when considering accidents which occur on remote rural roads or unmetalled footpaths which the highway authority has a duty to maintain. All writers on the subject have said that the highway authority is not obliged to maintain these to the same standards as urban pavements. This conclusion is supported not only by common sense, but by the test of reasonable foreseeability of danger. Although a one inch protrusion on a country footpath could cause a trip just as easily as on a city walkway, the reasonable man expects large footpath defects when on a country walk and he is not therefore taken dangerously by surprise by them, but might well be when running down the street to catch a bus.

In considering the reasonable foreseeability of danger on a particular highway, it is submitted that the degree of vigilance of the reasonable man when on *that* highway should be taken into account. It appears that Nield J in *Bird* did not consider this. He thought that the only relevant 'foreseeabilities' were the foreseeability of pedestrians crossing the carriageway and the foreseeability of a particular defect causing them injury. If these are the only relevant considerations, highway authorities would be under a duty to keep unmetalled country lanes in the same condition as city pavements, since it is foreseeable that a one inch defect on the country road could cause a trip, and foreseeable that people will walk along country lanes. It is submitted that this conclusion would be absurd, and that accordingly the approach adopted in *Bird* is wrong.

4.3.4 'Winter maintenance' cases: HA 1980, s 41 and s 150

Each year thousands of people are injured when they slip on ice and trip over uncleared snow on highways. Until the decision of the House of Lords in *Goodes v East Sussex CC* [2000] 1 WLR 1356 it was thought that the s 41 duty to maintain included a duty to take reasonable steps to keep the highway clear of snow and ice so that traffic, including pedestrian traffic, could use the highway for the purpose for which it was intended. *Goodes* said that it did not. Section 41(1A), inserted by the Railways and Transport Safety Act 2003, specifies that: 'In particular, a highway authority are under a duty to ensure, so far as reasonably practicable, that safe passage along a highway is not endangered by snow or ice.' Whether this has the effect of overruling *Goodes* is a moot point: see **4.2.3** above. If s 41(1A) does not put the law back into the position that it was understood to be in prior to *Goodes*, that is not necessarily the end of winter maintenance claims. Negligence is one (albeit difficult) possibility. It may help in cases of misfeasance. It is unlikely to help in cases of non-feasance. In *Sandhar v Department of Transport, Environment and the Regions* [2004] EWHC 28 (Appendix B, Case Summary 36) the claimant failed to persuade the judge that highway authorities had a common law duty to prevent ice forming on roads under their control, or to remove it once it had formed. The issue of liability in negligence is considered further in Chapter 5.

Section 150 of HA 1980 is another possible route of redress. This provides:

'(1) If an obstruction arises in a highway from accumulation of snow or from the falling down of banks on the side of the highway, or from any other cause, the highway authority shall remove the obstruction.

(2) If a highway authority fail to remove an obstruction which it is their duty under this section to remove, a magistrates' court may, on a complaint made by any person, by order require the authority to remove the obstruction within such period (not being less than 24 hours) from the making of the order as the court thinks reasonable, having regard to all the circumstances of the case.

(3) In considering whether to make an order under this section, and if so, what period to allow for the removal of the obstruction, the court shall in particular have regard to –

(a) the character of the highway to which the complaint relates, and the nature and amount of the traffic by which it is ordinarily used,

> (b)   the nature and extent of the obstruction, and
> (c)   the resources of manpower, vehicles and equipment for the time being available to the highway authority for work on highways and the extent to which those resources are being, or need to be, employed elsewhere by that authority on such work.
>
>   . . .
>
> (6)   The foregoing provisions of this section apply to a person liable to maintain a highway by reason of tenure, enclosure or prescription as they apply to a highway authority for that highway, and references in those provisions to a highway authority are to be construed accordingly.'

It is extremely rare to see this provision pleaded as giving rise to an action for damages when breached. The reluctance to do this probably arises from a cursory reading of *Haydon* (above). This case is principally cited as authority on the meaning of 'maintain' and 'repair' under HA 1980, s 41, but the claimant also contended that s 129 of the HA 1959 (which is, with a vitally important caveat, the statutory predecessor of s 150 of HA 1980), imposed on the highway authority a statutory duty, breach of which was actionable in damages, to remove highway obstructions. Section 129 states:

> '(1)   If an obstruction arises in a highway from accumulation of snow or from the falling down of banks on the side of the highway, or from any other cause, the highway authority for the highway shall cause the obstruction to be removed from *time to time*, and within 24 hours from the date of service of a notice from a justice of the peace . . . requiring the removal of the obstruction
>
>   . . .
>
> (3)   A highway authority . . . who fails to comply with the foregoing provisions . . . shall be guilty of an offence and shall be liable in respect to a fine . . .' (*author's emphasis*).

In *Haydon* Lord Denning MR held that HA 1959, s 129 did not give rise to an action in damages when breached. He said, at p 493:

> 'That section is very appropriate to deal with highways which get blocked or impeded by snow or ice, or by earth falling down from a bank or by a tree falling down and straddling the highway. It puts on the highway authority a duty to remove the obstruction, but it leaves it to the highway authority to carry out that duty at such time as it thinks best. To do it "from time to time". They have, therefore, a discretion: save that, if they delay too long, they can be brought to book by a magistrate's order. By no shadow of argument can it be called an absolute duty. Nor does it give rise to a civil action for damages if it is not performed.'

Lord Denning, in these final two sentences, is uncharacteristically obscure. He must mean, though, that the section does not give rise to a civil action for damages if not performed *because* it is does not impose an absolute duty.

Now compare and contrast HA 1959, s 129(1) with HA 1980, s 150(1). The important difference is that s 150(1) does not have the words 'from time to time', the very words which seem to have caused Lord Denning to conclude that s 129 did not impose a duty which, if breached, would give rise to an action in damages. As to the other two judges in *Haydon*, Goff LJ does not deal with s 129 at all, and Shaw LJ seems to agree with Lord Denning's reasons for concluding that s 129 does not lead to civil liability. At pp 498–499 Shaw LJ said:

> 'It is not without interest that to compare the procedure prescribed under section 129 with that set out in section 59 [the predecessor of HA 1980, s 41] in relation to what is described in general terms as "Enforcement of liability to maintain highway" but which is mainly directed to cases of want of repair. Although the procedure prescribed in section 129 exhibits a greater sense of the need for promptness it does not insist on an arbitrary or inflexible immediacy of action on the part of a highway authority. On the contrary it takes account of relevant considerations of practicability.'

It follows from this that HA 1980, s 150 may well impose an obligation, breach of which is actionable in damages. The point has not been decided. It should be. A precedent appears at Appendix A.19. Since it cannot be assumed that *Goodes* is the final nail in the coffin for all winter maintenance cases, there is at Appendix A.1 a questionnaire which will help in investigating such cases.

4.4   THE STATUTORY DEFENCE

Section 58(1) of HA 1980 states:

> 'In an action against a highway authority in respect of damage resulting from their failure to maintain a highway maintainable at the public expense it is a defence without prejudice to any other defence or the application of the law relating to contributory negligence) to prove that the authority had taken such care as in all the circumstances was reasonably required to secure that the part of the highway to which the action relates was not dangerous for traffic.'

By virtue of HA 1980, s 329(1), 'traffic' includes pedestrians.

Section 58 becomes relevant only where the claimant has succeeded in proving that the highway was not reasonably safe and that his accident was caused by the dangerous condition of it.

4.4.1   The burden of proof

The burden of proving the matters in s 58(1) rests on the defendant. The claimant does not have to prove that the highway authority did not take the requisite care. Nor, more surprisingly, does the claimant have to show that the lack of reasonable care was the cause of his injury. This is made clear in the judgment of Diplock LJ in *Griffiths v Liverpool Corporation* (see Appendix B, Case Summary 6). Diplock LJ further said: 'It may be that if the highway authority could show that no amount of reasonable care on their part could have prevented the danger the common law defence of inevitable accident would be available to them . . .' It is submitted that this is correct.

That said, where the defendant positively asserts that it was unreasonable to have a system in place to detect the specific defect which caused the claimant's injury, the defendant must produce evidence to support that proposition. Thus, in *Atkins v Ealing LBC* [2006] EWHC 2515 (QB) (see Appendix B, Case Summary 22), where the claimant was injured on a tilting manhole cover, it was not sufficient (without evidence) for the defendant to say that loose or tilting manhole covers were so rare that it was unreasonable to expect highway authorities to have a specific system in place to detect them.

4.4.2   The s 58(2) criteria

Section 58(2) sets out a number of matters to which the court is to have regard in deciding whether or not the highway authority has made out the defence. Note that s 58(2) is mandatory; the court *must* have regard to these factors. Counsel's submissions should therefore be built around these factors. Note that the following s 58(2) criteria are not exhaustive: the court is entitled to consider all relevant matters.

4.4.2.1   *The character of the highway and the traffic which was reasonably to be expected to use it (s 58(2)(a))*

The point has already been made that rural footpaths need not be maintained to as high a standard as busy city pavements. Even if the reasoning of Nield J in *Bird* was right and can be extrapolated to the remote footpath cases, s 58(2)(a) lets the highway authority escape.

Highway authorities have to take their highways as they find them. They do not have to make them better, but they must ensure that they do not make them worse. If a road is particularly old or fragile, the authority must take that into account. It is not enough for the authority to prove that there was in place in respect of that road, a system of maintenance, inspection and repair which would have been perfectly reasonable for a normal road. If a road demands a higher standard of caretaking because of special circumstances which the authority should have known about, the authority must apply a higher standard. Relevant factors may include the age of the road, the fragility of its surface, the drainage, the fact that it daily accommodates thousands of juggernauts or the fact that it is used only once a year by a pony and trap. Thus in *Jacobs v Hampshire County Council*, (1984) *The Times*, 28 May (QBD) (see Appendix B, Case Summary 16), where a roadway was particularly susceptible to water penetration, 6-monthly inspections were inadequate. See also *Bramwell v Shaw* [1971] RTR 167 (Appendix B, Case Summary 15); *Sharpness New Docks and Gloucester and Birmingham Navigation Co v Att-Gen* [1915] AC 654 (Appendix B, Case Summary 3). See also the discussion at **4.2.3** above, where the distinction between maintenance and improvements is examined.

Highway authorities commonly say that proof of their compliance with the major guidelines on highway maintenance (for instance the 1989 Code of Practice published by the Local Authorities Association) means that the s 58 defence has been made out. As a matter of fact, that will generally be correct, but this does not follow inexorably as a matter of law. In *Rance v Essex County Council* (unreported), 21 February 1997, Otton LJ said:

> ' . . . it is true that the Code of Practice sets down stringent obligations upon highway authorities, but it must be borne in mind that they are recognised as guidelines only and do not impose a rigid regime for the inspection and maintenance of roads. It does not follow that a breach of the code, however technical, creates a situation of negligence on the part of the highway authority or, conversely, as Miss Mishcon seemed to suggest, deprives them of the benefit of [the s 58] defence even though such a breach was not causative of the accident complained of . . .'

4.4.2.2   The standard of maintenance appropriate for a highway of that character and used by such traffic (s 58(2)(b))

The remarks above concerning s 58(2)(a) apply equally to s 58(2)(b).

4.4.2.3   The state of repair in which a reasonable person would have expected to find the highway (s 58(2)(c))

Obviously this criterion overlaps to some extent with that of *prima facie* breach – reasonable foreseeability of danger. Reasonable people expect highways to be kept in a state where danger is not reasonably foreseeable.

It is submitted, in the absence of authority, that the knowledge to be accredited to the reasonable person in this context should be the knowledge actually possessed by the highway authority. As Sauvain points out (*Highway Law and Practice* (Sweet and Maxwell, 1989), para.5–34), to hold otherwise could produce some curious results. Sauvain cites the example of a highway authority which, using its special knowledge of a highway, deliberately and intelligently adopts a standard of maintenance lower than is appropriate. A reasonable observer without the highway authority's special knowledge might well consider the highway to be in an unpardonably poor state of repair.

4.4.2.4 *Whether the highway authority knew, or could reasonably have been expected to know, that the condition of the part of the highway to which the action relates was likely to cause danger to users of the highway (s 58(2)(d))*

The question of whether the authority 'could reasonably have known' is, in part, a question about the adequacy of the highway authority's inspection system. It is also a question of common sense. Thus in *McKenna v Scottish Omnibuses* (1984) 134 NLJ 681 (QBD), a highway authority was held not to be liable to a claimant who was injured when a coach in which he was travelling skidded on black ice. It was held that the black ice was a purely temporary phenomenon which, without fault on the part of the highway authority, had not come to the authority's notice until after the accident. It would not be reasonable to expect the highway authority to patrol the district with a lorry full of warning signs whenever the temperature fell to near freezing, testing the co-efficients of friction on the roads.

However, where a local authority can predict the manner in which changes to the highway are likely to occur, it may be faced with increased difficulties when attempting to establish the s 58 defence. Thus in *West Sussex County Council v Sarah Caroline Russell* (see also **4.1.1** above), in circumstances where the safety of the highway required the verge to be level with the carriageway, the defendant should have known that a lower verge (caused by topsoil becoming more compact) was likely to be a danger to passing traffic.

In theory, the total absence of a system of inspection is not conclusive evidence of a breach of statutory duty (see *Whitaker v West Yorkshire Metropolitan County Council and Metropolitan Borough of Calderdale* [1982] CLY 1435 (Appendix B, Case Summary 17)). But highway authorities should not pin much hope on *Whitaker*; the decision not only confused what the claimant must prove with what the highway authority can raise in its defence, but it implied a standard of inspection and maintenance much lower than that which has generally been found necessary to absolve the highway authority.

The leading case on regularity of inspection is *Pridham v Hemel Hempstead Corporation* (1970) 69 LGR 523 (see Appendix B, Case Summary 14), in which it was decided that:

(a) if a highway authority has, after sufficiently careful consideration, adopted a system of maintenance and inspection, which includes checking the complaints book, and the system has been implemented, the authority has made out the s 58(2) defence;

(b) the statutory defence is based on reasonableness and not practicability. The trial judge had found that it was practicable for the highway inspector to examine the road in question more frequently than the defendant highway authority had considered reasonable, and had concluded from this that the defendant was liable. The Court of Appeal held that this was wrong. If the inspection regime was reasonable (and of course if it was in fact carried out), the defendant had made out the statutory defence;

(c)   expert evidence from an engineer was not necessarily essential for the court to be able to decide whether the interval between inspections was reasonable;

(d)   the court could be satisfied about the reasonableness of the decision-making process from an examination of the highway authority's minutes.

The comments in *Pridham* about how essential expert evidence is should, in today's culture of proportionality, be ignored. The (unusual) evidence in *Pridham* was that the relevant danger to pedestrians arose not from normal wear and tear to the footpath, but from unpredictable damage such as that caused by oil or acid spillage, deliberate damage or vehicles mounting the kerb. In most cases the highway authority will not have been able to make a reasonable decision about its inspection and maintenance regime without expert engineering advice about the fragility of the highway concerned. This advice should be before the court in the form of evidence from the engineer concerned so that the court can decide whether the conclusion which the highway authority came to was a reasonable one. It is unlikely to be reasonable to call independent engineering evidence to comment on what the highway authority's engineer has said.

The decision in *Pridham* turns many tripping cases into cases akin to judicial review. A crucial question in each case will be 'did the highway authority make a reasonable decision about what the system should be?' This will often be impossible to judge without examining how the decision-makers arrived at their conclusion. That may well mean examining critically the minutes of the highway authority. It is unclear whether the test to be applied is the *Wednesbury* one ('is this a conclusion to which no reasonable authority could have come?'); or one which demands rather more of the highway authority.

For examples of cases illustrating the court's approach to what constitutes adequate inspection, see *Whiting v Hillingdon London Borough Council* (1970) 68 LGR 437 (Appendix B, Case Summary 17); *Papworth v Mayor of Battersea* [1916] 1 KB 583 (Appendix B, Case Summary 18); *Whitaker v West Yorkshire Metropolitan County Council and Metropolitan Borough of Calderdale* [1982] CLY 1435 (Appendix B, Case Summary 20); *Birmingham v East Ham Corporation* (1961) 60 LGR 111 (Appendix B, Case Summary 21); and *Tarrant v Rowlands* [1979] RTR 144 (Appendix B,

Case Summary 24); *Rowe v Herman* [2000] CL 4243; *Garside v Bradford & Northern Housing Association Ltd* [2001] CL Nov; *Dingley v Bromley LBC* [2000] CL 4244; *Allen v Elmbridge BC* [1999] LGR 65.

It is now common for highway authorities to publish details of their inspection regimes, and in any event there is no difficulty obtaining these when an accident is being investigated. Most adopted the *Local Authority Association Code of Practice for Highway Maintenance*, 1989. It has been modernised by *Delivering Value in Highway Maintenance: Code of Practice for Maintenance Management*. The Codes contain criteria for grading the dangerousness of particular defects, and it specifies the urgency with which various types of defects should be repaired. While the courts have refused to adopt strict criteria for determining actionable dangerousness (rejecting the 'One inch rule', for example), it is often useful to see if the highway authority has met the standard it has set itself. A highway authority hoisted by its own petard is a highway authority which quietly writes a cheque.

An issue of increasing importance is whether the impecuniosity of a highway authority is a defence. Can an authority escape liability by asserting that it could not afford to do more by way of maintenance and repair than it in fact did, and that accordingly what it did satisfies the reasonableness criterion of s 58? It is submitted that the answer is no. The clear words of s 58(1) decree that, to be absolved from responsibility, the authority must prove that it took such care as in all the circumstances *was reasonably required* to secure that the relevant part of the highway was not dangerous. If the authority did not take such care as was reasonably required to make the highway safe, then the reasons why it did not, or could not, take such care are wholly irrelevant.

It should therefore never be necessary for the court to examine the way in which the budget for highway maintenance was drawn up and spent. Nor should it ever be necessary for an injured claimant to pursue the authority (which might not be the highway authority) which allocated the funds to the highway authority, contending that its decision to give the highway authority inadequate funds was reached negligently.

But an impecunious highway authority, found liable for failing to carry out repairs or maintenance which it could not afford, could arguably bite the hand that inadequately fed it – the authority which funds it – in Pt 20 proceedings for negligent decision-making.

4.4.2.5 *Where the highway authority could not reasonably have been expected to repair that part of the highway before the cause of action arose, what warning notices of its condition had been displayed (s 58(2)(e))*

Whether the highway authority's delay from the time it knew about the need for repairs is reasonable is a question to be decided after consideration of all relevant factors. These will include the magnitude of the defect, the amount of traffic using the stretch of highway concerned, and the danger posed by the defect. Obviously the greater the danger, the less tolerant of delay the court will be. In the course of serious defects, warning notices will be expected, (see *Morris v Thyssen (GB) Ltd*, unreported, but see 1983 Halsbury's Abridgement para 2418, (Appendix B, Case Summary 19)). The test of the adequacy of those notices will probably be akin to the corresponding test under the Occupiers' Liability Act 1957 – are the notices sufficient to enable road users to proceed in reasonable safety?

4.4.3   Independent contractors

The final part of s 58(2) states:

> ' . . . for the purposes of (the statutory) defence it is not relevant to prove that the highway authority had arranged for a competent person to carry out or supervise the maintenance of the part of the highway to which the action relates unless it is also proved that the authority had given him proper instructions with regard to the maintenance of the highway and that he had carried out the instructions.'

This section has the effect of giving statutory force to the common law rule that an authority which has been given a statutory duty to perform cannot escape liability for breach of the statutory duty by pleading the tort of an independent contractor engaged by the authority to carry out the statutory works (see *Hill v Tottenham Urban District Council* (1898) 79 LT 495; *Hardaker v Idle Urban District Council* [1896] 1 QB 356, (Appendix B, Case Summary 26)).

A claimant injured as a result of a breach of statutory duty is therefore at little risk of picking the wrong defendant. He should sue the highway authority. The claimant does not have to go to the trouble of finding out the identity, and the role in highway maintenance, of independent contractors.

But the claimant will have to make enquiries of this kind if he has been injured by negligence on the part of an independent contractor which is collateral to the vicarious performance of the statutory duty. The highway authority, as discussed in Chapter 1, will not be liable for such collateral negligence (*Dalton v Agnes* (1881) 6 App Cas 740). If there is no doubt about whether or not the negligence is collateral, both the highway authority and the independent contractor should be joined as defendants.

If the highway authority has engaged independent contractors who have failed to perform the works properly, the highway authority should consider Pt 20 proceedings against the contractors. Part 20 proceedings are likely to fail if the highway authority has not given the contractor proper instructions; and succeed if proper instructions were given but not carried out.

4.5   COMMON LAW DEFENCES

The statutory defence specifically does not exclude common law defences.

4.5.1   Contributory negligence

Contributory negligence is not, properly speaking, a defence, but it is a valid riposte in an action for breach of statutory duty (see *Caswell v Powell Duffry* [1939] 3 All ER 722 (HL) and the express words of HA 1980, s 58(1)). In practice, it is always pleaded by the highway authority in tripping cases, generally along the lines of 'He failed to look where he was going'. A deduction is occasionally made for contributory negligence, but on the reported authorities, highway authorities have little reason to feel confident about the plea. *Stowell v Railway Executive* [1949] 2 KB 519 (see Appendix B, Case Summary 31) sets out the standard which is expected of pedestrians. See also **4.2.2** above, and **5.3.6**.

4.5.2   Inevitable accident or act of God

It has been submitted above (at **4.4.1**) that Diplock LJ was correct in saying in *Griffiths v Liverpool Corporation* that the defence of inevitable accident could be invoked by a highway authority. Extreme weather conditions or a natural disaster may also defeat an action (see *Nicholas v Marsland* (1876) 2 Ex D 1 (a cloudburst)).

4.5.3   Act of a third party

If the claimant is injured as a result of the road subsiding suddenly because it has been undermined by a third party, the highway authority will not be liable to the claimant if the damage could not reasonably have been discovered in the time available. If the damage could be repaired by the highway authority, and sufficient time has elapsed since the subsidence for it to have been reasonable for the highway authority to repair the defect, the highway authority will be liable to the claimant, and should consider Pt 20 proceedings against the underminer. If the damage is such which could not be repaired by the highway authority, but could and should have been discovered, it is arguable that the highway authority would not be liable for a breach of the s 41 duty, but would be liable for causing or permitting a highway nuisance (by failing to fence off or highlight the defect), or in negligence.

4.5.4   Volenti non fit injuria

In practice, the doctrine of *volenti non fit injuria* has little relevance to normal tripping cases. It is impossible to imagine circumstances in which a pedestrian would consent to the poor maintenance and repair of the road. The plea may conceivably be relevant in cases of abnormal use of the highway, for instance when a skateboarder deliberately makes use of the defective part of the highway in order to perform more interesting stunts.

4.6   EVIDENCE

The collection and handling of evidence are discussed in Chapter 10. Obviously the following are important:

–   whether the highway in question is maintainable at the public expense: If not, by whom it is maintainable;

–   the size of the defect;

–   the shape of the defect;

–   the exact location of the defect;

–   the length of time that the defect has been present;

–   the nature, size and position of other nearby defects;

–   the weather conditions at the time of the accident;

–   detailed weather reports if the allegations include a failure adequately to clear snow, ice or water;

–   weather forecasts for the relevant period, again if failure to respond adequately or at all to such forecasts is to be alleged;

–   the time when the accident occurred;

–   the lighting of the *locus in quo*;

–   the manner in which the potential claimant was proceeding down the street;

– any disability which the potential claimant had;

– any complaint made about the incident by the claimant to the highway authority;

– any previous or subsequent complaints made by anybody in respect of the defect in question and/or the condition of the highway in general;

– the action, if any, specifically taken on such complaints;

– the records of inspection of the highway for five years before the accident;

– the records of maintenance of the highway for five years before the accident;

– the minutes of the meetings of the highway authority during which the inspection and maintenance policies were formulated;

– the claimant's medical records (both hospital and general practitioners' records);

– engineering reports relating to the state of the highway in question and the maintenance/repair appropriate.

Practitioners should remember the disapproval expressed by the courts of attempts to define, in terms of inches of defect, when a highway authority's liability can be assumed. Thus the mere fact that floodwater collected on a road after heavy rain is not in itself evidence of a breach of the s 41 duty or of negligence (*Pritchard v Clwyd County Council, The Times*, July 16, 1992). See also *Burnside v Emerson* [1968] 1 WLR 1490 (Appendix B, Case Summary 23).

CHAPTER 5

NEGLIGENCE

5.1 INTRODUCTION

If the tort of negligence features in a highway tripping case, it is usually the negligence of a statutory undertaker or contractor which is alleged. But there are exceptions. In particular there are two other categories of potential defendant. They are:

(1) the occupiers of premises upon which accidents occur; and

(2) persons responsible for accidents other than as occupiers.

5.2 DEFENDANTS OTHER THAN HIGHWAY AUTHORITIES

5.2.1 Occupiers

In practice, negligence is always pleaded as a cause of action against occupiers as an alternative to the statutory cause of action under the Occupiers' Liability Acts (see Chapter 7). This is a tactically sensible thing to do, because in some cases the claimant may not be able to satisfy the court that the defendant is an occupier. But 'occupation' is rarely in dispute, and if it is not, probably the common duty of care under s 2 of the Occupiers' Liability Act 1957, and the duty of care owed to trespassers under s 1 of the Occupiers' Liability Act 1984, are co-extensive with the common law duty of care in negligence. The liability of occupiers is discussed more fully in Chapter 7, which deals with these Acts.

5.2.2 Hybrid situations

Cases often arise, especially in the workplace, where a person is injured by the negligence of an employee of the occupier. Very often these cases can be pleaded against the occupier as straightforward occupiers' liability cases. Sometimes (and especially where the action rather than the inaction of an employee is responsible for the accident), it will make more sense to frame the case in terms of employers' liability in negligence, or breach of one of the multitude of statutory duties imposed on employers. Thus if a claimant trips over a rod which is being pulled across a factory walkway by a workmate, the claim could be expressed in a number of ways:

(a)   as a claim in negligence against the employer, who will be vicariously liable for the negligence of his employee, so long as the rod-pulling of the negligent employee was not wholly unrelated to his work;

(b)   as a claim under the Occupiers' Liability Act 1957. Such a claim may have force if there was evidence that rods frequently had to be pulled across this walkway because there was no alternative route;

(c)   as a claim for breach of statutory duty under s 28 and/or s 29 of the Factories Act 1961 (in a very elderly case), or under the Workplace (Health, Safety and Welfare) Regulations 1992.

5.2.3   Persons other than occupiers

In the rod-pulling example given above, the employee who was pulling the rod is unlikely himself to be the occupier, but he could be liable to his workmate in negligence. The injured worker would of course be well advised to sue his employer instead, simply because he will have a much better chance of executing any judgment in his favour. But the fact that the employer is also vicariously liable does not mean that the liability of the primary tortfeasor evaporates. And if the employer serves Part 20 proceedings on the negligent employee, that employee will be bound to reimburse the vicariously liable employer for the damages paid out on his behalf (*Lister v Romford Ice and Cold Storage Co Ltd* [1957] AC 555).

The special position of landlords so far as liability in negligence to tenants and third parties is concerned is discussed in Chapter 8.

5.2.4   Statutory undertakers

Statutory undertakers performing works on highways will be liable in negligence for injury resulting from the negligent execution of their statutory powers to do the work, or from the negligent performance of the works themselves. Thus if injury results from a failure to consider carefully:

(a)   the place where a statutory power will be exercised; or

(b)   the manner of its exercise; or

(c)   the way in which subsequent maintenance and use of whatever had been created under the statutory power will be carried out, an action will lie against the undertaker (see *McClelland v Manchester Corporation* [1912] 1 KB 118; *Manchester Corporation v Farnworth* [1930] AC 171).

If an undertaker interfering with a highway does not take reasonable care to ensure that the public are not injured by the works carried out under the statutory power, it will be liable in damages to a claimant so injured (see *Holliday v National Telephone Co* [1899] 2 QB 392 (laying of telephone wires); *Scott v Manchester Corporation* (1857) 2 H & N 204 (gas mains)).

If works done under statute result in the creation of a thing, the thing created must, usually, be maintained by its creator (see Chapter 1). It is submitted that this is an example of continuing statutory duty rather than negligence, and should be pleaded as such. In considering the continuing obligation to maintain, the decisions which relate to the highway authority's duty to maintain apply by analogy. Thus the undertaker will not be liable unless the defect in question is dangerous (see *Cohen v British Gas Corporation* [1978] CLY 2053 (Appendix B, Case Summary 43)). The general standard of care in maintaining and inspecting required of highway authorities under HA 1980, s 41 applies equally to statutory undertakers (see *Wells v Metropolitan Water Board* [1937] 4 All ER 639 (Appendix B, Case Summary 44); *Manchester Corporation v Markland* [1936] AC 360 (Appendix B, Case Summary 45); *Reid v British Telecommunications plc*, (1987) *The Times*, June 27 (Appendix B, Case Summary 46); *Longhurst v Metropolitan Water Board* [1948] 2 All ER 834 (Appendix B, Case Summary 47)).

The creators of statutory works may be liable for injury caused if the thing created is used negligently. It is arguable, for instance, that a railway authority which causes or permits water to drop onto a highway from one of its bridges is liable in damages to a claimant who slips on the verdigris which results (see *Great Western Railway Co v Bishop* (1872) LR 7 QB 550). It is submitted that this is an example not of continuing statutory duty, but of negligence, although both should be pleaded.

Independent contractors engaged by the highway authority to do maintenance works on the highway are discussed in Chapter 1.

For a remarkable case which should encourage the joinder by statutory undertakers of highway authorities (and vice versa) in the most improbable circumstances in the hope of getting a contribution, see *Nolan v Merseyside CC and North West Water Authority* (unreported), 17 July 1982, CA (see Appendix B, Case Summary 28).

5.2.5   The care people can be expected to take of themselves

In the absence of special knowledge about particular dangers or likelihood of danger, the law does not expect people to be looking down at their feet all the time; nor does it expect people to walk sedately all the time. For a discussion of what amounts to reasonable pedestrian behaviour, see **4.2.2** above and *Stowell v Railway Executive* [1949] 2 KB 519 (Appendix B, Case Summary 31).

5.3   NEGLIGENCE OF HIGHWAY AUTHORITIES

5.3.1   Pleading negligence

Cases of injury resulting from failure to maintain can be pleaded as cases of negligence, but, with the important caveat discussed at **5.3.4** below and Chapter 1, there will rarely be any point. Negligence and the s 41 duty relate to one another like negligence and the common duty of care under the Occupiers' Liability Act 1957. That there is no heresy in asserting such concurrent liability appears in the dictum of Lord Greene MR in *Hale v Hants & Dorset Motor Services Ltd* [1947] 2 All ER 628 where, in the context of a claim under the Road Improvement Act 1925, he said: ' . . . It does not appear to me to matter very much whether the action is regarded as an action based on breach of statutory duty or merely on nuisance or negligence at common law . . .'.

Note, though, that where a failure to maintain street furniture has caused injury, it has been held that the s 41 duty does not apply: see *Shine v Tower Hamlets LBC* [2006] EWCA Civ 852; at **4.2.6**). There the claimant, who was injured on a poorly maintained bollard, successfully brought his action in negligence, which was pleaded in the alternative to a s 41 claim.

5.3.2   Negligent performance of maintenance works

When a highway authority, in order to discharge its statutory duty to maintain the highway, itself undertakes works on a highway, it will be liable in negligence for injury caused in the course of the works by the negligent manner of performing those works. If, for example, a highway authority fails adequately to fence round an area of excavated highway upon which works are being performed, the highway authority will be liable in negligence to a claimant who is injured as a result of that failure to fence.

If it could be shown that the works which caused the injury were themselves necessitated by a previous failure on the part of the highway authority to discharge its statutory duty to maintain, it is submitted that there would be concurrent liability in negligence and for breach of the s 41 duty.

If a highway authority interferes with a highway, it is bound to reinstate it to its original condition, and will be liable for any subsequent deterioration of the reinstated section (see *Newsome v Darton Urban District Council* [1938] 3 All ER 93 (Appendix B, Case Summary 39)).

Highway authorities will also be liable in negligence for the later consequences of negligent performance. In *Capper and Lamb v Department of the Environment* [1984] 4 NIJB the defendant road authority had undertaken works to improve a road and in the course of those works had closed up a drain. As a result of this closure water accumulated on the road. The water froze, and the claimant lorry was damaged when it skidded on the ice which formed. It was held that the defendant was negligent in closing the drain and failing to make gullies or gratings to provide an escape route for the water.

5.3.3   Independent contractors

Where the highway authority engages an independent contractor to do the works necessary to discharge the authority's s 41 duty, the distinction between collateral negligence and negligence relating to essential parts of the maintenance work becomes crucial. This distinction and its consequences are dealt with in Chapter 1.

5.3.4   Negligent decision-making resulting in personal injury

It may sometimes be necessary or tactically wise for a claimant to allege that a local highway authority has been negligent in a decision-making process and that by such negligence he has suffered injury.

5.3.4.1   *Policy decisions and operational decisions*

The distinction between policy and operational decisions is old and very convenient. It was famously frowned on by Lord Hoffmann in *Stovin v Wise and Norfolk County Council* [1996] AC 923 (see Appendix B, Case Summary 34): but has gradually crept back into fashion: see *Phelps v Hillingdon London Borough Council* [2001] 2 AC 619, per Lord Clyde at 673; *Barrett v Enfield London Borough Council* [2001] 2 AC 550, per Lord Hutton at 586.

There is often prolonged and legitimate argument about whether a particular decision is a policy or an operational one, but once a decision is allocated to the right category, the legal consequences are fairly clear. A policy decision cannot be challenged unless it is unreasonable in the public law, *Wednesbury* sense. Operational decisions can be criticised using the ordinary rules of negligence.

An allegation that it was negligent to fail to exercise a statutory power is plainly an allegation of a negligent policy decision. This is squarely within *Stovin v Wise*. To succeed, a claimant must show (per Lord Hoffmann in *Stovin* at 953):

(a)   that it would have been irrational not to have exercised the power; and

(b)   that there are 'exceptional grounds for holding that the policy of the statute requires compensation to be given to persons who suffer loss because this power was not exercised'.

Criterion (a) is legally straightforward: it is familiar public law territory, but it is a hard criterion to satisfy.

Highway authorities classically rely on arguments about the funding of their many competing priorities: those arguments are often difficult or impossible to contradict.

Criterion (b) is legally much more difficult. The main 'exceptional ground' identified in *Stovin* was 'general reliance'. There are few mistier concepts in the entire law of England. Lord Hoffmann said, in *Stovin* at 954, that 'general reliance':

> ' . . . appears to refer to general expectations in the community, which the individual plaintiff may or may not have shared. A widespread assumption that a statutory power will be exercised may affect the general pattern of economic and social behaviour. For example, insurance premiums may take into account the expectation that statutory powers of inspection or accident prevention will ordinarily prevent certain kinds of risk from materialising. Thus the doctrine of general reliance requires an inquiry into the role of a given statutory power in the behaviour of members of the general public . . .'

This second criterion will arguably be met in many cases involving injury on roads. Winter maintenance cases are a classic example. Highway authorities have a statutory power to grit roads. There is certainly a general expectation that they will use that power. Unfortunately that general expectation does not seem to be shared by High Court judges.

Generally, claimants who cannot force their claims within HA 1980 should not be optimistic. *Stovin* is likely to frustrate them. A good example is *Sandhar v Department of Transport, Environment and the Regions* [2004] EWHC 28 (Appendix B, Case Summary 35). Here the claimant, trying to circumvent *Goodes* (above), contended that the highway authority was under a common law duty to remove ice from roads within its area, or prevent ice forming. The judge concluded that there was no such duty.

5.3.4.2   The effect of s 39 of the Road Traffic Act 1988

This provides, *inter alia*:

'(2)   Each local authority must prepare and carry out a programme of
measures designed to promote road safety and may make
contributions towards the cost of measures for promoting road safety
taken by other authorities or bodies.

(3)   Without prejudice to the generality of subsection (2) above, in
pursuance of their duty under that subsection each local authority –

(a)   must carry out studies into accidents arising out of the use of
vehicles on roads or parts of roads, other than trunk roads,
within their area,

(b)   must, in the light of those studies, take such measures as appear
to the authority to be appropriate to prevent such accidents,
including the dissemination of information and advice relating
to the use of roads, the giving of practical training to road users
or any class or description of road users, the construction,
improvement, maintenance or repair of roads for which they are
the highway authority (in Scotland, local roads authority) and
other measures taken in the exercise of their powers for
controlling, protecting or assisting the movement of traffic on
roads . . .'

The mandatory words of this section look, at first blush, hopeful for
claimants. The highway authority must take steps to avoid accidents. But
the words in subs (3) 'as appear to the authority to be appropriate . . .'
have lead the courts to construe the subsection as conferring a power
rather than imposing a duty: see *Gorringe v Calderdale MBC* [2004]
UKHL (Appendix B, Case Summary 35); *Larner v Solihull MBC* [2001]
RTR 469.

Once we are in the realm of powers rather than duties, *Stovin* tends to give
the kiss of death to claims.

5.3.5   Land not forming part of the highway

In *Stovin v Wise*, above, the House of Lords held that a highway authority
did have power to remove a dangerous obstruction near a road, but, as
discussed in detail above, that the preconditions to a private law right of
action in relation to non-performance were not established. This is likely
to be the case for most land not forming part of the highway.

5.3.6   Contributory negligence

As has been noted, contributory negligence is only occasionally
significant (see **4.5.1**). Generally speaking, pedestrians are not expected to
look 'down at the ground at every step they take' (*Stowell v Railway
Executive* [1949] 2 All ER 193, at 196).

However, where some degree of fault can be imparted upon the claimant, it is possible that a finding of contributory negligence may be made against him, although obviously the likelihood of such a finding turns upon the facts of the case.

Where a claimant has consumed a substantial amount of alcohol prior to the tripping accident, thereby adversely affecting his balance and judgment a finding of contributory negligence was viewed as being 'inevitable'. (See *Jonathan Harvey v Plymouth City Council* (unreported) 13 November 2009, QBD, at para 63.) The trial judge held the claimant to be 75% responsible, after he ran into a dark area and tripped over a fence while intoxicated.

If the claimant knows of a specific tripping/slipping risk, which then later causes their accident, there is a risk of a finding of contributory negligence being made against him. In the rather unfortunate case of *Susan Ellis v Bristol City Council* [2007] EWCA Civ 685, a care worker slipped on a patch of urine created by an incontinent resident. Most of the residents at the care home were incontinent, and so the claimant knew of the potential risk materialising. She had been warned of the danger (by way of a specific notice in the staff room) and could have kept 'a special look out [in the areas] where there was an increased risk of a hazard' (per Smith LJ at para 52). The claimant was held to be one-third responsible.

The Court of Appeal took a similar approach in *Wells v Mutchmeats and another* (unreported) 28 February 2006, CA), where a meat inspector tripped when he stepped into a tray of disinfectant in an abattoir during the nationwide outbreak of foot and mouth disease. A deduction was made of 40% in respect of contributory negligence. At paragraph 17, Gage LJ emphasised that this was 'not a standard tripping case'. The claimant had been specifically tasked with checking that the amount of disinfectant in the trays was appropriate. He should have known that the trays were liable to move if he stepped into them.

CHAPTER 6

NUISANCE

6.1 INTRODUCTION

Nuisance is out of fashion. As the tort of negligence has expanded, so nuisance has contracted. It has always tended to be a tort whose justification was the inadequacy of others. It is classically added in highway tripping claims as a make-weight: it is rarely the subject of detailed argument.

But since *Stovin* continues to maintain its grip on the law relating to the exercise of statutory powers, and since there is continued uncertainty about liability for winter maintenance cases despite s 41(1A) of HA 1980, nuisance is sometimes worth remembering.

The statutory nuisance provisions under HA 1980 are the most promising. Section 150 was considered at **4.3.4**; s 130 is considered below. But beneath the statutes there slumbers the law of public nuisance. It might wake up and do some good soon.

Private nuisance is mentioned here only for the sake of completeness. A private nuisance is an interference with a right of enjoyment of land. The claimant must have a right in the land. Only very occasionally will private nuisance feature in tripping cases. When it does, it is usually in the context of suits by tenants against landlords. Some of these possibilities are raised in Chapters 7 and 8.

Public nuisance is much more important in tripping cases. A public nuisance is a nuisance which materially affects the reasonable comfort and convenience of life of a class of Her Majesty's subjects who come within its sphere of influence (*Att-Gen v PYA Quarries Ltd* [1957] 2 QB 169 at 184). The remainder of this chapter is devoted to public nuisance.

6.2 THE 'CLASS' QUALIFICATION

So far as tripping cases on highways are concerned, pedestrians, as road users, constitute a 'class' within the meaning of the definition above. Whether membership of a class is established in other cases depends on the facts. In practice the point is rarely taken by defendants, and the courts are quick to infer membership for would-be claimants.

6.3   PUBLIC NUISANCE ON A HIGHWAY

A public nuisance on a highway involves an act or omission which prevents the convenient use of the way of passengers (per Byles J in *R v Mathias* (1861) 2 F & F 570). It can arise in two ways:

(a)   by an act or omission which makes the highway dangerous or less convenient for public passage (see *Dymond v Pearce* [1972] 1 QB 496 (Appendix B, Case Summary 58));

(b)   by the tortfeasor causing or permitting an unreasonable obstruction to the highway. The unreasonableness can consist of duration or degree or both (see *Harper v Haden & Sons Ltd* [1933] Ch 298 (Appendix B, Case Summary 56), and *Trevett v Lee* [1955] 1 WLR 113 (Appendix B, Case Summary 57)).

The distinction between these categories is blurred. In tripping cases the courts will almost always be working in the relatively uncharted no-man's land between them.

6.4   PARTIES TO AN ACTION

Anyone who is in a class as defined in **6.2** above who has suffered special damage caused by the nuisance can sue. Where no special damage is alleged the Attorney-General can bring proceedings in public nuisance; and so, by virtue of HA 1980, s 130(5), can the highway authority.

Anyone who has caused or authorised or continued or adopted a nuisance may be sued.

The meaning of 'caused' gives few problems. A person will be liable for a nuisance created by his independent contractor if he could reasonably have foreseen that the work he instructed the contractor to do was likely to result in a nuisance (see *Bower v Peate* (1876) 1 QBD 321; *Spicer v Smee* [1946] 1 All ER 489). In other words, he will be deemed to have caused the nuisance.

The meaning of 'authorised', other than in the context of an independent contractor, gives difficulties mainly in the area of landlord and tenant relations. This is discussed in Chapter 8. In the case of independent contractors, an act has been 'caused' if it has been authorised.

The meanings of 'continued' and 'adopted' were established by the House of Lords in *Sedleigh-Denfield v O'Callaghan* [1940] AC 880. An occupier of land 'continues' a nuisance if, with knowledge or presumed knowledge of its existence, he fails to take reasonable means to bring it to an end when he has ample time to do so. He has a duty to take such steps as in all the circumstances are reasonable, to prevent or minimise any risk, of which he knew or ought to have known, of injury or damage to suitably qualified claimants. See *Leakey v National Trust for Places of Historical Interest or Natural Beauty* [1980] QB 485 for a general summary of the nature of the duty (Appendix B, Case Summary 54).

An occupier 'adopts' a nuisance if he makes any use of the 'erection, building, bank or artificial contrivance' which constitutes the nuisance.

6.5 HIGHWAY NUISANCES

6.5.1 The highway authority's duty to abate nuisance

At common law, the obvious potential defendant in most cases is the highway authority, which has a common law duty to abate highway nuisances (see *Bagshaw v Buxton Local Board of Health* (1875) 1 Ch D 220).

Section 130 of HA 1980 states, inter alia:

'(1) It is the duty of the highway authority to assert and protect the rights of the public to the use and enjoyment of any highway for which they are the highway authority, including any roadside waste which forms part of it.

(2) . . .

(3) Without prejudice to [subsection (1)] above, it is the duty of a council who are a highway authority to prevent, as far as possible, the stopping up or obstruction of –

    (a) the highways for which they are the highway authority, and

    (b) any highway for which they are not the highway authority, if, in their opinion, the stopping up or obstruction of that highway would be prejudicial to the interests of their area.

(4) Without prejudice to the foregoing provisions of this section, it is the duty of a local highway authority to prevent any unlawful encroachment on any roadside waste comprised in a highway for which they are the highway authority.'

Section 130 thus imposes a statutory duty on the highway authority to prevent highway nuisances. Although it is unusual to see the causing or permitting of a public nuisance pleaded as a breach of statutory duty under s 130, it is submitted that it is technically correct to frame the cause of action in these terms, further or in the alternative to the ordinary nuisance pleading (see Appendix A.18).

'Roadside waste' may include strips of grass bordering the metalled part of a main road (see *Curtis v Kesteven County Council* (1890) 45 Ch D 504).

Note that the growth of vegetation off the highway which obscures the highway or pushes pedestrians over towards dangers amounts to an obstruction rather than rendering the highway out of repair: see *Thompson v Hampshire County Council* [2004] EWCA Civ 1016.

6.5.2   Owners of adjoining land

Under some circumstances the owners of land adjoining the highway can be liable in public nuisance. This matter is discussed in Chapter 1, and, in so far as it relates to landlords, in Chapter 8. Generally, there is no duty to fence off dangers adjoining the highway unless the danger is so close to the highway that a highway user might step inadvertently off the highway into the danger (*Caseley v Bristol Corporation* [1944] 1 All ER 14 (see Appendix B, Case Summary 53)).

6.5.3   Privately maintainable highways

Where a highway is privately maintainable, it is submitted that the person or body responsible for maintenance stands in the same position vis-à-vis potential claimants, so far as liability in public nuisance is concerned, as highway authorities in the case of highways maintainable at the public expense.

6.5.3.1   *Obstruction*

A claimant who contends that the highway was dangerous does not have to contend that the danger resulted from an obstruction on the highway (see *Almeroth v Chivers* [1948] 1 All ER 53 (Appendix B, Case Summary 60)). A great deal of judicial energy has been expended on this point (see, for instance, *Dymond v Pearce* [1972] 1 QB 496 (CA) (Appendix B, Case Summary 58)). The result has been that the cause of action can fall into either (a) or (b) set out in **6.3** above.

But, if the case is in fact based on the existence in the highway of an unreasonable obstruction, it will be necessary to prove not only the obstruction, but that the highway was dangerous as a result. The requirement of reasonable foreseeability must be met.

6.5.3.2   *Unreasonableness*

Establishing unreasonableness is crucial, and is the feature common to the two categories of action. For an obstruction to trigger liability it must be unreasonable. The 'dangerousness' criteria has been defined separately by the judges, but it is submitted that this criteria is only applicable to cases which have already passed the first test of unreasonable. It is not reasonable to cause or permit dangerous things in or on the highway. It is submitted that if there was anything which affected passage along a highway and which was neither dangerous nor an obstruction, but was unreasonable, the courts would find it to be a public nuisance.

Whether something is unreasonable is a question of fact and degree. The purpose for which the interference was created, any benefits which result from it, its size and duration, the identity of the person or body causing the interference, and the existence and degree of any fault may all be relevant.

6.5.3.3   Negligence

In theory, it is not necessary to prove negligence to establish public nuisance. This has been repeatedly emphasised by the courts (see, for instance, *Farrell v John Mowlem & Co Ltd* [1954] 1 Lloyd's Rep 437 and the judgment of Lord Reid in *The Wagon Mound (No 2)* [1967] 1 AC 617 (Appendix B, Case Summary 55)). But there are persuasive authorities which suggest the contrary (see, for example, *British Road Services v Slater* [1964] 1 WLR 498 (Appendix B, Case Summary 61) per Lord Parker CJ; *Maitland v Raisbeck & RT & J Hewitt Ltd* [1944] KB 689 (Appendix B, Case Summary 59) per Lord Greene MR at 691; and *Hudson v Bray* [1917] 1 KB 520).

It is nevertheless submitted that the law is clear – fault is not required. The authorities are easily reconciled. The cases which have suggested that fault is an element of public nuisance have all turned on the question of unreasonableness, and it is clear that fault is a relevant factor in deciding whether an obstruction (for instance) is unreasonable. The useful rule of thumb that nuisance requires fault is wrong as a proposition of substantive law, but unimpeachable as a statement of the evidence which will be required to make out the tort of nuisance. It is submitted that in so far as any authority suggests that fault should be elevated from the status of a relevant factor to an essential ingredient, it would not now be followed. In practice, as Lord Reid pointed out in *The Wagon Mound (No 2)* [1967] 1 AC 617 (Appendix B, Case Summary 55), it will be rare for there to be liability in public nuisance without some kind of fault. This is partly due to the confused dove-tailing of issues of fault and foreseeability, which is considered next.

6.5.3.4   Foreseeability

In *The Wagon Mound (No 2)*, inflammable oil had been discharged into Sydney harbour. The oil had ignited, damaging by fire the claimant's ships. The Privy Council held that the defendants were liable in nuisance. The case relates directly to highway nuisances, since it was about creating dangers to persons or property in navigable waters, which Lord Reid expressly said were 'equivalent to a highway'. He went on to say that although negligence in the strict sense was not necessary to establish nuisance, 'fault of some kind is almost always necessary and fault generally involves foreseeability . . .' It is not clear from the judgment whether he regarded fault or foreseeability as the vital ingredient. He said that they generally came together. There followed, at p 640, a passage of equivocation from which the law of nuisance has never recovered:

> 'It could not be right to discriminate between different cases of nuisance so as to make foreseeability a necessary element in determining damages in those cases where it is a necessary element in determining liability, but not in others. So the choice is between it being a necessary element in all cases or in none. In their Lordships' judgment the similarities between nuisance and other forms of tort to which *The Wagon Mound (No.1)* applies far outweigh any differences, and they must therefore hold that the judgment appealed from is wrong on this branch of the case. It is not sufficient that the injury suffered by the respondents' vessel was the direct result of the nuisance if that injury was in the relevant sense unforeseeable.'

As an expression of a legal axiom, Lord Reid's formulation is dismal. As a practitioner's advice on evidence, it is invaluable.

The Court of Appeal agreed with Lord Reid. In *Dymond v Pearce*, above and Appendix B, Case Summary 58, Sachs LJ, at 503, emphasised, uncontentiously, that a claimant who failed in negligence would only rarely succeed in nuisance. The reason is that ' . . . only rarely will that which was found not to be a foreseeable cause of an accident also be found to have been in law the actual cause of it'.

Although the law is not at all clear, the consequence for tripping cases is. It is difficult indeed to think of situations where it would not have been foreseeable that the thing which caused the accident could have done just that. For the liability in nuisance to be established, it must be shown that the danger or obstruction in fact caused the special damage complained of. When assessing foreseeability of damage, the focus is almost invariably on some kind of fault, if not negligence itself. In practice, if a claimant cannot prove fault on the part of the causer or permitter of the nuisance, he will fail.

6.5.3.5 *Non-dangerous obstructions*

There is much law about what constitutes an unreasonable obstruction. Personal injury lawyers can ignore it. If an obstruction is dangerous it will fail into the relatively simple class of obstructions which have passed the test of unreasonableness. If it is not dangerous, it will not be reasonably foreseeable that it can cause injury.

6.5.4 Dangerous nuisances affecting the highway

Generally, if there is a dangerous nuisance on a highway the highway authority will be liable for damage which foreseeably results from it, if it knew or could have known of the existence of the nuisance but failed to take reasonable steps to abate it.

Only highway users can sue for highway nuisance (*Bromley v Mercer* [1922] 2 KB 126 (CA) (Appendix B, Case Summary 62)). This is often relevant if the accident happened at the edge of a highway.

If the dangerous nuisance which forms the basis of the claimant's complaint was caused by an act or omission of an adjoining landowner, the landowner may be concurrently liable. An example of this might be where tree roots emerge from adjoining land and are themselves a tripping hazard, or break up the surface of the highway making it dangerous for pedestrians. In these circumstances the highway authority may succeed in Pt 20 proceedings against the landowner. The highway authority probably has a sufficient claim to ownership of the highway to give it *locus standi* in an action for nuisance against the tree owner. The fact of an adjoining landowner's fault does not itself absolve the highway authority from liability. For the general principle that damage caused by escaping tree roots can ground an action in nuisance, see *Butler v Standard Telephones and Cables Ltd* [1940] 1 KB 399.

In most cases the owners of land adjoining a highway, from which land emanates something which causes a public nuisance affecting the highway, will be liable for that nuisance on the same basis as that on which the highway authority would be liable. If they had actual or constructive knowledge of the thing causing the nuisance and failed to take reasonable steps to prevent it causing a nuisance, they will be liable. It seems that the requisite knowledge is knowledge that the thing constituted a nuisance, and not mere knowledge that the thing existed in the place where it existed (see *British Road Services v Slater*, above, and Appendix B, Case Summary 61).

A different and higher standard of care is imposed on landowners if the danger to highway users arises from dangerous structures adjoining a highway. This is not often relevant in tripping cases. The law is summarised in *Mint v Good* [1951] 1 KB 517 (Appendix B, Case Summary 65) and *Tarry v Ashton* (1876) 1 QBD 314 (Appendix B, Case Summary 66, and outlined in Chapter 8).

6.5.5 Dangers on land adjoining the highway

If a pedestrian steps accidentally from the limits of the highway and is injured by something on the adjoining land which would, had it been on the highway, have constituted a public nuisance, the owner of the adjoining land upon which the injury has occurred will be liable for the injury as if it were a highway nuisance.

A person who has left the highway deliberately will not be able to claim against the landowner in public nuisance (*Jacobs v LCC* [1950] AC 361 (Appendix B, Case Summary 63); *Creed v McGeoch & Sons Ltd* [1955] 1 WLR 1005). He may have a remedy under the Occupiers' Liability Act 1984.

6.5.6   Animals and their products

See **1.3.2.7** for a discussion on liability for animals and their products. In *Kent CC v Holland* (1997) 161 JP Rep. 558 rottweiler dogs in a property adjoining a highway barked and jumped up against wire mesh which formed the boundary of the property and the highway. Pedestrians were scared. It was contended that the fear constituted a physical obstruction to the highway. This was rejected. Fear could not amount to an obstruction within the meaning of HA 1980, s 137(1), and the protrusion of the dogs' heads into the highway was minimal and therefore not actionable as a nuisance.

6.5.7   Liability of occupiers for nuisance caused by independent contractors

Section 2(4)(b) of the Occupiers' Liability Act 1957 provides that:

> 'Where damage is caused to a visitor by a danger due to the faulty execution of any work of construction, maintenance or repair by an independent contractor employed by the occupier, the occupier is not to be treated without more as answerable for the danger if in all the circumstances he had acted reasonably in entrusting the work to an independent contractor and had taken such steps (if any) as he reasonably ought in order to satisfy himself that the contractor was competent and that the work had been properly done.'

It is unclear whether or not there is a general principle that an occupier is liable in nuisance for the nuisance of his independent contractor but *Spicer v Smee* [1946] 1 All ER 489 suggests that there is. *Matania v National Provincial Bank Ltd* [1936] 2 All ER 633 suggests that there will only be such liability if the work done by the contractor created a particular risk of the creation of a nuisance. It is submitted that *Matania* is the better view, and is more likely to be followed.

6.6   RELATIONSHIP BETWEEN PUBLIC NUISANCE AND THE DUTY UNDER HA 1980, S 41

Very often, public nuisance and the duty under HA 1980, s 41 cover exactly the same ground. An unrepaired defect in the road surface may constitute an unreasonable obstruction, and be a breach of the authority's duty to maintain. But there will also be instances where a nuisance is not a s 41 breach, for instance where an obstruction is caused by something placed on the surface of the highway without damaging it. In this context the cases on the highway authority's obligation to clear snow and ice are interesting. In those cases there was no consideration of whether snow or ice on a road constituted obstructions amounting to public nuisances on the highway for which the highway authority, by failing to remove them in good time or at all, was liable. There is no reason in principle why such an argument should not succeed (see **4.2.3**).

Where a breach of the s 41 duty identical with public nuisance is alleged, both causes of action should be pleaded in the alternative.

6.7   REMEDY

The only public nuisance remedy relevant to personal injury tripping cases is damages. Sometimes communities will want to have the danger or obstruction removed. An action in public nuisance for an injunction is the right procedure.

CHAPTER 7

THE LIABILITY OF OCCUPIERS

7.1 INTRODUCTION

This chapter deals with the liability of the occupier of premises to people injured in tripping or slipping accidents on the premises. If the premises are industrial or commercial, there is a galaxy of specific statutory duties which may give an injured claimant a remedy. The most commonly relevant are set out in Chapter 9.

This chapter deals with the liability of occupiers under the two Occupiers' Liability Acts of 1957 and 1984. Other possible causes of action against occupiers (such as negligence, nuisance or breaches of other statutory duties) are dealt with elsewhere. Landlords, who may or may not be occupiers, have Chapter 8 to themselves.

Parliament imposes a general statutory duty (the common duty of care) on all occupiers. The existence of this general duty does not abrogate the common law duty of care (breach of which is negligence), although for most practical purposes the common duty of care is co-extensive with the common law duty of care, (a point recently reiterated by the Court of Appeal in *Cole v Davis-Gilbert & Ors* [2007] EWCA Civ 396).Nor, more importantly, does it abrogate or exclude the other more specific statutory duties commonly applying to the workplace. A worker who slips on a factory floor may be able to invoke (for example) the Workplace (Health, Safety and Welfare) Regulations 1992, as well as s 2 of the Occupiers' Liability Act 1957.

7.2 THE MEANING OF 'OCCUPIER'

The Occupiers' Liability Act 1957 contains no definition of occupier. The common law rules therefore apply. The test is to be found in *Wheat v Lacon* [1966] AC 552 (HL). The case concerned the meaning of 'occupier' under the 1957 Act, but the definition formulated was intended by their Lordships, and has been taken by courts and commentators, to apply to the associated common law too. Lord Pearson, at p 589, said: '[t]he foundation of occupier's liability is occupational control, i.e. control associated with and arising from presence in and use of or activity in the premises'.

The 'occupational control' need not be complete to qualify its possessor as an occupier. Lord Denning said, at p 578:

> '... wherever a person has a sufficient degree of control over premises that he ought to realise that any failure on his part to use care may result in injury to a person coming lawfully there, then he is an "occupier" and the person coming lawfully there is his "visitor" ... In order to be an "occupier" it is not necessary for a person to have entire control over the premises. He need not have exclusive occupation. Suffice it that he has some degree of control. He may share the control with others. Two or more may be "occupiers". And whenever this happens, each is under a duty to use care towards persons coming lawfully on to the premises, dependent on his degree of control. If each fails in his duty, each is liable to a visitor who is injured in consequence of his failure, but each may have a claim to contribution from the other.'

When a landlord lets premises by a lease to a tenant, he is presumed to have parted with all control over those premises, even if he has undertaken to repair the premises. But if the landlord has let only part of a building, and has retained other parts, he will be in control, for the purposes of the 1957 Act, of the un-let parts (see *Wheat v Lacon*, above). Thus, for example, landlords have been held to be occupiers of a staircase in the common parts of a block of flats (see *Miller v Hancock* [1893] 2 QB 177; *Fairman v Perpetual Investment Building Society* [1923] AC 74).

A brewery and a licensee may both be occupiers of a public house (*Wheat v Lacon*, above).

Club proprietors and the managers of a restaurant on the club premises may both occupy the restaurant (*Fisher v CHT* [1966] 2 QB 475).

A local authority which has requisitioned a house occupies it (*Hawkins v Coulsdon and Purley Urban District Council* [1954] 1 QB 319).

A local education authority occupies its schools (*Fryer v Salford Corporation* [1937] 1 All ER 657); and a local authority may occupy the parks it owns and maintains (*Glasgow Corporation v Taylor* [1922] 1 AC 44).

A corporation which has given notice of entry under a compulsory purchase order, but has not yet entered the property is an occupier (*Harris v Birkenhead Corporation* [1976] 1 All ER 341).

Highway authorities do not occupy roads which they have a statutory duty to maintain (*Whitting v Hillingdon LBC* (1970) 68 LGR 437).

7.3   THE DUTIES OF AN OCCUPIER

7.3.1   To visitors

To a visitor (see below) an occupier owes, by s 2 of the Occupiers' Liability Act 1957, a duty: '. . . to take such care as in all the circumstances of the case is reasonable to see that the visitor will be reasonably safe in using the premises for the purposes for which he is invited or permitted by the occupier to be there', except in so far as the occupier has validly extended, restricted, modified or excluded that duty by agreement or otherwise.

7.3.1.1   *Children*

Section 2(3)(a) of the 1957 Act states that an occupier must be prepared for children to be less careful than adults.

7.3.1.2   *Workmen and other visitors who know how to take care of themselves*

Section 2(3)(b) of the 1957 Act states that 'an occupier may expect that a person, in the exercise of his calling, will appreciate and guard against any special risks ordinarily incident to it, so far as the occupier leaves him free to do so'.

7.3.1.3   *Warnings*

By s 2(4) of the 1957 Act:

> 'In determining whether the occupier of premises has discharged the common duty of care to a visitor, regard is to be had to all the circumstances, so that (for example) –
> (a)   where damage is caused to a visitor by a danger of which he had been warned by the occupier, the warning is not to be treated without more as absolving the occupier from liability, unless in all the circumstances it was enough to enable the visitor to be reasonably safe . . .'

Section 2(4)(a) speaks for itself, and is commonly called on in tripping actions. Often the issue for the judge will be whether a warning given about spilt oil in a corridor was sufficient to enable the corridor used to be reasonably safe. The judge in such a case will consider the words used, the specificity of the description of the danger, the place where warning signs are sited and their number, and the earnestness of oral warnings. Sometimes a flippant delivery of otherwise perfectly adequate words will render a warning insufficient (see *Bishop v JS Starnes & Sons Ltd* [1971] 1 Lloyd's Rep 162).

7.3.1.4   *Dangers created by independent contractors*

Section 2(4)(b) of the 1957 Act provides that:

> 'where damage is caused to a visitor by a danger due to the faulty execution
> of any work of construction, maintenance or repair by an independent
> contractor employed by the occupier, the occupier is not to be treated
> without more as answerable for the danger if in all the circumstances he had
> acted reasonably in entrusting the work to an independent contractor and
> had taken such steps (if any) as he reasonably ought in order to satisfy
> himself that the contractor was competent and that the work had been
> properly done.'

Section 2(4)(b) often gives rise to debate between defendants or between a
defendant and a Pt 20 defendant in tripping cases. It is submitted that,
ideally, the words of this subsection should be recited in statements of
case such as the occupier's Pt 20 Particulars of Claim served on builders
engaged by him, since the subsection effectively outlines a statutory
defence.

The words 'faulty execution' in subs (4)(b) include work which is
incidental to the construction which the independent contractor is
contracted to do (see *AMF International Ltd v Magnet Bowling Ltd* [1968]
2 All ER 789).

As to whether occupiers are liable in nuisance for the nuisance created by
an independent contractor see **6.5.7**.

7.3.2   **To non-visitors**

To a person other than a visitor an occupier owes, by s 1 of the Occupiers'
Liability Act 1984, a duty: ' . . . to take such care as is reasonable in all the
circumstances of the case to see that (the person) does not suffer injury on
the premises by reason of the danger concerned'.

The duty is owed in respect of risk of non-visitors suffering injury on the
premises by reason of any danger due to the state of the premises or to
things done or omitted to be done on them (s 1(1)), if:

> '(a)   . . . [the occupier] is aware of the danger or has reasonable grounds to
> believe that it exists;
> (b)   [the occupier] knows or has reasonable grounds to believe that the
> other is in the vicinity of the danger concerned or that he may come
> into the vicinity of the danger (in either case, whether the other has
> lawful authority for being in that vicinity or not); and
> (c)   the risk is one against which, in all the circumstances of the case, [the
> occupier] may reasonably be expected to offer the other some
> protection.'

7.4 VISITORS AND NON-VISITORS

By s 1(2) of the 1957 Act, visitors, for the purposes of the Act are: ' . . . the same (subject to subsection (4) of this section) as the persons who would at common law be treated as . . . [the occupier's] invitees or licensees'.

7.4.1 Implied licences and invitees of holders of rights of way

The effect of the statutory definition is fairly self-evident. It follows, for instance, that a person using land pursuant to an implied licence, or at the invitation of a third party who has a right of way over the land, is not a visitor under the 1957 Act (see *Holden v White* [1982] QB 679; *Greenhalgh v British Railways Board* [1969] 2 QB 286; *Gautret v Egerton* (1867) LR 2 CP 371).

It is curious that the rule in *Gautret v Egerton* has rested in the common law apparently unnoticed since 1867. When the House of Lords said in *McGeown v Northern Ireland Housing Executive* [1994] 3 WLR 187 that this entirely uncontroversial doctrine still represented the law, personal injury lawyers realised with panic that they had been getting lots of cases wrong over the years, and tried to pretend that *McGeown* was a significant and new milestone. This was not true.

The rationale of the rule was well stated by Lord Keith in *McGeown* at p 193. He reviewed the authorities on the rule and continued:

> 'These authorities, though there are others, are sufficient to show that the rule in *Gautret v Egerton* is deeply entrenched in the law. Further, the rule is in my opinion undoubtedly a sound and reasonable one. Rights of way pass over many different types of terrain, and it would place an impossible burden upon landowners if they not only had to submit to the passage over them of anyone who might choose to exercise them but also were under a duty to maintain them in a safe condition. Persons using rights of way do so not with the permission of the owner of the solum but in the exercise of a right. There is no room for the view that such persons might have been licensees or invitees of the landowner under the old law or that they are his visitors under the English and Northern Irish Acts of 1957.'

It followed, said the House, that the landowner was not liable to the user of a public right of way for negligent nonfeasance. Although the claimant in *McGeown* would have been a licensee of the housing authority in respect of the path on which she had fallen before it had become a public right of way, that licence had merged in the right of way subsequently established. It was therefore irrelevant to the liability of the landowner that the path had formed part of a means of access for the claimant to and from the house of which her husband was tenant. As to whether any duty at all is owed, see **7.6**.

7.4.2   Access agreements and orders under the National Parks and Access to the Countryside Act 1949

Section 1(4) of the 1957 Act reads:

> 'A person entering any premises in exercise of rights conferred by virtue of an access agreement or order under the National Parks and Access to the Countryside Act 1949, is not, for the purposes of this Act, a visitor of the occupier of those premises.'

The 1984 Act applies to persons who do not qualify as visitors.

Sections 60 and 64–66 of the National Parks and Access to the Countryside Act 1949 define access agreements and orders, delineate the rights of the public where an access agreement or order is in force, and set out the effect of access agreements or orders on the rights and liabilities of owners. The net effect of these sections, together with s 1(4) of the 1957 Act, is that where someone enters land pursuant to an access agreement or order and is injured while on it, his cause of action as against the owner of the land is common law negligence and/or a breach of the 1984 Act, and not a breach of the common duty of care under the 1957 Act.

Section 5(1) of the 1957 Act implies the common duty of care into any contract pursuant to which a person may enter the premises of the contracting occupier.

If the injured party entered the premises pursuant to a contract between the occupier and a third party, the contract cannot exclude the duty of care owed by the occupier to the injured party (as a visitor). Subject to any contrary provision in the contract, the occupier will also owe to the injured party any increased duty which he, the occupier, has contractually bound himself to perform (see s 3(1) of the 1957 Act). The same applies to non-contractual tenancies (s 3(4) and (5)).

If the injury is caused by the negligence of independent contractors, s 3(2) of the 1958 Act should be noted. This provides that:

> 'A contract shall not by virtue of this section have the effect, unless it expressly so provides, of making an occupier who has taken all reasonable care answerable to strangers to the contract for dangers due to the faulty execution of any work of construction, maintenance or repair or other like operation by persons other than himself, his servants and persons acting under his direction and control.'

7.5   ACCIDENTS IN SHOPS

Ordinary law-abiding shoppers are visitors. The common duty of care is owed to them.

A fleeing shoplifter is probably owed the common duty of care under the 1984 Act. Whether the common duty of care is owed to a person who enters the shop with the intention of stealing but before he has stolen is a moot point.

A lower court dealing with a tripping or slipping accident in a shop would probably consider itself bound by *Ward v Tesco Stores Ltd* [1976] 1 All ER 219 (see Appendix B, Case Summary 33). This was not, oddly, a case brought under the Occupiers' Liability Act 1957; it was pleaded purely in negligence. Nonetheless a court would readily be persuaded that the case really defines the common duty of care owed by shopkeepers to their customers. It sets a very high standard and has some significant ramifications for trial procedure.

In *Ward* the claimant who was shopping in the supermarket owned and managed by the defendants, slipped on some yoghurt which had been spilt on the floor. The defendants' evidence was that such spillages occurred about 10 times a week and that their staff had been instructed that if they saw spillages on the floor they were to stay where they were and call somebody to clear up the spillage. Apart from general cleaning, the floor of the supermarket was brushed five or six times every day. There was no evidence about when the floor was last brushed before the claimant's accident. The trial judge held that the claimant had made out a prima facie case and that accordingly the defendants were liable.

On appeal, the defendants contended that the onus was on the claimant to show that the yoghurt had been on the floor for an unduly long time, and that there had been opportunities to clear it up which had not been taken; and that unless there was some evidence about when the yoghurt had been spilt there could be no prima facie case of negligence.

The Court of Appeal held that the defendants had a duty to keep the floors clean and free from spillages. Because the claimant's accident was not one which, in the ordinary course of events, would have happened if the floor had been kept clean and spillages dealt with as they occurred, the onus was on the defendants to provide some explanation and to show that the accident had not occurred because of any want of care on their part. Since it was probable that, by the time of the accident, the yoghurt had been on the floor long enough for it to have been cleared up had there been an adequate inspection and clearance system, the judge could properly infer negligence.

There has been considerable academic and judicial disapproval of *Ward*. In *Bell v Department of Health and Social Security*, (1989) *The Times*, June 13, which involved a slipping accident in an office, Drake J was very ready to distinguish *Ward* into irrelevance. He said: ' . . . [i]n my judgment the situation in a supermarket is clearly different from that in an office block. I think that *Ward v Tesco Stores Ltd* depends very much on the facts of that particular case'. While it is true that each case turns on its own facts, and the situation in, for example, a home, will be very different to that in a shop (see *Fryer v Pearson*, (2000) *The Times*, April 4), there is no doubt that *Ward* still represents the law. It has been repeatedly endorsed by the appellate courts: see, for example, *Jacob v Tesco Stores Ltd* (unreported) 19 November 1998; *Furness v Midland Bank PLC* (unreported) 10 November 2000; *Hall v Holker Estate Co Ltd* [2008] EWCA Civ 1422.

Ward turned on whether inferences about negligence could in the circumstances be properly drawn, and so is best seen as a case more about evidence than about the substantive law of the common duty of care. Unfortunately it has not been used that way in and by the courts. If it is about the common duty of care, it imposes an exceptionally heavy burden on shopkeepers. A similar case, *Turner v Arding & Hobbs Ltd* [1949] 2 All ER 911 (see Appendix B, Case Summary 32), is similarly best regarded as a strong judicial comment about how cases are proved rather than the substantive law.

7.6   USERS OF PUBLIC RIGHTS OF WAY NOT MAINTAINABLE AT THE PUBLIC EXPENSE

People who use public rights of way which are not maintainable at the public expense are in an odd legal position. Unlike users of private rights of way, they are not visitors within the 1957 Act. Indeed, the 1957 Act does not apply to them at all (see *Greenhalgh v British Railways Board* [1969] 2 QB 286). Possibly the common duty of care under the 1984 Act applies (see *British Railways Board v Herrington* [1972] AC 877; *Thomas v British Railways Board* [1976] QB 912 (CA) and the discussion in Buckley, *The Modern Law of Negligence*, (Butterworths, 2nd edn, 1993) at 16.35–36). The point was not decided in *McGeowan* (above) and seems still arguable.

7.7   EXCLUSION AND RESTRICTION OF LIABILITY

By s 2(1) of the Unfair Contract Terms Act 1977: '[a] person cannot by reference to any contract term or to a notice given to persons generally or to particular persons exclude or restrict his liability for death or personal injury'. And that, so far as tripping cases are concerned, is that.

CHAPTER 8

THE LIABILITY OF LANDLORDS

8.1 INTRODUCTION

Landlords deserve a chapter of their own. In negligence and nuisance, some quirky common law rules apply to them. The repairing obligations imposed on landlords by leases and/or by operation of statute do not apply to other classes of defendant. Landlords may or may not be occupiers. When a landlord is an occupier, he is in the same position as any other occupier. Thus if someone trips on a common staircase the Occupiers' Liability Acts should be considered. The principles which apply are dealt with in detail in Chapter 7.

Only someone who is a party to a contract can sue under it. Leases are contracts. An action against a landlord framed as a breach of an obligation under a lease will succeed only if it is brought by the tenant. Section 8.5 of this chapter deals with matters of this kind. The first part of this chapter deals with causes of action which are independent of the lease and can therefore be invoked by third parties as well as by tenants who otherwise qualify.

8.2 NEGLIGENCE

Landlords owe no general duty of care either to their tenants or to third parties (see *Cavalier v Pope* [1906] AC 428; *Travers v Gloucester Corporation* [1947] KB 71; *Ball v London County Council* [1949] 2 KB 159). This rule really says no more than that the Occupiers' Liability Act 1957 has codified the common law. It would be absurd for the non-occupying landlord to be guiltless under the Act but liable under the residual common law.

Where there is only a licence, the landlord will owe the 'tenant' and others a duty of care (see *Greene v Chelsea Borough Council* [1954] 2 QB 127). Similarly, the landlord will owe a duty to both tenants and non-tenants where, as well as being the landlord, he built the premises (*Rimmer v Liverpool City Council* [1985] QB 1).

Where a landlord retains control or possession of part of the premises, he can be liable in negligence in failing to keep in repair that part which is within his control, if someone is injured as a result (see *Cockburn v Smith* [1924] 2 KB 119, cp *Duke of Westminster v Guild* [1985] QB 688), but obviously such control or possession will usually qualify the landlord as an occupier within the 1957 and 1984 Acts.

8.3   NUISANCE

The ordinary rules apply to a landlord's liability in nuisance. A landlord, just like anyone else, will be liable for a nuisance if he causes or continues or authorises or adopts it. The meanings of these words are discussed in Chapter 6.

It follows that a landlord who has presumed or actual knowledge of a nuisance on land that is subsequently let will be liable, usually concurrently with the tenant, for that nuisance (see *Todd v Flight* (1860) 9 CBNS 377: landlord liable for damage to a claimant caused by the falling of chimneys on a house knowingly let in a dangerous state by the landlord; *Gandy v Jubber* (1864–65) 5 B & S 78: landlord liable for knowingly letting a building with a defective grating which caused injury).

If a nuisance on land continues after letting, the tenant will be liable as occupier for it, but the landlord will probably be concurrently liable. If a landlord has an obligation or a right to repair, there will be little doubt that he will be liable for the continuing nuisance, again concurrently with the tenant (see *Mint v Good* [1951] 1 KB 517, (Appendix B, Case Summary 65). If the nuisance has been allowed to continue by reason of a breach by the landlord of an obligation in the lease to repair, the tenant, if sued, may well succeed in Pt 20 proceedings against the landlord.

If a landlord has authorised a nuisance he will be liable for it, concurrently with the tenant. A nuisance will be authorised by the landlord if the lease authorises it, but it is often unclear whether or not a lease in fact authorises a nuisance. It certainly does so if a nuisance is certain to result from using the premises as allowed by the lease (see *Smith v Scott* [1973] Ch 314), but some authorities suggest that a landlord will be liable if it is reasonably foreseeable that a nuisance will result from the specifically authorised use (see *Tetley v Chitty* [1986] 1 All ER 663).

Normally only the tenant, and not the landlord, will be liable for a nuisance which arises after the grant of a lease. There are two important exceptions. The first is that where premises abut the highway, the landlord will be liable to third parties for a nuisance created by the state of the premises (see *Howard v Walker* [1947] 1 KB 860). The second is that where the lease obliges or enables a landlord to repair, and a nuisance arises by failure to discharge the duty or exercise the right, the landlord will probably be liable in nuisance to a third party who sustains damage by reason of that failure (see *Nelson v Liverpool Brewery Co* (1877) 2 CPD 311; *Mint v Good*, above; *Heap v Ind Cooper & Allsopp* [1940] 2 KB 476).

If a landlord owns property adjoining a highway, and those premises constitute a highway nuisance, the landlord will be liable if he has an obligation to repair. He need not know of the matters constituting the nuisance (*Wringe v Cohen* [1940] 1 KB 229 (see Appendix B, Case Summary 64).

8.4   THE DEFECTIVE PREMISES ACT 1972

By s 4(1) of this Act, even where a landlord is not an occupier within the *Wheat v Lacon* definition, he will, where the tenancy obliges him to maintain or repair the premises, owe a duty to all persons who might reasonably be expected to be affected by defects in the state of the premises. The duty is to take such care as is reasonable in all the circumstances to see that those persons are reasonably safe from personal injury or from damage to their property caused by a relevant defect. Section 4(2) provides that the s 4(1) duty is owed if the landlord either knows or ought in all the circumstances to have known of the relevant defect.

Section 4(3) defines 'relevant defect' as a defect in the state of the premises which exists at or after the 'material time' (see below). The defect must arise from, or continue because of, an act or omission of the landlord which constitutes or would, if the landlord had had notice of the defect, have constituted, a failure by him to carry out his obligation to the tenant for the maintenance or repair of the premises.

'Material time' is defined in ss 4(3)(a) and (b). Where the tenancy commenced before the Act, the material time is the date of commencement of the Act, which was 1 January 1974. Where the tenancy commenced after the Act, the material time is the earliest of:

(i)   the time of commencement of the tenancy;

(ii)   the time when the tenancy agreement is entered into; or

(iii) the time when possession of the premises is taken in contemplation of the letting.

Where premises are let under a tenancy which expressly or impliedly gives the landlord the right to enter the premises to carry out maintenance or repair, the general s 4 duty arises as soon as the landlord is in a position to exercise the right, or can put himself in a position to exercise the right. The landlord is not, however, under any such duty (under this Act) in respect of any defect in the premises which arises from or continues because of a failure to carry out an obligation which the tenancy expressly imposes on the tenant.

The Act interprets 'tenancy' very broadly. Section 4(6) provides that s 4 applies to a right of occupation which is given by contract or by any enactment even if it does not technically amount to a formal tenancy.

Where the person suing a landlord under s 4 is the tenant, it is a moot point whether he is suing in contract (s 4 having been statutorily incorporated into the tenancy agreement), or in tort. Probably the best view is that this is a claim in tort, but both causes of action should be pleaded.

Other sections in the Defective Premises Act 1972 relate to the liability of non-landlords, and are considered in Chapter 9.

For the relationship between s 4 of the Defective Premises Act and s 11 of the Landlord and Tenant Act 1985, see **8.5.2.5** below.

8.5   CONTRACTUAL LIABILITY OF LANDLORDS

Obviously only tenants can invoke causes of action against their landlords based in contract.

8.5.1   At common law

Unless the lease or a statute specifically provides otherwise, a landlord is under no duty to put leased premises into repair at the start of the tenancy; nor is he under a duty to carry out repairs during the continuation of the tenancy. In the absence of specific provision, a landlord is not liable to keep the premises habitable. Even if a tenant has covenanted to repair 'damage by fire and tempest' or 'fair wear and tear' excepted, the landlord has not impliedly covenanted to make good such damage or wear and tear (see *Arden v Pullen* (1842) 10 M & W 321).

There is now an important qualification to this general principle. It is contained in the House of Lords decision in *Liverpool City Council v Irwin* [1977] AC 239. Council flats in a high-rise block were let. Tenants had the use of common lifts, stairs and rubbish chutes. The premises were regularly vandalised and the tenants did not cooperate in the maintenance of the common facilities. The House of Lords held that the tenancy agreement conferred on the tenants implied easements or quasi-easements to use the lifts, the stairs and the chutes; and that in the circumstances it had to be inferred that the landlords had an obligation to maintain and repair the lifts, stairs and chutes. This included, since natural light was absent or inadequate, a duty to provide sufficient lighting. The obligation was an obligation to take reasonable care to maintain the facilities in reasonable condition.

The breadth of this decision is hotly debated. It does not change the general common law rule that a landlord owes no duty, independently of the lease, to repair or maintain demised premises. Nor does it change the principle that the grant of an easement does not impose on the servient owner a duty to maintain the subject matter of the easement.

The courts have been wary of *Irwin*. It was distinguished by the Court of Appeal in *Duke of Westminster v Guild* [1985] QB 688, when the court refused to say that, pursuant to *Irwin*, a landlord was obliged to repair a drain. The court emphasised the general principle that contracts were presumed to be definitive of the relationship between contracting parties, and appeared to suggest that *Irwin* should be restricted to situations where access to the premises concerned, or control over the particular facility in respect of which complaint was made, remained in the control of the landlord. Similar sentiments were expressed by the Court of Appeal in *Gordon v Selico Co Ltd* (1986) 18 HLR 219.

This interpretation is supported by *King v South Northamptonshire District Council* [1992] 1 EGLR 53, in which the Court of Appeal followed *Irwin*, holding that where a house was let with a rear entrance used for servicing and deliveries, the landlord had an implied duty to maintain and repair a path which led to the rear entrance.

There are two exceptions to the common law rule. First, if a house is purchased or, probably, leased while it is being constructed, the vendor/lessor impliedly warrants that the builder will perform the work in a good and workmanlike manner and use good and proper materials (see *Lawrence v Cassel* [1930] 2 KB 83; *Hancock v Brazier* [1956] 1 WLR 1317).

Secondly, where the landlord retains possession of something ancillary to the demised premises, which is necessary for the enjoyment of the demised premises, he is under a duty to take reasonable care that the ancillary thing will not cause damage to the lessee or the demised premises. This duty exists in contract, not tort (see *Gordon v Selico Co* [1985] 2 EGLR 79).

8.5.2 Under the Landlord and Tenant Act 1985

8.5.2.1 The implied duty

By s 11(1)(d) of the Landlord and Tenant Act 1985 there is implied into a lease of less than 7 years of a dwelling house an obligation to keep in repair the structure and exterior. This obligation does not apply to a new lease granted to an existing tenant or to a former tenant still in possession if the previous lease was not a lease to which s 11 applied or, in the case of a lease granted before 24 October 1961, would have applied (see s 14 of the 1985 Act).

The obligation to keep in repair includes an obligation to put the structure and exterior into repair if they are not in repair at the start of the tenancy. It does not require a landlord to eradicate inherent design faults (*Quick v Tarf-Ely Borough Council* [1986] QB 809).

The obligation to keep the exterior in repair does not generally include an obligation to keep in repair a garden attached to the dwelling (*McAuley v Bristol CC* [1991] 3 WLR 968) or a garage (*Irvine v Moran* [1991] 1 EGLR 261). But it may include an essential means of access (see *Brown v Liverpool Corporation* [1969] 3 All ER 1345, where a landlord was held to be obliged to repair steps leading to the house). It does not include a back yard or access to the back yard (*Hopwood v Cannock Chase District Council* [1975] 1 All ER 796).

Where the dwelling in question is a flat in a block, the 'structure and exterior' to which the repairing covenant relates is, generally, the structure and exterior of the flat itself, not of the block (*Campden Hill Towers v Gardner* [1977] QB 823). But if the tenancy was entered into on or after 15 January 1989 (provided that the lease was not pursuant to a contract made before that date), the landlord's obligation extends to any part of the building in which the lessor has an estate or interest (s 11(1A) of the 1985 Act, inserted by Housing Act 1988, s 116).

8.5.2.2   The statutory defence

Section 11(3A) of the 1985 Act (inserted by Housing Act 1988, s 116) provides the lessor with a statutory defence. It applies where the obligation on the lessor is the new, extended (s 11(1A)) obligation, and in order to comply with it the lessor needs to carry out works or repairs otherwise than in or to an installation in the dwelling house, and he does not have a sufficient right in the part of the building or the installation concerned to enable him to carry out the required works or repairs. It is a defence for him to prove that he has used all reasonable endeavours to obtain, but was unable to obtain, such rights as would be adequate to enable him to carry out the works or repairs.

8.5.2.3   Notice of the defect

For a s 11 implied covenant to ground an action against a landlord, the landlord must have notice of the defects to be remedied (see *Morgan v Liverpool Corporation* [1927] 2 KB 131; *McCarrick v Liverpool Corporation* [1947] AC 219; *O'Brien v Robinson* [1973] AC 912).

8.5.2.4 *Basis of claim*

Note that a claim under this section is a claim in contract under the lease. There is no reason why a breach of an implied term should not ground a personal injury action, but the privity of contract rules decree that only a tenant could recover damages for a breach of the term resulting in injury.

8.5.2.5 *Relationship with s 4 of the Defective Premises Act 1972*

The relationship between the duty under the 1985 Act and that under s 4 of the Defective Premises Act 1972 may be important when a tenant has not given notice to his landlord of a defect which the landlord, under s 11 of the 1985 Act, has a duty to repair. If the tenant is injured by that defect, he will not be able to sue the landlord for breach of the covenant implied into the lease under s 11 because the landlord does not have notice of the defect (see *Morgan v Liverpool Corporation*, above). Can the tenant rely on breach of the duty owed in tort under s 4 of the Defective Premises Act?

It is submitted that the answer is yes. The Lloyd's names cases make it reasonably clear, despite an impressive rearguard action by the opponents of a general law of obligations, that there is a general rule of concurrent liability in tort and contract. Cases such as *Greater Nottingham Co-operative Society Ltd v Cementation Piling and Foundations Ltd* [1989] QB 71 and the famous judgment of Lord Scarman in the Privy Council case of *Tai Hing Cotton Mill Ltd v Liu Chong Hing Bank Ltd* [1986] AC 80 must be regarded with suspicion if indeed they are to be regarded at all.

Critics of the proposition that the tenant can rely on breach of the duty owed in tort would say that to assert that the tenant had a right in tort when he had failed to give notice of the defect would make redundant s 11 of the 1985 Act, and make otiose the decisions of the courts indicating that notice was necessary in order to activate s 11. If the duties imposed by s 11 of the 1985 Act and s 4 of the 1972 Act were the same, those critics would be right.

But the duties are not identical. The duty imposed by s 11 is more onerous than that imposed by s 4. Section 11 requires the landlord, once he has been given notice of a defect, to keep in repair the structure and exterior of the dwelling house. He is accordingly required actually to keep it in repair, not merely to take reasonable steps to keep it in repair. Section 4 is less demanding. It imposes on landlords a duty to all persons who might reasonably be expected to be affected by defects in the state of the premises to take such care as is reasonable in all the circumstances to see that those persons are reasonably safe from personal injury or from damage to their property caused by a relevant defect, provided that the landlord knows or ought in the circumstances to have known of the relevant defect. A landlord can escape from s 4 by taking reasonable care, but he cannot satisfy s 11 by doing anything less than fully performing all his obligations. Section 11 is absolute, s 4 is not.

It follows that a claimant who has failed to give notice of a defect so as to enable him to sue under s 11 is not in exactly the same position, in relying on s 4, as he would have been if he had not defaulted by failing to give notice. He is at a disadvantage, and would be better off if he had given notice and could use s 11.

Since the two duties are different in both nature and scope, it is submitted that any residual doubts about non-concurrence of liability in contract and tort should not prevent a non-notifying tenant from suing his landlord under the Defective Premises Act.

8.5.3   Under the Agricultural Holdings Act 1986, s 7

Section 7 of the Agricultural Holdings Act 1986 has the effect of imposing on landlords of agricultural holdings liability for the repair and maintenance of the items of fixed equipment, including buildings, which are specified as the responsibility of landlords in Pt 1 of the Schedule to the Agriculture (Maintenance, Repair and Insurance of Fixed Equipment) Regulations 1973, SI 1973/1473. The tenant can, by written agreement, shoulder this liability himself.

In so far as generally relevant to tripping cases, the Regulations provide that the landlord is liable:

(a)   to repair and replace floors, floor joists, ceiling joists and timbers, exterior staircases and fixed ladders of farmhouse and cottages;

(b)   to execute all repairs and replacements to underground water pipes, wells, bore-holes and reservoirs and all underground installations connected therewith and to sewage disposal systems, including septic tanks, filtering media and cesspools (but excluding covers and tops).

But the landlord is under no obligation:

(a)   to repair or replace buildings or fittings which are the property of the tenant;

(b)   (subject to a duty to make good damage by fire) to repair or replace when that is made necessary by the wilful act or the negligence of the tenant or any members of his household or his employees;

(c)   to execute any work if and in so far as the execution of such work is rendered impossible (except at prohibitive or unreasonable expense) by reason of subsidence of any land or the blocking of outfalls which are not under the control of either the landlord or the tenant.

CHAPTER 9

MISCELLANEOUS STATUTORY DUTIES IN THE WORKPLACE

9.1   INTRODUCTION

The four major statutory duties relevant to tripping cases have been dealt with in other chapters. These are the duties under s 41 of HA 1980, s 2 of the Occupiers' Liability Act 1967, s 1 of the Occupiers' Liability Act 1984, and ss 3 and 4 of the Defective Premises Act 1972. This chapter deals with other statutory duties which are often relevant in tripping and slipping cases, with a particular emphasis on duties which are likely to apply in the workplace.

9.2   GENERAL PRINCIPLES

Each statutory duty which it is proposed to invoke must be looked at carefully. Particulars of Claim are often full of allegations of breaches of statutory duty which have no relevance to the premises where the accident in question occurred, or breaches which do not give rise to an action for damages. The corresponding defences are often full of deafening failures to point the defects out.

All the examples of statutory duty discussed in this chapter give rise to civil liability in damages. The general principles which determine whether a statutory duty sounds in damages were set out by the House of Lords in *Lonrho Ltd v Shell Petroleum Co Ltd (No 2)* [1982] AC 173. Generally, where the performance of a statutory obligation required by an Act is also enforced by the Act in a particular manner (eg by the imposition of a criminal penalty for non-compliance), the performance cannot be enforced in any other way (see *Solomons v R Gertzenstein Ltd* [1954] 2 QB 243). Where an Act provides only a criminal sanction for non-compliance, there can only be civil liability in two exceptional cases. These are:

> 'Where on the true construction of the Act it is apparent that the obligation or prohibition was imposed for the benefit or protection of a particular class of individuals, as in the case of the Factories Acts and similar legislation . . . The second exception is where the statute creates a public right (i.e. a right to be enjoyed by all those of Her Majesty's subjects who wish to avail themselves of it) and a particular member of the public suffers what Brett J. in *Benjamin v Storr* (1874) L.R. 9 CP 400 at 407 described as "particular

direct and substantial" damage "other and different from that which was common to all the rest of the public".' (per *Lonrho* above at p.185)

It follows that to succeed in an action for damages for breach of statutory duty the claimant must establish:

(a)   that the statutory provision was intended to protect an ascertainable class of persons; and

(b)   that the claimant was a member of that class at the material time; and

(c)   that the provision has been breached; and

(d)   that the claimant has suffered damage of a kind which the provision was intended to prevent; and

(e)   that the damage was caused by the breach.

An employer cannot escape civil liability for breach of statutory duty by delegating the duty (*Lochgelly Iron and Coal Co Ltd v M'Mullan* [1934] AC 1) unless the claimant is the person to whom the duty was delegated clearly and definitely, the accident was the claimant's fault, and the obligations of the employer under the relevant statute are co-extensive with the obligations delegated to the claimant (see *Vyner v Waldenburg Brothers Ltd* [1946] KB 5; *Ginty v Belmont Building Supplies Ltd* [1959] 1 All ER 14; *Ross v Associated Portland Cement Manufacturers Ltd* [1964] 2 All ER 452).

9.3   THE WORKPLACE (HEALTH, SAFETY AND WELFARE) REGULATIONS 1992

It is these Regulations (SI 1992/3004) which have caused and will cause problems in the realm of personal injury cases in the workplace. The Regulations are intended to implement Workplace Directive 89/654. They replace much of the old law. What they replace it with is sometimes unclear. Probably many of the principles used in deciding the old statutory duty cases will survive. The Regulations are supplemented by the Workplace Health, Safety and Welfare Approved Code of Practice.

9.3.1   Commencement

The Regulations generally came into force on 1 January 1993, but those which create duties relevant to tripping and slipping cases came into force on 1 January 1996 with respect to any workplace or part of a workplace which is either a workplace used for the first time as a workplace after 31 December 1992, or a modification, extension or conversion.

The Regulations had the effect of repealing a number of previously relevant provisions contained within the Factories Act 1961. For the purpose of tripping and slipping claims in a modern context, the practitioner is unlikely to bring many (if any) actions under the Factories Act 1961. The Workplace (Health, Safety and Welfare) Regulations 1992 are likely to be the applicable Regulations for the vast majority of claims. Sometimes they may be joined by others. A fuller explanation of the Factories Act 1961 regime is contained within previous versions of this work: see Foster, *Tripping and Slipping: A Practitioner's Guide* (Sweet and Maxwell, 2005).

9.3.2   Application

The Regulations apply to every workplace *except* (by reg.3):

'(a)   a workplace which is on a ship;
(b)   a workplace where the only activities being undertaken are building operations or works of engineering construction within section 176 of the Factories Act 1961 and activities for the purpose of or in connection with these activities;
(c)   a workplace where the only activities being undertaken are the exploration for or the extraction of mineral resources;
(d)   a workplace which is situated in the immediate vicinity of another workplace or intended workplace where exploration for or extraction of mineral resources is being or will be undertaken, and where the only activities being undertaken are activities preparatory to, for the purposes of, or in connection with such exploration or extraction of mineral resources at that other workplace.'

A workplace is defined by reg 2(1) as any premises or part of premises which are not domestic premises and are made available to any person as a place of work. The definition expressly includes any place within the premises to which a worker has access while at work and any room, lobby, corridor, staircase, road or other place used as a means of access to or egress from that place of work or facilities provided for use in connection with the place of work other than a public road. The definition does not include a modification, extension or conversion of any of these things until the modification, extension or conversion is completed.

9.3.3   The duties

9.3.3.1   General maintenance and repair

Regulation 5(1) provides that '[t]he workplace and the equipment, devices and systems to which this regulation applies shall be maintained (including cleaned as appropriate) in an efficient state, in efficient working order and in good repair'.

It is clear from the Code of Practice that 'efficient' here does not have its usual meaning and is nothing to do with economics or levels of productivity, but instead with health, safety and welfare. And so, surprisingly, it can probably be invoked by a claimant who trips on a floor where a tool has been inefficiently left.

9.3.3.2   *Lighting*

Regulation 8 provides that:

> '(1)   Every workplace shall have suitable and sufficient lighting.
> (2)   . . .
> (3)   Without prejudice to the generality of paragraph 1, suitable and sufficient emergency lighting shall be provided in any room in circumstances in which persons at work are specially exposed to danger in the event of failure of artificial lighting.'

9.3.3.3   *Waste materials on floors*

Regulation 9(3) provides that: 'So far as is reasonably practicable, waste materials shall not be allowed to accumulate in a workplace except in suitable receptacles.'

9.3.3.4   *Condition of floors and 'traffic routes'*

Regulation 12 provides that:

> '(1)   Every floor in a workplace and the surface of every traffic route in a workplace shall be of a construction such that the floor or surface of the traffic route is suitable for the purpose for which it is used.
> (2)   Without prejudice to the generality of paragraph 1, the requirements in that paragraph shall include requirements that –
>   (a)   the floor, or surface of the traffic route, shall have no hole or slope, or be uneven or slippery so as, in each case, to expose any person to a risk to his health or safety and
>   (b)   every such floor shall have effective means of drainage where necessary.
> (3)   So far as is reasonably practicable, every floor in a workplace and the surface of every traffic route in a workplace shall be kept free from obstructions and from any article which may cause a person to slip, trip or fall.
> (4)   In considering whether for the purpose of paragraph (2)(a) a hole or slope exposes any person to a risk to his health or safety –
>   (a)   no account shall be taken of a hole where adequate measures have been taken to prevent a person falling; and
>   (b)   account shall be taken of any handrail provided in connection with any slope.

(5)   Suitable and sufficient handrails and, if appropriate, guards shall be provided on all traffic routes which are staircases except in circumstances in which a handrail can not be provided without obstructing the traffic route.'

By reg 2, a 'traffic route' is a route for pedestrian traffic, vehicles or both, and includes any stairs, staircase, fixed ladder, doorway, gateway, loading bay or ramp.

Note that reg 12 removes the distinction, enshrined in ss 28 and 29 of the Factories Act 1961, between places of work and means of access to and egress from them.

The criterion of reasonable practicability in reg 12(3) was considered by the Court of Appeal in *King v RCO Support Services Ltd and Yorkshire Traction Co Ltd*, (2001) *The Times*, February 7. It makes comforting reading for employers, but emphasises that each case turns on its own facts. There is no judicial comment on the regulation which says much more than the regulation itself says.

9.4   CONSTRUCTION SITES

Trips and falls in the construction sector continue to provide the source of many (potentially high value) claims. Thirty-four of the 72 worker deaths in construction in 2007/08 resulted from a fall from height. In addition c 4,000 major injuries resulting from tripping/slipping accidents on a construction site were reported to the Health and Safety Executive,:see http://www.hse.gov.uk/construction/tripsandfalls/index.htm.

Given these statistics, it is unsurprising that two key sets of Regulations are in place in order (inter alia) to reduce the risk of tripping and slipping accidents in the construction industry.

The Construction (Design and Management) Regulations 2007 repeal and replace the earlier obligations imposed by the Construction (Health, Safety and Welfare) Regulations 1996. Falls from a height are governed by the Work at Height Regulations 2005. Both sets of regulations might apply simultaneously, for example, if the worker falls from scaffolding or a working platform at a height.

9.5   CONSTRUCTION (DESIGN AND MANAGEMENT) REGULATIONS 2007 (SI 2007/320)

9.5.1   Commencement

These regulations came into force on 6 April 2007. They are accompanied by an Approved Code of Practice.

Check the date of the accident. Make sure that you do not plead the 2007 Regulations when the Construction (Health, Safety and Welfare) Regulations 1996 (the previous set of applicable regulations) were in force. That said, the two sets of Regulations impose very similar obligations.

9.5.2   Application

The regulations apply in respect of all work done on 'construction sites' in Great Britain. The definition of a construction site is contained within reg 2(1). The definition is broad, and will apply to almost any situation where construction work is taking place. For instance, redecoration work is likely to fall within the ambit of the Regulations (see *Matthews v Glasgow City Council* [2006] CSIH 1).

Regulation 25 imposes the obligiations under Part IV of the regulations on two classes of people:

(a)   by virtue of reg 25(1), 'Every contractor carrying out construction work shall comply with the requirements of regulations 26 to 44 insofar as they affect him or any person carrying out construction work under his control or relate to matters within his control.'

(b)   by virtue of reg 25(2) 'Every person (other than a contractor carrying out construction work) who controls the way in which any construction work is carried out by a person at work shall comply with the requirements of regulations 26 to 44 insofar as they relate to matters which are within his control.'

The concept of 'employment status' is irrelevant when considering whether a potential defendant owed obligations to the proposed claimant (although it may have probative value when considering whether the regulations apply). The key issue is whether the potential defendant had control of the construction work which the claimant was undertaking when the accident occurred.

9.5.3   Obligations: safe place of work, traffic routes & lighting

A full account of the regulations falls outside the scope of this book. Below, we highlight the regulations which are likely to be of relevance in a tripping/slipping claim on a construction site.

9.5.3.1   Safe place of work

Regulation 26 is crucial. It states as follows:

'(1)   There shall, so far as is reasonably practicable, be suitable and sufficient safe access to and egress from every place of work and to and from every other place provided for the use of any person while at work, which access and egress shall be properly maintained.

(2)   Every place of work shall, so far as is reasonably practicable, be made and kept safe for, and without risks to health to, any person at work there.

(3)   Suitable and sufficient steps shall be taken to ensure, so far as is reasonably practicable, that no person uses access or egress, or gains access to any place, which does not comply with the requirements of paragraph (1) or (2) respectively.

(4)   Every place of work shall, so far as is reasonably practicable, have sufficient working space and be so arranged that it is suitable for any person who is working or who is likely to work there, taking account of any necessary work equipment present.'

It will almost always be necessary to plead a breach of reg 26 where a tripping or slipping accident occurs on a construction site. The broad obligations imposed by this regulation include a duty to eliminate tripping and slipping hazards '*so far as is reasonably practicable*'.

9.5.3.2   *Traffic routes*

Under reg 2, a 'traffic route' is defined as 'a route for pedestrian traffic or for vehicles and includes any doorway, gateway, loading bay or ramp'.

Regulation 36(1) stipulates that construction sites should be organised in such a way (so far as is reasonably practicable) as to ensure that pedestrians and vehicles can move safely and without risks to health. There is a further obligation to ensure that traffic routes are suitable for the persons or vehicles using them, sufficient in number, in suitable positions and of sufficient size (reg 36(2)).

Regulation 36 may apply where an accident has been caused by a tripping/slipping hazard on a traffic route. The contractor (and/or person in control of the work) is under a positive obligation, so far as is reasonably practicable, to ensure that any traffic route on a construction site is in such a state that workers can move safely, and without risk to their health.

9.5.3.3   *Lighting*

Consider a breach of reg 44 where poor lighting contributed to the claimant's trip, slip or fall.

The lighting must be 'suitable and sufficient', and so far as is 'reasonably practicable' should be provided by natural light (reg 44(1)). Secondary lighting should be provided in circumstances where the health or safety of a person is put at risk in the event of failure of primary artificial lighting (reg 44(3)).

9.6   THE WORK AT HEIGHT REGULATIONS 2005 (SI 2005/735)

9.6.1   Application

The regulations apply regardless of the distance from which the person is likely to fall. By virtue of reg 2:

' "work at height" means –
(a)   work in any place, including a place at or below ground level;
(b)   obtaining access to or egress from such place while at work, except by a staircase in a permanent workplace,
where, if measures required by these Regulations were not taken, a person could fall a distance liable to cause personal injury.'

9.6.2   Obligations

A full account of the terms and effect of the Work at Height Regulations 2005 is beyond the scope of this book. Where the regulations apply, all work at height must be properly planned and appropriately supervised so as to ensure that the work is carried out in a safe manner (reg 4).

Regulation 6(2) dictates that 'every employer shall ensure that work is not carried out at height where it is reasonably practicable to carry out the work safely otherwise than at height.' Where it is necessary to carry out work at height, reg 6(3) imposes a general duty to 'take suitable and sufficient measures to prevent, so far as is reasonably practicable, any person falling a distance liable to cause personal injury'.

The provisions made in respect of 'working platforms' are likely to be of particular relevance to a tripping/slipping claim. Regulation 2(1) provides a broad definition for 'working platforms'. They are defined as being any platform used as a place of work or as a means of access to or egress from a place of work. The definition also refers to any scaffold, suspended scaffold, cradle, mobile platform, trestle, gangway, gantry or stairway as amounting to a 'working platform'.

By virtue of reg 8(b), any working platform must comply with the standards stipulated within Sch 3, Part 1 to the Regulations. Paragraph 5 of Sch 3, Part 1 is of particular note. It is set out in full below:

'A working platform shall–
(a)   be of sufficient dimensions to permit the safe passage of persons and the safe use of any plant or materials required to be used and to provide a safe working area having regard to the work being carried out there;
(b)   possess a suitable surface and, in particular, be so constructed that the surface of the working platform has no gap –

(i) through which a person could fall;

(ii) through which any material or object could fall and injure a person; or

(iii) giving rise to other risk of injury to any person, unless measures have been taken to protect persons against such risk; and

(c) be so erected and used, and maintained in such condition, as to prevent, so far as is reasonably practicable –

(i) the risk of slipping or tripping; or

(ii) any person being caught between the working platform and any adjacent structure.'

Schedule 3, Part 2 of the Regulations sets out the necessary standards required of scaffolding. No direct reference is made in Part 2 to slipping/tripping risks.

9.7 THE DOCKS REGULATIONS 1988 (SI 1988/1655)

9.7.1 Application

By reg 3, these Regulations apply to and in relation to all dock operations in Great Britain and outside Great Britain but within territorial waters, to and in relation to the loading, unloading, fuelling or provisions of a vessel, as ss 1–59 and 80–82 of the Health and Safety at Work Act 1974 apply. Regulation 2, in defining 'dock operations' provides an extensive catalogue.

9.7.2 Access to dock premises

Regulation 7 provides:

'(1) Subject to paragraph (2), there shall be provided and properly maintained safe means of access to every part of dock premises which any person has to visit for the purpose of dock operations, and in particular floors, decks, surfaces, stairs, steps, passages and gangways comprised in dock premises shall not be used unless they are of adequate strength for the purpose required, of sound construction and properly maintained.

(2) So far as is reasonably practicable, all floors, decks, surfaces, stairs, steps, passages and gangways in dock premises shall be kept free from any substance or obstacle likely to cause persons to slip or fall or vehicles to skid.'

The general comments on the construction of words and phrases in ss 28 and 29 of the Factories Act apply equally here.

9.7.3 Lighting

Regulation 6 provides:

'(1) Each part of dock premises which is being used for dock operations
      shall be suitably and adequately lighted.
(2) Every obstacle or hazard in dock premises which is likely to be
      dangerous when vehicles, lifting appliances or people move shall be
      made conspicuous by means of colouring, marking, lighting, or any
      combination thereof.'

It is submitted that this section should give rise to civil liability and that
the authorities relating to s 5 of the Factories Act 1961 apply.

9.8 STATUTORY DEFENCES

Many statutes which impose a duty also provide an escape route. If there
is a statutory defence it must be specifically pleaded. If not, the pleader is
likely to find himself the subject of a wasted costs order if an
adjournment is required to investigate the matters which should have been
pleaded. If the court refuses leave to amend to add the statutory defence,
an adviser at fault may face a professional negligence suit.

It is not good enough merely to refer to the section in the statute which
provides the defence. The words of the statute should be incorporated
into the defence and particulars of the reasons why the defendant alleges
that the statute absolves him should be set out. Thus if it is a defence that
the defendant has taken all steps which are reasonably practicable to
prevent a breach of the statutory duty, the defence should detail the steps
taken and assert with reasons why it was not reasonably practicable to do
more. Sometimes this can become ridiculously tautological where a
pleader says that it was not practical to do more simply because it was not
practical to do so. But an effort must be made to explain why this is so.

9.8.1 'Reasonably practicable'

A number of the Regulations cited above provide an implicit statutory
defence, in that the employer will escape liability, if it can be established
that it did all that was reasonably practicable to avoid the risk.

Whether it is reasonably practicable to keep the floor, etc free from
obstruction and from any substance likely to cause a person to slip is a
question of balancing the magnitude of the risk against the sacrifice, in
terms of time, trouble or money, which would be required to avert it. If
the risk is insignificant in comparison with the sacrifice, the defendant will
succeed in proving that it was not reasonably practicable to comply with
the regulation. The burden of proving that compliance was not reasonably
practicable lies with the person on whom the duty to comply is placed

(*Nimmo v Alexander Cowen & Sons Ltd* [1968] AC 107). The 'reasonably practicable' criterion gives defendants a statutory defence. If it is relied on it must be specifically pleaded. It is not enough merely to state that there was no breach of statutory duty.

It may be that when considering whether steps taken were 'reasonably practicable,' the courts may decide to apply a test akin to that applied when considering 'reasonable care' in the tort of negligence. This to some extent may import issues and questions surrounding acceptable 'industry standards'. It may be necessary to resort to expert opinion when considering whether a potential defendant did all that was 'reasonably practicable' to avoid the risk posed.

CHAPTER 10

PREPARING A CASE

10.1 INTRODUCTION

This chapter is not a general guide to the practice and procedure of personal injury litigation. It assumes that readers know very well how to issue county court proceedings and prepare a brief. The chapter looks instead at certain stages of the litigation process where special considerations might apply to tripping or slipping cases.

The CPR Personal Injury Pre-Action Protocol ('the PI protocol') applies. The relevant parts are at Appendix D below. Particularly significant are the Standard Disclosure Lists which set out the classes of documents which the defendant would normally be expected to provide on receipt of the letter of claim and which should be specifically requested in the letter of claim. The pre-action protocols have made formal application for pre-action disclosure (previously so common in tripping and shipping cases), very unusual.

10.2 FIRST STEPS FOR THE CLAIMANT

10.2.1 Photographs, measurements and weather conditions

Immediately after taking initial instructions, the most urgent priority is to gather evidence about the circumstances of the accident. This is particularly urgent if a complaint about the state of a highway or other site has already been lodged. Defects in pavements where a person has been injured disappear miraculously quickly. A camera loaded with film should be in every solicitor's office, so that the solicitor can go immediately to the site and take photographs of the defect. A ruler or other clearly visible scale should appear in the photograph. The defect should be measured carefully at a number of points. Dividers are useful. Measurements should be taken to the nearest millimetre. The height of the alleged defect in a tripping case has to be given in any application for legal aid. A protractor may be necessary to measure angles. The details taken should be sufficient to enable an accurate scale plan to be drawn.

Where the allegation involves slipping on ice and snow, a sharp probe should be pushed through the ice or snow to measure its depth. A careful note of the quantity of ice or snow, and of the weather conditions at the time the measurements were taken, should be made. If there are grit or salt boxes nearby, what, if anything is in them, and how much? Is there any sign of gritting near the accident? Questionnaires such as that set out in Appendix A.1 should be readily available and used to elicit information from witnesses.

10.2.2   Medical records

The claimant's hospital and general practitioner records should be obtained. The time of admission to the Accident and Emergency Department should tie in with the client's account. If the complaint is a non-specific injury to the back or neck (extremely difficult injuries to disprove), the client should be asked detailed questions about the exact circumstances of the accident. Are subsequent visits to the GP consistent with the alleged injuries? It is better for both client and solicitor if any malingering is unveiled now rather than later.

10.2.3   Proofs of evidence

Detailed proofs of evidence should be taken as soon as possible after the event, not left until there is pressure for the exchange of witness statements under automatic directions. By then, memories will have faded and innocent lapses can be made to look sinister by a good cross-examiner.

10.2.4   Selecting the defendant

The right defendant must be identified. Chapter 1 should help. If the accident happened on a road which is not obviously a highway, a visit to the office of the district or county council should elicit a list of highways maintainable at the public expense. County and district councils are required to keep these lists, and they must be available for inspection by anyone at all at reasonable hours free of charge (see HA 1980, s 36(6) and (7)).

If the relevant highway was recently adopted, a copy of the adoption agreement, if any, should be requested. The date on which the highway became maintainable at the public expense may be crucial. If the adoption was under s 40 of HA 1980, confirmation of the date of adoption should be sought. If the highway authority was not responsible for the highway at the material time, it will no doubt be very quick to say so.

If the accident occurred on a walkway, a copy of the relevant walkway agreement is essential (see HA 1980, s 35). If the walkway was created by a local Act, the Act must be consulted.

In non-highway accidents, or accidents on highways involving non-highway authorities as potential defendants, door-to-door enquiries may be the only way to find out who to sue. The identity of statutory undertakers and independent contractors will be, or should be, within the knowledge of the highway authority. Again, pre-action disclosure should be formally sought if necessary, but this should now be very rare.

Once all the basic evidence is collected, two copies of the letter of claim should be sent to the defendant. One copy is for the defendant; the second copy is for the defendant's insurer. The protocol emphasises the importance of passing the letter of claim to the insurer (see PI protocol, at paragraphs 2.7 and 3.4). The letter of claim should contain a clear summary of the facts, together with an indication of the injuries suffered and the extent of any financial loss incurred (PI protocol, at paragraph 3.2). An example of an appropriate letter is in Appendix A.4. A further example is contained at Annex A of the PI protocol itself. The PI protocol recommends that solicitors use a 'standard format' akin to that used at Annex A (see paragraph 3.3).

The PI protocol advocates a 'cards on the table' approach (see PI protocol, at paragraph 2.4), particularly in cases which are likely to be allocated to the fast track. The partial aim of the protocol is to resolve litigation quickly. Matters should be ready for trial within 30 weeks of allocation. As is well known, ideally the protocol seeks to resolve disputes without recourse to formal litigation at all.

The letter should ask for the details of the defendant's insurer (paragraph 3.4).

Generally, practitioners should not be overly worried if their position changes from that stated in the letter of claim/response. Letters of claim and responses do not have the same status as pleadings. The guidance notes to the PI protocol acknowledge that matters may come to light prior to the issue of proceedings which to some extent may move the goalposts. It is not within the spirit of the protocol 'to take a point' on this in the formal proceedings, 'provided that there was no obvious intention by the party who changed their position to mislead the other party' (see PI protocol, at paragraph 2.12).

Because there are a number of ways that defendants can escape liability (for example via the s 58 defence in a highway maintenance/repair case), and because most of these escape routes lie in territory to which the claimant has no access until disclosure, it is wise not to be over-enthusiastic (or at least over-vocal) in assessing a client's chances at this stage.

10.2.5   Documents routinely disclosed in highway tripping cases

10.2.5.1   Records of highway inspections

The local highway authority's records of inspections of the stretch of highway in question may help decide whether a court is likely to accept the authority's statutory defence, even if the claimant establishes that there is a prima facie case.

They may indicate whether the pattern of inspection has changed. If a highway authority, until 2000, inspected a particular stretch of highway once a fortnight, and then reduced the frequency to once every 3 months, the reasons for that reduction need to be looked at carefully. Has the status of the road changed? Has it, since 2000, carried a lower volume of traffic (which might justify a lower standard of maintenance and repair)? Or was the pre-2000 inspection regime immoderately over-enthusiastic and the post-2000 regime sensible?

10.2.5.2   Maintenance records

The local authority's maintenance records, including the records of independent contractors working in the relevant area, again may indicate the s 58 defence. However unbeatable the claimant's case may seem when viewed in isolation, the records may still show that the highway authority is legally blameless.

Changes in patterns of maintenance work over the past few years may be important. If there have been, in the late winter and early spring of the past 5 years, flurries of maintenance activity on the stretch of highway in question, it may be possible to infer that the stretch of road is vulnerable to winter damage by flood or frost. And if the potential claimant has been injured in the first spring after that maintenance ceased, useful conclusions may follow.

Maintenance records should also deal specifically with the system for providing warnings of road works and for fencing them off.

10.2.5.3   Minutes of highway authority meetings

Minutes of highway authority meetings where maintenance or repair policy has been discussed or decided, together with the consultation papers used, can easily be obtained without any process of formal discovery. See Chapter 3 for the provisions for public access to local government documents. These records should reveal details of the budget for highway maintenance. If independent contractors have been engaged, the criteria by reference to which they were selected may be relevant.

10.2.5.4 Complaints records

If it seems that the potential claimant has a good prima facie case, but it is known that a regular and, on the face of it, adequate inspection and maintenance regime existed, then records of complaints about the state of the stretch of highway in question can be conclusive in establishing that the apparently reasonable regime was in fact so inadequate that s 58 cannot shield the authority.

10.2.5.5 Accident records

Records of other accidents which have occurred on the relevant stretch of highway are admissible in evidence in road traffic accident cases where it is alleged that the highway authority has been negligent (see *William Alexander & Sons v Dundee Corporation* 1950 SC 123, Court of Session). The same rule should apply in negligence and s 41 highway tripping cases, and indeed the inclusion of accident records in the standard disclosure writ seems to imply that this is the case.

10.2.5.6 Records of the location of grit and salt boxes

These may still be relevant if *Goodes* can be circumvented. Often, a claimant claims that there should have been a grit or salt box near where he fell, and that if there had been, that grit and salt would have been used on the relevant patch of road and prevented the accident. The difficulties in such cases are obvious. Since grit boxes are sometimes moved when warm weather arrives, it may be necessary to determine, before beginning an action, just where the nearest salt box was. Claimants relying on such tenuous causes of action usually have slender recollection of the location of boxes, and so the official records will be needed.

The records should also show the amounts of grit, salt or both which have been used, and the activities of the vehicles used to spread them, including tachograph records, all of which may be important.

10.2.5.7 Other records

Documents which may help in non-highway cases include records of accidents and records of cleaning and safety procedures in shops and other premises.

10.3   FIRST STEPS FOR THE DEFENDANT

10.3.1   The site

As soon as a claim has been notified, the defendant's solicitor should go immediately to the site where the accident is alleged to have occurred. He should take the same measurements and make the same observations as the claimant's solicitor.

10.3.2   Records and proofs

Voluntary disclosure of the medical records should be requested. But if it is not granted, it will rarely be worth seeking an order for early disclosure. The relevant inspection and maintenance records should be obtained. Does the regime look reasonable? Detailed proofs from all personnel involved should be taken.

10.3.3   Repairs

Do not be afraid to advise the client to make good the defect after all necessary photographs and measurements have been taken. It is politic to ask the claimant's solicitor if he wants any further inspection before the making good; the allegation that there was a wilful destruction of evidence will not help. Equally there is little force in the submission, often made on behalf of claimants, that the fact that something has been made safer than it was before necessarily means that before the repair it was culpably unsafe.

10.4   STATEMENTS OF CASE

These should be specific and detailed. Their content is now defined by the CPR.

Where measurements are given (for example, of a pavement defect) those measurements should ideally appear in both metric and imperial units in the pleadings. There is a conversion table at Appendix I of this book. If one system only is used, the judge trying the case will certainly know only the other.

Special particularity is required if the defendant alleges that the claimant failed to have regard to warnings.

10.4.1   Particulars of Claim

The Particulars should give the exact position of the place where the accident occurred. The defect should be described in detail, giving measurements of all relevant dimensions. If it is alleged that the defendant failed to have regard to relevant complaints previously made to it, the claim should give the names of the complainants and the way the complaints were made, identifying documents if relevant, and saying what words were used, to whom, by whom, when and where. A medical report must be annexed to the Particulars of Claim unless there are special reasons for not doing so. If no medical report is annexed, an application should be made to the court for permission to serve the Particulars of Claim without it.

10.4.2   Defence

If a statutory defence is to be pleaded, the words of the statute itself should be followed closely. A statutory defence must be pleaded with particularity. In pleading the defence under s 58 of HA 1980, for instance, the way in which the defence is made out should be detailed, using the words of each criterion under s 58(2) which is relied on. An example appears in Appendix A.8. It is too general to aver that 'the defendant took such care as in all the circumstances was reasonably required to secure that the part of the highway to which the action relates was not dangerous for traffic'. A well-justified Request for Further Information would follow. To be fair to counsel who plead the s 58 defence, the information necessary to particularise the s 58(2) criteria is often not provided to them by the instructing solicitor. The moral for defence solicitors is: before drafting the defence, or sending it to counsel to be drafted, solicitors should go through s 58(2) asking of each criterion, 'can this help us, and if so, what needs to be pleaded to make out or justification under this heading?'

If the information needed to draft the defence will not be available in time for the deadline for the service of the defence an extension should be sought.

A properly particularised defence under s 41 or 58 of HA 1980 should be very frightening. No one, quite rightly, will be much concerned by the mere recital of s 58 in the middle of a standard defence generated from a word processor.

10.4.3   Requests for Further Information

A defendant is entitled to know exactly where, when and how an accident is alleged to have happened. It is entitled to have allegations of negligence, nuisance or breach of statutory duty particularised so that it can respond specifically. It should understand, however, that it will have in its own custody much of the information required to paint the full picture of the genesis of an accident.

A claimant is entitled to assert that the defendant 'failed to institute any or any adequate system of inspection of a road' without knowing what the system actually was. If the claimant reasonably considers that the fact of the accident suggests that there was no such adequate system, the allegation is honestly pleaded, and the defendant will not be entitled to ask, in a Request, what system the claimant thinks would have been adequate. The defendant would arguably be entitled to seek, in a Request for Further Information relating to the Particulars of Claim, knowledge of just what the claimant considers would have constituted an adequate system, but a district judge could find little to criticise in an answer which stated:

(a)   An adequate system would have been one which would have caused the said road to be reasonably safe.

(b)   Without prejudice to the generality of the aforesaid such a system would have been one which detected and eliminated the said defect before the date of the accident.

(c)   The question of the appropriate regularity and method of conducting such an inspection is a matter for expect evidence.

All of these answers would have got the defendant nowhere.

As mentioned above, defendants who plead the general s 58 defence should be served with a request for further information, seeking a statement of which s 58(2) criteria are relied on, together with details of the elements within each criterion which substantiate the averment that the s 58 defence is made out. An example of such a request is found in Appendix A.12.

10.4.4   Replies

A Reply should be drafted if the defence makes significant substantive factual assertions rather than merely taking issue with what appears in the Particulars of Claim. A defendant may allege that the claimant caused or contributed to her own accident by running over ice, drunk, wearing stiletto heels and failing to heed the oral warning from a nearby council workman who shouted out, long before the claimant ever reached the excavation in the pavement which injured her, 'watch out for that hole'. The reply will need to assert the claimant's case that she was walking soberly in flat shoes, and that if, which is denied, there was such a workman who shouted any such thing, the claimant could not hear it because she is congenitally deaf.

It is good practice, wherever there are allegations of contributory or causative negligence, to serve a Reply. Failure to plead a claimant's case properly can result in penalties in costs if the claimant is ultimately successful, and in extreme cases, robust judges may refuse to allow last minute amendments and refuse to admit important evidence, which can be fatal to a tripping case.

10.5   PREPARING A CASE FOR THE CLAIMANT

In theory all the claimant has to prove in a highway tripping case is:

(a)   that the defendant highway authority was responsible for the repair and maintenance of the highway where the accident happened;

(b)   that the accident actually happened on the highway;

(c)   that the highway was dangerous; and

(d)   it was a result of the dangerousness that the accident happened.

If this can be shown, the ball is then in the highway authority's court. The highway authority will have to show, on the balance of probabilities, that the statutory defence under s 58 of HA 1980 is made out. The claimant does not have to disprove the statutory defence, but should be in a position to contradict the allegations which the defendant says constitute its statutory defence.

If the defendant states only that an inspection once every 6 months was sufficient to secure that the highway was reasonably safe, there will generally be no need for a claimant to call expert evidence. The only question in issue is a legal one which the judge should be able to answer unaided, namely was the road in fact reasonably safe. If not, forbidden words like res ipsa loquitur will spring immediately and conclusively to mind. Even in these fast-track, proportionate, post CPR days there will sometimes be a place for experts in tripping and slipping cases.

If, the highway authority contends that the road in question crumbled away wholly unpredictably, it will no doubt seek to call expert evidence to support these conclusions. If it does not it should fail. The claimant should consider engaging experts of his own to maintain that any competent highway engineer could and should have foreseen that the road in question would crumble at this time, and that such-and-such a step should have been taken 3 months earlier to avoid it.

10.5.1   Instructing an expert

Sometimes it is obvious that an expert is needed. But some experts can make the simplest tripping accidents bristle with breaches of statutory duty. In a tripping accident on stairs, for instance, it may be worth instructing a health and safety expert who will be able to assess whether the stairs meet the relevant building regulations and whether the carpet on them satisfies the appropriate British standard. These experts can make Particulars of Claim or Defence look much more formidable; and even if they do not force an early settlement, they will provide superb cross-examination material. Remember proportionality, though, and Lord Woolf's loathing of experts.

The PI protocol gives guidance on the instruction of experts (see paragraphs 3.15–3.21). Before instructing an expert, the instructing party should send a list of proposed experts to the other side. The other party may indicate an objection to the proposed expert. The safest course is the course of least resistance – ie to instruct an appropriate alternative and mutually agreed expert. If the instructing party does not follow this route, it will be for the court to determine whether either party has acted unreasonably.

Where the other party has agreed to the instruction of an expert, it will not be permitted to rely on its own expert in that field unless:

(a)   the first party agrees;

(b)   the court so directs; or

(c)   the first party's expert report has been amended, and the first party is not prepared to disclose the original report (paragraph 3.19).

The PI protocol encourages joint instructions where possible, particularly in respect of matters allocated to the fast track (paragraph 2.14).

As a general rule, whenever a breach of statutory duty is alleged, other than under s 41 of HA 1980 or under the Occupiers' Liability Acts, think about instructing an expert. Of course there will be cases where allegations of breaches of common law duties, of s 41 of HA 1980, or of the Occupiers' Liability Acts will need to be supported by expert evidence.

Conferences with counsel and any expert witness should always be held well before the trial takes place. An expert who is robust and elegant on paper may be fumbling, incoherent and profoundly embarrassing in the witness box. It is better to find this out before he goes into the witness box. In the initial conference, counsel should cross-examine the expert along the lines of the expected cross-examination. If the expert becomes upset about this, do not use him.

Experts can give useful advice on the additional evidence which needs to be obtained before the case is ready for trial. But experts tend to neglect the basic and crucial common-sense points on which the judge will focus: do not hold them in too much awe.

The expert should see and expressly comment in his report on *all* the relevant documents. The expert will have a view on what documents are relevant, and so should see everything which is obtained from the defendant. To ensure that nothing has been missed, and to avoid unexpected and damaging questions later, it is wise to ask the expert to comment orally on every document not expressly referred to in the report. The report should be amended to include further references to these documents if necessary. Even a statement that a particular document is irrelevant, stating why it is irrelevant, can be useful.

Beware of medical reports which, when dealing with the circumstances of the accident, contradict the account given in the witness statements.

10.5.2   Using the disclosed documents

There seems to be an unhealthy and irrational presumption among personal injury solicitors that documents do not matter. Some solicitors may deal splendidly and minutely with whole rainforests of paper in a contract case but not bother to read what is disclosed to them from the highway authority. This is partly because:

(a)   they do not know about the mechanics of the highway authority apparatus, and so do not know what they are looking at or for; and

(b)   of a deep-seated presumption, held unconsciously or consciously by some of the best and worst solicitors respectively, that personal injury cases are about sordid, undocumented details like blood, bones and roads.

Innumerable opportunities are lost because of such attitudes.

The ways in which discovered documents can be useful, and the points to look for when they become available, are discussed in detail at **10.2.5** above. The checklist below shows what a claimant in a highway tripping case can expect to get in discovery, either routinely or by way of specific application. Not all these documents are, of course, pursuant to disclosure under the pre-action protocol standard disclosure writ on subsequent disclosure, relevant to all cases. For example, there is no need to demand information on how many tonnes of grit were deposited on a stretch of highway in December if the accident occurred on a sunny day in August; it is surprising how many legal advisers feel they need it!

10.5.3   Checklist of records

–   The local authority's records of inspection for the relevant stretch of highway.

— The local authority's maintenance records, including those of independent contractors working in the relevant area.

— Records of minutes of highway authority meetings where maintenance or repair policy has been discussed or decided, together with the consultation papers used. This class includes details of the budget for highway maintenance. If independent contractors have been engaged, look carefully at the criteria used in the selection of those contractors.

— Inspection and maintenance protocols issued to highway inspectors and independent contractors undertaking repairs. This class of documents should deal specifically with protocols for provision of warnings/fencing of works.

— Records of complaints about the state of the highways.

— Records of other accidents which have occurred on the relevant stretch of highway.

— Records of the location of grit and salt boxes, the amount of grit/salt deposited on roads, and the activities of gritting and salting vehicles including, where appropriate, tachograph records.

10.5.4   Seeking counsel's advice

If there has been proper disclosure there may well be a large number of documents. The solicitor may benefit from independent advice on liability and evidence once the first rash of discovery is complete. This will be most useful if it is sought as soon as possible after disclosure. Since counsel tend to do exactly as they are told and no more, a good bottom line of instructions to counsel at this stage might read as follows:

Counsel is asked:

(i)   To advise on liability on the basis of the documents already disclosed.

(ii)   To advise on whether any further documents should be sought, and if so to identify those documents and state their importance [and if necessary draft the necessary application to the court with a supporting statement].

(iii)   To advise whether any information should be sought from the defendant by way of a request for further information, and if so to draft that request.

(iv) To indicate what, if any, other information should be sought at this stage by instructing solicitors and to indicate where appropriate the steps which should be taken to obtain it.

(v) To consider whether any expert evidence should be sought at this stage and if so, to indicate what should be obtained and why. It would be helpful if counsel could suggest an appropriate expert and draft a list of questions to be put to that expert. If counsel considers that no expert should be instructed at this stage but that it is likely that one will eventually be necessary, it would again be helpful if the name of an expert could be suggested so that instructing solicitors can ascertain approximately how much that expert would charge for a report.

(vi) To advise on evidence generally.

10.5.5   The trial bundle

The claimant is responsible for bringing the action to trial, and for preparing a common trial bundle for use by both sides and by the court. It should contain all documents to be used by both sides. Inclusion of a document in the bundle does not mean that its contents are agreed. In an action with two parties, at least six bundles should be prepared (one each for counsel and solicitors on each side, one for the judge and one for the witness box).

The bundle should contain:

–   statements of case;

–   all applications and orders made in the interlocutory stages of the action;

–   inspection and maintenance records and any other similar documents (such as local authority minutes) relied upon by either side;

–   medical reports;

–   other expert reports;

–   witness statements;

–   any relevant correspondence, carefully excluding all the 'without prejudice' correspondence such as Pt 36 offers;

–   photographs of the locus in quo. In practice it will often be useful to include the photographs in separate bundles.

The bundle should be bound in some way which makes all its pages easily accessible. A ring-binder is fine. A spiral spine is even better. The pages should be numbered. The bundles should be delivered to the court and to the defendant in good time before the trial. The morning of the trial is not acceptable.

The names and references of the authorities to be relied on should be notified to the other side not later than the night before the trial. It is good practice to send a fax to the court notifying it of the authorities to be relied on, but since the libraries of most county courts are poorly stocked, copies of the authorities or the original reports must always be brought for the judge. It is courteous to bring copies for the opponent also. If the copies of the authorities can be spirally bound or put into a ring-binder, so much the better. If a case is reported in more than one report, the official law reports are to be preferred. It is not enough to rely on summaries of and quotations from the authorities.

10.6 PREPARING A CASE FOR THE DEFENDANT

10.6.1 The statutory defence

Section 58(2) of HA 1980 is a useful and practical checklist for investigations and lines of argument which can help defendants. Examine each of the criteria and ask 'could this possibly apply? If so, how is this element to be proved?' Since the burden of making out the statutory defence lies on the defendant, defendants in highway tripping cases tend to be more proactive than defendants in other areas of personal injury litigation, but it should of course be borne in mind that the claimant has first to establish breach of the statutory duty before s 58 becomes at all relevant.

10.6.2 Experts

The same comments apply here as apply to the use of experts by claimants.

10.6.3 Giving disclosure

Everything which is hidden is likely to be made known. It is difficult to keep anything undisclosed when faced with an application for specific disclosure, and a coy defendant is likely to be penalised in costs. Worse still, it will seem sinister to the trial judge if a defendant (even if perfectly properly) at first refused to hand over a document which later became the subject of an order for specific disclosure. It will only play into the claimant's hands to withhold anything unnecessarily.

10.6.4 Contributory negligence

Allegations of contributory negligence are difficult to sustain. But they will often, and properly, appear in the defence. They may help if the judge takes a particular, personal dislike to the claimant.

10.7 TRIAL AND AFTERWARDS

Once a case comes to trial and to consideration of appeals, tripping and slipping litigation has no particularly special features.

APPENDIX A

PRECEDENTS

A.1 QUESTIONNAIRE FOR POTENTIAL WITNESSES

[Solicitors' address and reference]

We act for [name] who was injured in a [tripping] accident on [date] at about [time] on [name of road]. We understand that you may have witnessed the accident, and would be very grateful if you will answer the following questions on the form provided and return the form in the enclosed stamped addressed envelope.

1. Did you see the accident? If you did not, and cannot help us in any other way, we would be grateful if you will still return the form to us. If you did not see the accident yourself, but know of someone else who did, would you please complete the 'Other witnesses' section at paragraph 16 below.

2. What time did the accident happen?

3. Being as precise as you can, where did it happen?

4. Where were you at the time you saw the accident?

5. How far was this from the accident?

6. Was your view of the accident obstructed in any way? If so, by what and for how long?

7. Please describe in your own words what you saw happen. A sketch plan would be helpful. Please use the reverse side of the form for this.

8. If the accident occurred by tripping in or over a defect in the highway:

(a)   How was the defect created (e g was one corner of a paving stone sunk below the neighbouring paving stones? Was the edge of the road worn away? Was a grating standing proud of the rest of the pavement?)

(b)   How long, how wide and how deep, at the deepest, was the defect?

(c)   Please use the reverse side of the form to draw the defect.

(d)   Do you have any idea how long the defect has been present in the pavement?

(e)   Have you seen the defect before?

(f)   If so, when did you first see it?

(g)   When, before the time of the accident, did you last notice the defect?

(h)   Do you think that the defect was dangerous to pedestrians?

9. How often do you use the stretch of pavement where the accident happened?

10. When, before the accident, was the last time you used that stretch?

11. What happened after the accident? (eg did anyone help [   ] to her feet? Did anyone call an ambulance?)

12. What was the weather like at the time of the accident?

13. If the accident did not occur during the day, what was the lighting like at the place where the accident occurred? Where did artificial light come from?

14. Was the defect over which [   ] fell fenced or guarded in any way? If so, please describe just how it was fenced or guarded.

15. Were there any notices giving warning of the existence of the defect over which [   ] fell? If so:

(a)   How many were there?

(b)   Where were they?

(c)   What did they say?

(d)   How long had they been in place?

(e)   Had you noticed them before the accident happened and if so, how long before?

16. Do you know of any other people who you think could help us in our investigation? (eg other people who have tripped at or near the place where this accident occurred). If so please tell us:

(a)   the names and addresses of those people and

(b)   how you think they could be helpful.

17. Would you be prepared to give evidence in court?

Thank you for the time you have taken to complete this form.

A.1.1 Additional Questions for Accidents Involving Street Works

We understand that the accident involved street works. Please answer as many of the following questions as you can:

1. Who were the contractors doing the work?

2. What works were they doing?

3. How long had they been working at the site of the accident?

4. Were any workmen or other officials involved in the works present at the time of the accident?

5. If so, please identify each of them by name and/or description and say in what capacity you understood each to be at the site of the accident.

6. Did any of them say anything to you or to anyone else in your hearing or knowledge about the accident? If so, please state what was said to whom, and when and where it was said.

7. Do you know if, at any time, anyone has lodged any complaints about the street works? If so, please tell us the names and addresses of the person making the complaint, and, if you know, to whom the complaint was made, when it was made, about what it was made and what the response, if any, was.

A.1.2 Additional Questions for Accidents Involving Slipping on Ice and Snow

We understand that [   ] slipped on some [compacted snow or ice]. Please answer as many of the following questions as you can:

1. Did you see exactly where [   ] slipped? Please describe as well as you can what was underfoot.

2. If there was snow or ice on the ground:

(a)   how thick was it?

(b)   how long had it been there?

(c)   what state was it in? (eg was the snow melting? Was there free water on the top layer of any ice?)

3. If [   ] slipped on ice, was it black ice, or was it clearly visible?

4. If [   ] slipped on ice, do you know where the water which formed the ice came from? (eg did it come from a broken drain pipe or an overflowing stream?)

5. If the ice was formed from water from any premises, do you know who owns or occupies those premises? If so, please give us their name(s) and address.

6. When was the road where [   ] fell last gritted or salted?

7. Did the grit/salt reach the part of the road where [   ] fell?

8. Where was the nearest grit or salt bin?

9. Was there grit/salt in it at the time of the accident?

10.

(a)   Have there recently been any changes in the number and/or position of grit bins in the area where the accident occurred? If so, what changes have there been?

(b)   Did this result in less grit/salt being available near to the place where the accident occurred?

(c)   If this change had not occurred, do you think that the spot where [   ] fell would have been gritted? Or were the grit bins not in practice used?

(d)   Do you know of any complaints which have been made about the changes in grit bins? If so, please tell us who made those complaints, the names and addresses of the people making them, and what each complaint was about.

11. Do you know of anyone else who has slipped on ice or snow near where the accident occurred? If so, please give us their names and addresses and tell us whatever you know about their accident, including the time when it happened, exactly where it happened, what injuries (if any) were suffered, whether any complaints were lodged (and if so with whom) and whether any legal proceedings resulted.

A.2   GENERAL ENDORSEMENT

The Claimant's claim is for personal injuries suffered and losses sustained as a result of an accident on 2 March 2008 in Main Street, London WC1 caused by the negligence and/or breach of statutory duty of the Defendants, their servants or agents.

A.3   CERTIFICATE OF VALUE

A certificate of value is mandatory in a personal injury action commenced in the High Court (see *Practice Direction* [1991] 1 WLR 642).

> This writ includes a claim for personal injury but may be commenced in the High Court because the value of the action for the purposes of article 5 of the High Court and County Courts Jurisdiction Order 1991 exceeds £50,000.

This certificate must be signed by the claimant's solicitor.

A.4 LETTER OF CLAIM

The Chief Clerk
Blankshire County Council
County House,
Blank BL1 4XX

Dear Sir,

Re Alan Smith
100 High Street, Blank, BL4 5EE, Blankshire
Employed by Vlad Impalers Inc, 1 The Pit, London SW1X 4XZ

We are instructed by the above named ('the claimant') to claim damages in connection with a tripping accident which occurred on 14 January 2008 outside the main entrance to the Dog's Home, Low Street, Blank.

Please confirm the identity of your insurers. Please note that the insurers will need to see this letter as soon as possible and it may affect your insurance cover and/or the conduct of any subsequent legal proceedings if you do not send this letter to them.

The circumstances of the accident are that at about 4.30 pm the claimant was walking along the northern side of Low Street, Blank, when, at a point opposite the main entrance to the dog's home, he tripped over a defect in the pavement and fell.

The reason we are alleging that you are liable to the claimant is that the accident was caused by your breach of your statutory duty to maintain the highway under section 41 of the Highways Act 1980 and/or by your negligence and or by you causing or permitting a nuisance. The defect was formed by the sinking of one paving stone relative to another. It presented a trip of 1.5 inches. It is obviously dangerous and our enquiries suggest that it had been present for some months. It would have been detected by a competent regime of inspection. It amounted to an obstruction to safe passage along the highway.

A description of the claimant's injuries is as follows:

Comminuted fracture of the right humerus.

The claimant is employed as a security guard. As a result of the accident he went off work on 14 January 2008 and has not returned since. He earns about £245 net per week and there has been a total loss of earnings since 14 January 2008. That loss continues. The claimant is unlikely ever to work again. He is certainly at a disadvantage on the labour market.

At this stage of our enquiries we would expect the documents contained in the 'Highway Tripping Claims' part of the CPR standard disclosure list to be relevant to this action.

A copy of this letter is enclosed for you to send to your insurers. Finally we expect an acknowledgment of this letter within 21 days by yourselves or your insurers.

Yours faithfully,

A.5 LETTER TO METEOROLOGICAL EXPERT REQUESTING WEATHER RECORDS

Note: The Meteorological Office no longer provides historic weather information upon request. However, a number of private companies offer similar services. A letter akin to that below should assist in ensuring that the relevant meteorological data is obtained.

Meterological Services Limited
123 Anystreet
Anytown
AN1 2NS

Dear Sir,

We act on behalf of Gladys Green who was injured in a slipping accident on the High Street, Greater Danger, Berkshire, at about 10.30 pm on 28 December 2008.

Mrs Green alleges that she slipped on compacted ice and snow which had lain uncleared for several days.

We understand that you provide historic meteorological data. We would be grateful if you could prepare a [report/witness statement] indicating the following details:

(a)   the maximum and minimum and mean temperatures in Greater Danger or your nearest monitoring point from 20 December to 29 December 2008 inclusive.

(b)   what forecasts the Meteorological Office issued:
   (i)   earlier in the year, for the winter of 2008–2009 in general, stating when this forecast was issued, and via what media;
   (ii)   for the period 20 December to 29 December 2008 inclusive, stating when such forecasts were issued, and via what media.

(c)   When the snow which was on the ground on 28 December 2008 was first recorded as falling in Greater Danger, and what reports of the depth and state of that snow you received from the time of the first fall of snow until 29 December 2008.

[In the event that a formal expert report is required; set out an expert's obligations to the Court below, in the usual manner.]

Yours faithfully,

A.6 LETTER TO AUTOMOBILE ASSOCIATION REQUESTING INFORMATION ABOUT THE STATE OF ROADS

Automobile Association
Carr Ellison House
William Armstrong Drive
Newcastle Upon Tyne NE4 7YA

Dear Sirs,

We act on behalf of Gladys Green who was injured in a slipping accident on the High Street, Greater Danger, Berkshire, at about 10.30 pm on 28 December 2008.

Mrs Green alleges that she slipped on compacted ice and snow which had lain uncleared for several days.

We would be grateful if you will please indicate:

(a)   What your 'state of the road' reports for the Greater Danger area were from 20 December to 29 December 2008 in so far as those reports dealt with adverse weather conditions.

(b)   What, if any, warnings you would have given to road users about using roads in the Greater Danger area from 20 December to 29 December 2008 in so far as the warnings resulted from adverse weather conditions.

A.7 PARTICULARS OF CLAIM IN A CASE OF BREACH OF STATUTORY DUTY OF A HIGHWAY AUTHORITY; NEGLIGENCE; NUISANCE

IN THE COUNTY COURT CLAIM No. 1234567

BETWEEN: A.B. Claimant

and

C. COUNTY COUNCIL Defendant

Particulars of Claim

1. The Defendant is and was at all material times the highway authority responsible for a highway known as High Street, Greater Stumbling (hereinafter referred to as 'the street').

2. At about 4.30 pm on 23 March 2009 the Claimant was walking along the pavement of the north side of the street when, at a point opposite the main gate of the Greater Stumbling Infant School, she tripped on a defect ('the defect') in the said pavement and fell.

3. The defect was formed by the sinking of the corner of one flagstone and was 4.6 centimetres (1.81 inches) deep at its deepest point and was triangular in shape, the sides of the said triangle being 5 centimetres (1.96 inches), 7.8 centimetres (3.07 inches) and 13.2 centimetres (5.20 inches) long.

4. The Claimant said accident was caused by the Defendant's breach of its statutory duty under section 41 of the Highways Act 1980 to repair or maintain the street.

5. Further or in the alternative the said accident was caused by the negligence of the Defendant.

Particulars of Breach of Statutory Duty and/or Negligence

(a) Failing adequately or at all to repair and/or maintain the street.

(b) Failing to raise the corner of the said paving stone to the level of the surrounding pavement or fill in the defect or otherwise render the street safe for pedestrians passing along it.

(c) Failing to institute and/or maintain any or any adequate regime for the inspection of the condition of the street.

(d) Failing to fence off or guard the defect.

(e) Failing to provide any warning, by means of bollards skirting the defect or by way of written notices or otherwise, of the existence of the defect.

(f) Failing to take any or any sufficient heed to the complaints about the dangerous condition of the part of the street where the accident happened which were notified to the Defendant as follows:
  (i) By letter dated 23 January 2009 to the Defendant from Miss Cee Dee. The said letter complained generally about loose and sinking paving stones on the pavement of the street opposite the Greater Stumbling Infant School, and commented specifically on the danger to pedestrians which these defects posed.
  (ii) Orally by telephone in or around December 2008 from Mr Gee Aitch to a male employee at the Defendant's Greater Stumbling offices who did not identify himself.

This complaint concerned loose paving stones outside the Raj Tandoori Restaurant, which is on the street about 25 yards south from the place where the Claimant's accident occurred, on the same side of the street. This complaint specifically mentioned a tripping accident outside the said restaurant sustained by the said Gee Aitch as a result, inter alia, of the said paving stones about 2 days prior to the complaint being lodged by him.

6. Further or in the alternative the defect constituted a nuisance which was caused or permitted by the Defendant, and the said accident was caused by that nuisance.

7. By reason of the matters aforesaid the Claimant, who was born on 12 August 1930, sustained personal injuries, loss and damage.

Particulars of Personal Injuries

(a) The Claimant fell heavily on her left side. She sustained a comminuted fracture of her left ulna and radius. She was badly shocked.

(b) She was taken by ambulance to the Greater Stumbling District Hospital. On 24 March 2009 she underwent an operation for internal fixation of the radical fracture with a plate. She was placed in an above-elbow plaster. She was discharged from the said hospital on 30 March 2009.

(c) The plaster was removed on 23 May 2009. The Claimant attended a total of 14 times at the said hospital for out-patient and physiotherapy appointments between May and October 2009.

(d) Between the date of the said accident and October 2009 the Claimant was in considerable but decreasing discomfort and was unable to do ordinary household chores. Her sleeping was disturbed by the pain, and she had to take sleeping tablets. Her hobbies of bridge and knitting were severely affected and her social life suffered in consequence.

(e) The left arm fractures have healed well. The Claimant has a normal range of movement in her left arm. She has some stiffness and aching in cold weather. This will persist for the rest of her life. No other long term sequelae are expected.

(f) Further details are set out in the medical report of Mr John Smith, Consultant Orthopaedic surgeon, dated 11 December 2009, which is annexed hereto.

Particulars of Special Damage

These are set out in a separate Schedule annexed hereto.

9. Further the Claimant is entitled to and claims interest on the sum found due to her for such period and at such rate as the court may think fit, pursuant to section 69 of the County Courts Act 1984.

AND the Claimant claims:

1. Damages in excess of £5000 but limited to £50,000.

2. Interest pursuant to statute as aforesaid.

A. BARRISTER

DATED this 23rd day of January 2010

By A. Solicitor & Co, 12 High Street, Greater Stumbling, GS1 1OO, Solicitors for the Claimant.

Statement of Truth

I believe that the facts stated in these Particulars of Claim are true.

Signed . . . .

A.8 DEFENCE IN A CASE OF BREACH OF STATUTORY DUTY OF A HIGHWAY AUTHORITY; NEGLIGENCE; NUISANCE

IN THE COUNTY COURT CLAIM No. 1234567

BETWEEN: A.B. Claimant

and

C. COUNTY COUNCIL Defendant/Part 20 Claimant

and

D. PLC Part 20 Defendant

Defence

1. In the Defence, wherever anything is said to be not admitted, the Claimant is required to prove it.

2. Paragraph 1 of the Particulars of Claim is admitted.

3. Save that it is admitted that on or around 23 March 2009 the Claimant sustained an accident (the place, time, manner and cause of which are specifically not admitted), no admissions are made as to paragraph 2 of the Particulars of Claim.

4. It is not admitted that the alleged defect at any material time existed.

5.

(a) No admissions are made as to paragraph 3 of the Particulars of Claim

(b) Without prejudice to the generality of the aforesaid if, which is not admitted, the defect existed at the material time, no admissions are made as to its cause or any of its characteristics.

6. It is denied that the Defendant was in breach of its statutory duty and/or was negligent as alleged in paragraphs 4 and 5 of the Particulars of Claim, and the causation alleged therein is denied.

7. Without prejudice to the generality of the aforesaid the Defendant:

(a) denies that the complaints set out at paragraph 5(f) of the Particulars of Claim were ever made and

(b) contends that if, contrary to the aforesaid, either or both of the said complaints were made, there was no substance whatever therein.

8. Further or in the alternative if, which is denied, the street was in a dangerous condition, the Defendant contends that at all material times it took all such care as in all the circumstances was reasonably required to secure that the part of the highway to which the action relates was not dangerous for traffic.

Particulars

(a) The part of the street where the said accident is alleged to have occurred (hereinafter referred to as 'the site') is only rarely used by pedestrians, and never by other traffic. Those pedestrians who use the relevant part of the street can reasonably be assumed to know the street well and avoid any defects therein. The Defendant will rely on section 58(2)(a) of the Highways Act 1980 (hereinafter referred to as 'the Act').

(b) The site was regularly maintained. The surface of the street was completely resurfaced in May 2007. Because the site is rarely used, and is not subject to the pooling of surface water or other significant erosive factors, no further active maintenance was required. The Defendant will rely on section 58(2)(b) of the Act.

(c) The site was in a reasonable state of repair. The Defendant will rely on section 58(2)(c) of the Act.

(d) The Defendant instituted and maintained a system of inspection of the highway which included the site. Inspections were carried out once every three months, the last relevant inspection being 23 February 2009. The Defendant will rely on section 58(2)(d) of the Act.

9. As to paragraph 7 of the Particulars of Claim:

(a)   If, which is not admitted, the said defect existed, it is denied that it constituted a nuisance.

(b)   If, contrary to the above, the said defect did constitute a nuisance, it is denied that the nuisance was caused or permitted by the Defendant.

(c)   It is denied that the Claimant's accident was caused by any nuisance.

10. The accident was caused or materially contributed to by the Claimant's own negligence.

Particulars of Claimant's Negligence

If, contrary to the aforesaid, the said accident occurred in the circumstances set out in the Particulars of Claim, the Claimant was negligent in:

(a)   Failing to look where she was going.

(b)   Failing to place her feet carefully.

(c)   Wearing high stiletto heeled shoes.

(d)   Running over the site while carrying heavy bags.

(e)   Being at all material times drunk.

(f)   Failing to heed the presence of the said defect, despite going over or past the site most days.

(g)   Failing to take the shorter alternative route to and from her home through New Street, which route is entirely on a metalled surface smoother than that at the site.

11. Further or in the alternative the accident was caused by the negligence of the Part 20 Defendant (who was the independent contractor engaged by the Defendant to perform the repairs required at the site), as appears in the Part 20 claim form and Particulars of the Part 20 Claim.

12. As to paragraph 8 of the Particulars of Claim:

(a)   No admissions are made as to the alleged or any personal injuries, loss or damage.

(b)   The causation alleged therein is denied.

13. No admissions are made as to the Claimant's entitlement to interest on any sum found due to her, on the basis pleaded at paragraph 9 of the Particulars of Claim or at all.

B. COUNSEL

DATED this 10th day of February 2010.

By B. Attorney, 23 Low Street, Greater Stumbling, GS1 4WF, Solicitors for the Defendant.

Statement of Truth

I believe that the facts stated in this Defence are true.

Signed . . . .

A.9 REPLY IN A CASE OF BREACH OF STATUTORY DUTY OF A HIGHWAY AUTHORITY; NEGLIGENCE; NUISANCE

IN THE COUNTY COURT CLAIM No. 1234567

BETWEEN: A.B. Claimant

and

C. COUNTY COUNCIL Defendant/Part 20 Claimant

and

D. PLC Part 20 Defendant

Reply

1. Save insofar as the same consists of admissions or is hereinafter specifically admitted or expressed to be not admitted, the Claimant denies each and every contention made by the Defendant in its Defence.

2. Paragraph 7 of the Defence is denied in its entirety, and without prejudice to the generality of this denial the Claimant contends:

As to Particulars (a)

(i)   That the site is used daily and often by a large number of pedestrians passing between Bank Street and High Street.

(ii)   That the site is further used regularly and often by motorised vehicles delivering goods to the Crown Public House.

As to Particulars (b)

(i)   That it is not admitted that the surface of the street was completely re-surfaced or re-surfaced at all in May 2007.

(ii)   That if the street was re-surfaced in May 2000 that re-surfacing did not extend to the site.

(iii)   That no maintenance or repair work has been done on the site since about 1970.

(iv)   That the site is subject to pooling of water after moderate rain fall.

(v)   That in cold weather the surface of the site is particularly subject to disruption from frost and ice because of the pooling of water as aforesaid and because of water vapour emerging from the ventilation ducts of the Crown Public House which freezes on the site.

As to Particulars (c)

That it is denied that the site was in a reasonable state of repair.

As to Particulars (d)

(i)   That no admissions are made as to the facts alleged therein.

(ii)   That if such a system was instituted and maintained, the said system either failed to include the site within its ambit or was manifestly inadequate.

3. As to paragraph 10 of the Defence:

(a)   It is denied that the Claimant was negligent as alleged or at all.

(b)   If, contrary to the aforesaid the Claimant was negligent, such negligence was not in any way causative of the said accident and did not contribute to it.

(c)   Without prejudice to the generality of the aforesaid the Claimant pleads to the Particulars of alleged negligence as follows.

As to Particulars (a) and (b)

These are denied.

As to Particulars (c)

(i)   It is admitted that the Claimant was wearing stiletto-heeled shoes at the time of her accident.

(ii)   It is denied that these shoes could properly be described as being high heeled, the heels thereof being 3.5 centimetres high.

As to Particulars (d)

(i)   It is denied that the Claimant ran over the site.

(ii)   It is averred that the Claimant was at all material times walking slowly with appropriate care.

(iii) It is admitted that the Claimant was carrying heavy bags when going over the site.

As to Particulars (e)

(i)   It is denied that the Claimant was drunk.

(ii)   The Claimant is a teetotaler and was returning home from a Prayer meeting at St Luke's Church.

As to Particulars (f)

(i)   It is denied that the Claimant goes over or past the site most days.

(ii)   The Claimant would normally take the alternative route described in Particulars of Claimant's Negligence (g), but on 23 March 2009 the said alternative route was impassable because of the erection of police barricades across the junction of New Street and Old Street.

As to Particulars (g)

(i)   It is admitted that the said alternative route is shorter and passes along an entirely metalled road with a smoother surface than that of the site.

(ii)   For the reasons set out above, it is denied that on 23 March 2009 the said route was an alternative one.

(iii) The Claimant in any event contends that the existence of an alternative route is wholly irrelevant to the issue between the Claimant and the Defendant.

A. BARRISTER

DATED this 23 day of March 2010.

By A Solicitor & Co, 12 High Street, Greater Stumbling, GS1 1OO, Solicitors for the Claimant.

Statement of Truth

I believe that the facts stated in this reply are true.

Signed . . . .

A.10   PART 20 PARTICULARS OF CLAIM IN A CASE OF BREACH OF STATUTORY DUTY OF A HIGHWAY AUTHORITY; NEGLIGENCE; NUISANCE

IN THE COUNTY COURT CLAIM No. 1234567

BETWEEN: A.B. Claimant

and

C. COUNTY COUNCIL Defendant/Part 20 Claimant

and

D. PLC Part 20 Defendant

Part 20 Particulars of Claim

This action has been brought by the Claimant against the Defendant Part 20 Claimant (hereinafter 'the Defendant'). In it the Claimant claims against the Defendant damages for personal injuries resulting from an accident which is alleged to have occurred on 23 March 2009 as appears from the claim form, a copy of which is served herewith together with the Particulars of Claim. If, contrary to its Defence, the Defendant is found liable to the Claimant, the Defendant claims to be entitled against the Part 20 Defendant to an indemnity against the Claimant's claim together with the costs of the action or alternatively a contribution thereto on the grounds that:

1. By a written contract ('the contract') dated 3 February 2006 made between the Part 20 Defendant and the Defendant the Part 20 Defendant agreed to undertake the work of repaving a 150 metre length of pavement on the East side of a highway known as High Street, Greater Stumbling.

2. The following were, inter alia, express terms of the contract:

(a) By clause 2(4)(a)

That the Part 20 Defendant would place the new paving stones on a newly dug foundation.

(b) By clause 2(4)(b)

That the Part 20 Defendant would ensure that the new paving stones were embedded firmly on a base of a type of cement which accorded with British Standard TSX 12345.

(c) By clause 4(3)(c)

That the Part 20 Defendant would use all reasonable care and skill in the performance of the contract.

3. In May 2006 the Part 20 Defendant performed the said re-paving works.

4. The Part 20 Defendant re-paved the part of the said highway where it is alleged the Claimant sustained injury.

5. The Part 20 Defendant was in breach of the terms of the contract set out in paragraph 2 hereof.

Particulars of Breach of Contract

(a)   In breach of clause 2(4)(a) the Part 20 Defendant failed to dig out any foundations, but merely place the new paving stones on the original base upon which the old paving stones, which the Part 20 Defendant removed, had been lying.

(b)   In breach of clause 2(4)(b) the Part 20 Defendant failed:
  (i)   to embed the new paving stones in cement which accorded to the said British Standard. The Part 20 Defendant used instead an inferior brand called 'Amber Nectar'.
  (ii)   to embed the new paving stones firmly. The layer of cement the Part 20 Defendant used was 1 centimetre (0.39 inches) thick: It should have been at least 3 centimetres (1.18 inches) thick.

(c)   In breach of clause 4(3)(c) the Part 20 Defendant failed in the respects particularised in paragraphs 5(a) and 5(b) hereof to use reasonable care and skill.

6. Further or in the alternative the Part 20 Defendant was negligent, and the Defendant repeats the allegations in paragraph 5 hereof as Particulars of Negligence.

7. If the defect referred to in the Particulars of Claim existed, and if it caused the personal injuries, loss or damage referred to therein, or any part thereof, such was caused by the Part 20 Defendant's breach of contract and/or negligence aforesaid, and the Part 20 Defendant is liable to indemnify the Defendant against any sum awarded to the Claimant whether by way of damages or costs, together with the costs of defending this action or to pay the Defendant damages commensurate with such sum.

8. Further or alternatively the Part 20 Defendant is liable to the Claimant in respect of such damage as she may prove at trial, and is accordingly liable to contribute towards such sum as may be awarded to the Claimant whether by way of damages or costs, together with the costs of defending this action.

B. COUNSEL

DATED this 10 day of February 2010

By: B Attorney, 23 Low Street, Greater Stumbling, GS1 4WF, Solicitors for the Defendant.

Statement of Truth

I believe that the facts stated in these particulars of the Part 20 Claim are true.

Signed . . . .

A.11   DEFENCE TO PART 20 PARTICULARS OF CLAIM IN A CASE OF BREACH OF STATUTORY DUTY OF A HIGHWAY AUTHORITY; NEGLIGENCE; NUISANCE

IN THE COUNTY COURT CLAIM No. 1234567

BETWEEN: A.B. Claimant

and

C. COUNTY COUNCIL Defendant/Part 20 Claimant

and

D. PLC Part 20 Defendant

Defence of the Part 20 Defendant

1. In this Defence, whenever anything is said to be not admitted, the Part 20 Defendant requires the Claimant and the Defendant/Part 20 Defendant ('the Defendant'), (as appropriate) to prove it.

2. No admissions are made as to the fact of the Claimant's accident or any of the pleaded circumstances or consequences of it.

3. It is denied that the Part 20 Defendant is liable:

(a)   to indemnify the Defendant or

(b)   contribute at all in respect of the action between the Claimant and the Defendant.

4. Paragraphs 1, 2 and 3 of the Part 20 Particulars of Claim are admitted.

5. It was further an express term of the said contract, by clause 5(3)(c) hereof, that the said works would at all material times be supervised by an employee of the Defendant and that the said employee would make the final decision about the manner in which the said works were to be performed.

6. It was an implied term of the said contract (to be implied in order to give the said contract business efficacy, and to reconcile clause 5(3)(c) with the other clauses thereof referred to in the Part 20 Particulars of Claim), that the express stipulations in the said contract about the mode of performance thereof would be subject to variation at the direction of the Defendant's supervising representative.

7. At all material times, pursuant to the terms set out at paragraph 5 hereof, the performance of the said works was supervised by the Defendant's representative, one David Brown.

8. Paragraph 4 of the Part 20 Particulars of Claim is not admitted.

9. As to paragraph 5 of the Part 20 Particulars of Claim:

(a)   It is admitted that no new foundations were dug out, but that the new paving stones were placed on the base upon which the old paving stones had been lying.

(b)   It is admitted that 'Amber Nectar' cement was used to embed the new paving stones.

c)   It is admitted that 'Amber Nectar' cement does not conform to the said British Standard, but it is denied that the brand is an inferior brand.

(d)   It is admitted that the layer of cement used was 1 centimetre (0.39 inches) thick.

(e)   It is denied that the new paving stones were not embedded firmly and it is averred that they were embedded firmly.

(f)   All the practices particularised in paragraphs 7(a), 7(b), and 7(d) above were known to and expressly authorised by the said David Brown and accordingly, by operation of the term set out in paragraph 4 hereof, the Part 20 Defendant was not in breach of the said contract by adopting them.

(g)   At all material times the Part 20 Defendant exercised reasonable care and skill in the performance of the said contract.

(h)   In the premises it is denied that the Part 20 Defendant was in breach of contract or negligent as alleged in the Part 20 Particulars of Claim or at all.

10. Paragraphs 7 and 8 of the Part 20 Particulars of Claim are denied.

D. ADVOCATE

DATED this   day of   2010 by

Berry & Co, 123 Middle Road, London WC1, Solicitors for the Part 20 Defendant.

Statement of Truth

I believe that the facts stated in this Defence to the Part 20 Particulars of Claim are true.

Signed . . . .

A.12 REQUEST FOR FURTHER INFORMATION RELATING TO THE DEFENCE WHERE THE DEFENDANT HAS MERELY PLEADED THE GENERAL WORDS OF S 58(1) OF HA 1980

IN THE COUNTY COURT CLAIM No. 1234567

BETWEEN: A.B. Claimant

and

C. COUNTY COUNCIL Defendant

REQUEST DATED 18 JANUARY 2010

FOR FURTHER INFORMATION RELATING TO

DEFENCE, SERVED PURSUANT TO CPR PART 18

Under paragraph 3

Of: 'The defendant took such care as in all the circumstances was reasonably required to secure that the part of the highway to which the action relates was not dangerous for traffic.'

Request

State:

1. Which of the criteria under section 58(2) of the Highways Act 1980 are relied upon.

2. For each criterion relied upon, with the particularity to be relied upon at trial each and every fact and matter relied upon in support of the contention that that criterion assists the defendant in establishing the statutory defence under section 58 of the said Act.

The Claimant expects a response to this request by 18 February 2010.

A.13   REQUEST FOR FURTHER INFORMATION RELATING TO THE DEFENCE SEEKING INFORMATION ABOUT STREETWORKS

IN THE COUNTY COURT CLAIM No. 1234567

BETWEEN: A.B. Claimant

and

C.D. Defendant

REQUEST DATED 14 DECEMBER 2009

FOR FURTHER INFORMATION RELATING TO

DEFENCE, SERVED PURSUANT TO CPR PART 18

1. Was the purpose of the works referred to in paragraph 3 of the Defence to repair a broken gas main?

2. Did the works involve the excavation of a trench in the carriageway of High Street, Blank, opposite the main entrance to the Cold Plunge Swimming Pool?

3. If the answer to question 2 above is yes, was the trench created in the course of those works still unfilled when work finished on 7 January 2008?

4. What if any precautions did you take on the night of 7–8 January 2008 to ensure that the wooden fencing around the trench was not removed during the night by vandals whose threats are referred to in paragraph 6 of the Defence?

The Claimant expects a response to this request by 14 January 2010.

A.14   REQUEST FOR FURTHER INFORMATION FROM THE CLAIMANT

IN THE COUNTY COURT CLAIM No. 1234567

BETWEEN: A.B. Claimant

and

C.D. Defendant

REQUEST DATED 19 JUNE 2009

FOR FURTHER INFORMATION FROM THE

CLAIMANT, SERVED PURSUANT TO CPR PART 18

1. Were you wearing high-heeled shoes at the time of the accident?

2. Were you running at the time of the accident?

3. Had you come out of the Fractured Arms public house about 5 minutes before the accident?

4. Were you involved in a road traffic accident in May 2005?

5. If the answer to question 4 above is yes, did you sustain a lower back injury in the course of that road traffic accident?

6. Did you suffer from lower back pain during the time between the road traffic accident and the time of the accident complained of in these proceedings?

The Defendant expects a response to this Request by 19 July 2009.

A.15   PARTICULARS OF CLAIM IN AN ACTION AGAINST INDEPENDENT CONTRACTORS ENGAGED BY A HIGHWAY AUTHORITY IN RESPECT OF INJURIES CAUSED BY COLLATERAL NEGLIGENCE

IN THE COUNTY COURT CLAIM No. 1234567

BETWEEN: A.B. Claimant

and

C. LIMITED Defendant

Particulars of Claim

1. At all material times the Defendant was an independent contractor engaged by the D County Council to conduct works connected with the maintenance and repair of water pipes running beneath a highway known as High Street, Greater Stumbling (hereinafter referred to as 'the street').

2. On 4 May 2009 the Claimant was walking along the northern side of the street towards Greater Stumbling and was passing some trenches which had been dug by the Defendant in the course of the execution of the said works, when she tripped and fell over a hammer which had been left by the Defendant in the centre of the pavement.

3. The said accident was caused by the negligence of the Defendant, its servants or agents.

Particulars of Negligence

(a) Leaving the hammer on the pavement.

(b) If the working area necessarily included the area where the hammer was left, failing to fence off or guard the said area so as to prevent the Claimant from walking into the said area.

(c) Failing to give any warning, whether oral or written or otherwise, of the presence of the said hammer.

4. The Claimant will rely on the manner of the said accident as evidence of negligence.

5. By reason of the matters aforesaid the Claimant who was born on 23 January 1944, sustained personal injuries, loss and damage.

Particulars of Personal Injuries

[Set out details, and refer to the supporting medical report.]

Particulars of Special Damages

Particulars are served in a separate schedule annexed hereto.

6. Further the Claimant is entitled to and claims interest on the sum found due to her for such time and at such rate as the court may think fit, pursuant to section 69 of the County Courts Act 1984.

AND the Claimant claims:

1. Damages in excess of £5,000 but limited to £50,000.

2. Interest pursuant to statute as aforesaid.

A. BARRISTER

DATED etc.

Statement of Truth

I believe that the facts stated in these Particulars of Claim are true.

Signed . . . .

**A.16   PARTICULARS OF CLAIM IN A HIGHWAY
TRIPPING CASE INVOLVING A HIGHWAY
AUTHORITY, A STATUTORY UNDERTAKER AND A
BUILDING CONTRACTOR: BREACH OF
STATUTORY DUTY, NEGLIGENCE, NUISANCE**

IN THE COUNTY COURT CLAIM No. GS123456

BETWEEN: MARY SMITH Claimant

and

GRIMESHIRE

COUNTY COUNCIL First Defendant

and

MEGABUCK

TELECOMMUNICATIONS

PLC Second Defendant

and

GREED LIMITED Third Defendant

Particulars of Claim

1. At all material times the First Defendant was the highway authority
responsible, by operation of section 41 of the Highways Act 1980 ('the Act') for
the maintenance and repair of Somme Road, Passchendale, Grimeshire ('the
street').

2. At all material times the Second Defendant was a statutory undertaker
empowered to effect necessary works on and in the street, and had a duty to
reinstate any part of the street disrupted by such works.

3. At all material times the Third Defendant was a building contractor responsible
for works on a site known as and situate at Huge Manor (hereinafter referred to as
'Huge Manor') on the street.

4. At a time unknown, but shortly prior to the accident which is the subject of this
action, the Second Defendant carried out works on the street (the exact nature of
such works being unknown to the Claimant), at a point on the street (hereinafter
referred to as the 'accident site') opposite an entrance from the street to Huge
Manor.

5. At all material times the Third Defendant used the accident site as a route of passage from the street to Huge Manor, and caused or permitted vehicles, including heavy vehicles, to pass across the pavement of the street to Huge Manor.

6. At about 6 pm on 8 August 2009 the Claimant walked across the pavement at the accident site, and tripped on the pavement there, and fell.

7. The pavement at the point where the Claimant fell is dangerous by reason of its rough surface and the erosion at the edges thereof/excessive additions to the centre thereof, the nature of which is shown on the photographs annexed hereto, and it was because of the said dangerous state of the said pavement that the Claimant fell.

8. The Claimant's accident was caused by the breach of its statutory duty under section 41 of the Act and/or negligence of the First Defendant and/or by the negligence of the Second and/or Third Defendant.

Particulars of Breach of Statutory Duty and/or Negligence of the First Defendant

(a)   Failing to institute and/or maintain any or any adequate system for the inspection and/or maintenance and/or repair of the pavement at the accident site.

(b)   Failing to heed the danger which the roughened/otherwise defective surface of the pavement posed to pedestrians.

(c)   Failing to fill in the defects shown on the annexed photographs and remove the surface debris and level the pavement.

(d)   Failing to fence, guard or otherwise prevent access to the said dangerous area of pavement.

(e)   Failing to give any or any adequate warning of the dangerous condition of the pavement at the accident site.

(f)   Failing, by the institution of proceedings under the Act or otherwise to compel the Second and/or Third Defendant to make good the surface of the pavement and/or abate the highway nuisance which the condition of the pavement at the accident site constituted.

Particulars of Negligence of the Second Defendant

(a)   Failing, having performed statutory works on or in the said pavement, to reinstate the same to a condition which would make the pavement safe for pedestrians to walk over.

(b)   Without prejudice to the generality of the aforesaid, failing to fill in the defects shown on the annexed photographs and remove the surface debris and level the pavement.

(c)   Failing to heed the danger which the roughened/otherwise defective surface of the pavement posed to pedestrians.

(d)   Failing to fence, guard or otherwise prevent access to the said dangerous area of pavement.

(e)   Failing to give any or any adequate warning of the dangerous condition of the pavement at the accident site.

Particulars of Negligence of the Third Defendant

(a)   Causing or permitting the break up of the surface of the pavement at the accident site by causing or permitting vehicles, including heavy vehicles, to pass over the pavement without protecting the pavement by the placement of ramps, boards or otherwise.

(b)   Failing to heed the danger posed by the roughened/otherwise defective surface of the pavement to pedestrians.

(c)   Failing to fill in the defects shown on the annexed photographs and remove the surface debris and level the pavement.

(d)   Failing to notify the First Defendant of the condition of the pavement.

(e)   Failing to fence, guard or otherwise prevent access to the said dangerous area of pavement.

(f)   Failing to give any or any adequate warning of the dangerous condition of the pavement at the accident site.

9. Further or alternatively the said roughened/otherwise dangerous surface of the pavement at the accident site, and the surface debris thereon, constituted a nuisance which was caused or permitted by the First and/or Second and/or Third Defendant, and the Claimant's accident was caused thereby.

10. By reason of the matters aforesaid the Claimant, who was born on 4 May1924, has sustained personal injuries, loss and damage.

Particulars of Personal Injuries

[Summarise the injuries and set out the prognosis.]

Further details are set out in the report of Mr Sawbone, Consultant Orthopaedic Surgeon, dated 1 October 2009.

Particulars of Special Damages

These are set out in a separate schedule annexed hereto.

11. Further the Claimant is entitled to and claims interest on the sum found due to her, for such period and at such rate as the court may think fit, pursuant to section 69 of the County Courts Act 1984.

AND the Claimant claims:

1. Damages in excess of £5000.

2. Interest pursuant to statute as aforesaid.

FLASH LONDON-COUNSEL (Ms)

DATED etc.

By Ambulance, Chaser & Co, Twenty-Fifth Floor, Trotter House, Independent Trading Building, Peckham, London SE22, Solicitors for the Claimant.

Statement of Truth

I believe that the facts stated in the Particulars of Claim are true.

A.17   DEFENCE: INVOKING THE RULE IN GAUTRET V EGERTON/MCGEOWN V NORTHERN IRELAND HOUSING EXECUTIVE

1. As to paragraph 1 of the Particulars of Claim:

(a)   It is admitted that the Claimant sustained an accident on the said footpath on the Claimant's land near the Stone Cross on 3 February 2009.

(b)   No admissions are made as to the circumstances of the said accident.

(c)   It is admitted that the Defendant was an occupier of the said land.

(d)   The Claimant's said accident took place on a public right of way, and accordingly the Defendant owed the Claimant no duty of care, whether under the Occupiers' Liability Act 1957, or at all.

2. [Continue as before.]

A.18   PARTICULARS OF CLAIM, CONTENDING, INTER ALIA, THAT BREACHES OF HA 1980, S 130 CONSTITUTE BREACHES OF STATUTORY DUTY ACTIONABLE IN DAMAGES

1. At all material times the Defendant was a highway authority which owed a duty:

(a)   pursuant to section 41 of the Highways Act 1980 ('the Act') to repair and maintain the street; and

(b)   pursuant to section 130 of the Act:
    (i)   to assert and protect the rights of the public to use and enjoyment of the street; and
    (ii)   to prevent, as far as possible, the stopping up or obstruction of the street.

2. As the Defendant well knew or ought to have known, that part of the street which abuts the Abattoir had been, for several months prior to the accident which is the subject of this action, stopped up and obstructed by animal bones and other debris, rendering pedestrian access along the pavement on the north side of the street (which was and is the only pavement on the street at that point) difficult.

3. On 1 April 2009 the Claimant was walking along the said pavement of the street and, immediately opposite the Abattoir, when she was trying to negotiate the said animal bones and other debris, tripped over a cow skull and fell.

4. The Claimant's said accident was caused by the breach of statutory duty under the said sections of the Act, and/or the negligence of the Defendant, its servants or agents.

Particulars of Breach of Statutory Duty and/or Negligence

(a)   Failing, despite numerous complaints, details of which cannot at present be given, to remove or cause to be removed the said animal bones or other debris.

(b)   Accordingly failing to assert and protect the public's rights to enjoyment of the street, and failing to prevent, so far as possible, the stopping up or obstruction of the street.

(c)   For the avoidance of doubt the Claimant will contend that the failure detailed in Particulars a) above amounted to a breach of its duty to maintain the street.

5. Further, the said animal bones and other debris constituted a nuisance which the Defendant caused, permitted, or failed to abate, and the Claimant's said accident was caused thereby.

6. By reason of the matters aforesaid, the Claimant, who was born on 23 August 1921 has suffered personal injuries and sustained loss and damage.

[Continue as before.]

A.19 CONTENTION IN PARTICULARS OF CLAIM THAT BREACHES OF HA 1980, S 150 CONSTITUTE BREACHES ACTIONABLE IN DAMAGES

[Note, in practice such a claim would always be supplemented by allegations of breach of HA 1980, s 41 duty, negligence, common law nuisance, and often by an allegation of breach of HA 1980, s 130 duty.]

1. At all material times the Defendant was the highway authority responsible for High Street, Fracture, Wiltshire ('the street'), and accordingly, by virtue of section 150 of the Highways Act 1980 ('the Act'), owed a duty, if an obstruction arose in the street from the accumulation of snow, to remove the obstruction.

2. On the night of 22 December 2008 there was a heavy fall of snow on the street, and this fall of snow caused an obstruction on the pavement of the street opposite the Post Office.

3. At about 10 am on the morning of 24 December 2008 the Claimant was walking down the said pavement, and in trying to climb over a mound of snow which was obstructing the street at the foresaid location, she tripped and fell.

4. The Claimant's said accident was caused by the breach by the Defendant, its servants or agents, of its duty under the said section of the Act.

Particulars of Breach of Statutory Duty

Although it knew or ought to have known of the presence of the said obstruction, failing to take any or any adequate steps to remove it. The obstruction was never removed by the Defendant: the snow was left to melt, which it had done by mid-February 2009.

[Continue as before.]

A.20 PARTICULARS OF CLAIM: CUSTOMER SLIPPING IN A SHOP

[Heading as before.]

Particulars of Claim

1. The Defendant is and was at all material times the owner and occupier within the meaning of the Occupiers' Liability Act 1957 ('the Act') of premises known as A-Team Stores, High Street, London WC1 (hereinafter referred to as ('the premises').

2. At about 2.30 pm on 3 June 2009 the Claimant lawfully entered the premises as a visitor within the meaning of the Act and, while looking at the wine display on the second floor of the premises, slipped on some yoghurt which was on the floor, and fell.

3. The said accident was caused by the negligence and/or breach of its statutory duty under section 2 of the Act of the Defendant, its servants or agents.

Particulars of Negligence/Breach of Statutory Duty

(a)   Failing to clear up the said yoghurt.

(b)   Failing to note the presence of the said yoghurt on the floor.

(c)   Failing to institute and/or maintain any or any adequate system for the regular inspection of the floors of the premises and the removal therefrom of anything likely to cause harm.

(d)   Failing to give any or adequate warning, orally or by written notice or otherwise, of the presence of the said yoghurt.

(e)   Failing to fence off the area where the yoghurt was until such time as it was removed.

(f)   In the premises failing to take reasonable care to ensure the safety of the Claimant while on the premises.

4. By reason of the matters aforesaid the Claimant, who was born on 30 July 1967, has sustained personal injuries, loss and damage.

[Continue as before.]

A.21   PARTICULARS OF CLAIM IN TRIPPING ACCIDENT IN A FACTORY: BREACHES, (INTER ALIA) OF THE WORKPLACE (HEALTH, SAFETY AND WELFARE) REGULATIONS 1992

[Heading as before.]

1. The Defendant is and was at all material times the owner and occupier within the meaning of the Occupiers' Liability Act 1957 of premises known as the Pie Factory, East Road (hereinafter referred to as 'the premises').

2. At all material times the Claimant was employed by the Defendant as a machine operator at the premises.

3. At about 2.30 pm on 8 April 2008 the Claimant was walking across the main processing floor at the premises (which was a workplace within the meaning of Workplace (Health, Safety and Welfare) Regulations 1992 and a place to which

the said Regulations at all material times applied) when, at a point 3 metres (3.3 yards) south of the crank-shaft of the beef dicing machine, she tripped over a pile of discarded beef bones which were lying on the floor and forming an obstruction about 30 centimetres (11.8 inches) long, 6 centimetres (2.4 inches) wide and 12 centimetres (4.7 inches) high, and fell.

4. The said accident was caused by the negligence and/or breach of statutory duty under section 2 of the said Act and/or Regulation 5(1) and/or Regulation 8(1) and/or Regulation 9(3) and/or Regulation 12(3) of the said Regulations.

Particulars of Neligence/Breach of Section 2 of the said Act

(a) Causing or permitting the accumulation of the said bones on the floor of the said workplace.

(b) Failing to institute and/or maintain any or any adequate system for the inspection of the said floor and/or the removal of the said bones.

(c) Failing to provide bins or other receptacles at or near the said beef dicing machine for the safe disposal or collection of waste products (including bones) resulting from the work carried out thereon or from work carried on elsewhere in the said workplace.

(d) Failing to provide any warning whatsoever of the presence of the said bones on the floor.

(e) Failing to fence off the area where the said bones were lying.

(f) Failing to provide suitable or sufficient lighting of the part of the floor where the bones were lying so that the Claimant could note their presence. It is the Claimant's case that the said bones were lying in a dark area in deep shadow created by the cutting head of the said machine, and that the only illumination came from a fluorescent strip light which hung over the chicken packing plant some 13 metres (14.2 yards) to the east of where the said bones lay.

(g) Failing to take any or sufficient heed of the complaints about bones being allowed to accumulate in the said area by the said beef dicing machine. The said complaints were as follows:
   (i) A written complaint lodged by A. Smith on 3 May 2007 in the Defendant's complaints book lodged in the works office, which complaint read: 'Today I fell over some bones by the beef dicing machine. It is very dark there. Please see to it'.
   (ii) An oral complaint made in or about August 2007 by R. Brown to the Defendant's then Senior Works Manager George Black. R. Brown said that bones were allowed to accumulate by the pie stamping press and that they were very dangerous. George Black said that he 'would deal with it'.

(h) Accordingly failing to take reasonable steps to ensure that the premises were reasonably safe for the Claimant.

Particulars of Breach of Regulation 5(1) of the said Regulations

(a)   Particulars of Negligence (etc) (a), (b), (c), (d), (e), (f) and (g) above are repeated.

(b)   Accordingly failing to maintain the said workplace and/or the beef dicing machine in an efficient state and/or in efficient working order.

Particulars of Breach of Regulation 8(1) of the said Regulations

Particulars of Negligence (etc) (f) and g(i) above are repeated.

Particulars of Breach of Regulation 9(3) of the said Regulations

(a)   Particulars of Negligence (etc) (a), (b), (c), and (g) above are repeated.

(b)   Accordingly allowing waste materials to accumulate in the said workplace other than in suitable receptacles.

Particulars of Breach of Regulation 12(3) of the said Regulations

(a)   Particulars of Negligence (etc) (a), (b) and (c) above are repeated.

(b)   Accordingly failing to keep the said floor of the workplace free from obstructions and/or from articles which may cause a person to slip, trip or fall.

5. The Claimant further contends that the said accumulation of bones constituted a nuisance, and that the said nuisance was causative of his accident.

6. By reason of the matters aforesaid the Claimant has sustained personal injuries, loss and damage.

[Set out details and continue as before.]

A.22   PARTICULARS OF CLAIM: TRIPPING ACCIDENT AT PREMISES WHICH THE CLAIMANT HAS PAID TO ENTER

[Heading as before.]

1. At all material times the Defendant was the owner and occupier within the meaning of the Occupiers' Liability Act 1957 of the Crown Theatre, High Street, Blackstone (hereinafter referred to as 'the theatre').

2. On 23 January 2008 the Claimant bought a ticket for the 8 pm performance of Romeo and Juliet at the theatre on that date (hereinafter referred to as 'the performance'), and attended the performance.

3. The Claimant accordingly entered the theatre on the said date pursuant to a contract ('the contract') between himself and the Defendant, which contract was contained in, alternatively evidenced by, the said ticket.

4. By the operation of section 5 of the Occupiers' Liability Act 1957 it was a term of the contract that the Defendant owed to the Claimant the common duty of care under the said Act at all times when the Claimant was at the theatre pursuant to the contract.

5. When walking down the south aisle at the start of the first intermission during the performance the Claimant tripped over a large fold in the carpet in the said aisle, which fold protruded about 3 inches (7.6 centimetres) above the level of the surrounding carpet and formed an obstacle about 2 feet (0.61 metres) long, running transversely from the seat pillars of row D forwards towards row C at an angle of about 45 degrees from the said row D seat pillars.

6. The said accident was caused by the breach of contract/and or negligence and/or breach of statutory duty under section 2 of the Occupiers' Liability Act 1957 of the Defendant, its servant or agent.

Particulars of Breach of Contract/Negligence/Breach of Statutory Duty

(a)   Causing or permitting the carpet to the condition described.

(b)   Failing to take any or any sufficient steps to prevent the said carpet from folding up in the way described, whether by tacking it to the floor, applying adhesive to the back of the said carpet and sticking it to the floor or otherwise.

(c)   Failing to institute and/or maintain any or any adequate system of inspection and/or maintenance of the floors in the theatre.

(d)   Failing to provide any warning of the said fold of carpet, whether oral, written or otherwise.

(e)   Failing to fence off or otherwise prevent access to the area where the said fold was.

(f)   In the premises failing to take reasonable steps to ensure that the Claimant was safe while in the theatre.

7. Further or alternatively the said fold of carpet constituted an obstructive nuisance which was caused or permitted by the Defendant, and the said accident was caused by such nuisance.

8. By reason of the matters aforesaid the Claimant, who was born on 23 October 1951, sustained personal injuries, loss and damage.

[Set out details.]

10. [Claim for interest.]

[Prayer.]

[Signed.]

DATED etc.

A.23 DEFENCE BY THE THEATRE OWNER/OCCUPIER IN THE ABOVE CASE, PLEADING THAT A WARNING WAS GIVEN

[Heading as before.]

1. In this Defence, where anything is said to be not admitted, the Claimant is required to prove it.

2. Paragraphs 1, 2, 3 and 4 of the Particulars of Claim are admitted.

3. As to paragraph 5 of the Particulars of Claim:

(a)   It is admitted that there was a fold in the carpet in the south aisle ('the aisle').

(b)   No admissions are made as to the position or dimensions of the said fold.

(c)   It is admitted that the Claimant tripped in the aisle.

(d)   Save that it is admitted that the accident occurred at the evening performance of Romeo and Juliet on 23 January 2008, no admissions are made as to the manner, cause, time or place of the Claimant's accident.

4. It is denied that the Defendant was in breach of contract and/or in breach of statutory duty and/or negligent as alleged in paragraph 6 of the Particulars of Claim or at all, and the causation alleged therein is denied.

5. As to paragraph 7 of the Particulars of Claim:

(a)   It is denied that the said fold constituted an obstructive or any nuisance.

(b)   If, contrary to the aforesaid, the said fold did constitute a nuisance, it is denied that it was caused or permitted by the defendant.

(c)   The causation alleged therein is denied.

6. Without prejudice to the generality of the aforesaid, it is expressly denied that no warning was given to the Claimant and it is averred that the Defendant's employee, Donna Kebab, who was working at the material time as an ice cream vendor in the said south aisle said to the Claimant about one minute before the

said accident occurred: 'Watch out. Someone has just kicked up the carpet just there. I will get it fixed, but until I do, be careful not to trip on it.'

7. The said Donna Kebab indicated the position of the said fold by pointing and the Claimant indicated his understanding of the warning by nodding.

8. The Defendant contends that the warning was sufficient to enable the Claimant to be reasonably safe.

9. The Defendant further contends that the said fold in the said carpet had been caused about 2 minutes before the Claimant's said accident by another patron of the theatre, whom the Defendant cannot at this stage identify, kicking at the carpet and causing it to fold.

10. The said fold was recognised within one minute of its creation by the said Donna Kebab who issued (as aforesaid) all necessary warnings and would shortly have remedied the defect.

11. The Claimant's accident was caused or contributed to by his own negligence.

Particulars of Claimant's Negligence

(a)   Failing to look where he was going.

(b)   Failing to place his feet with sufficient care.

(c)   Failing to have any or any adequate regard to the aforesaid warning given by the said Donna Kebab.

(d)   If, contrary to the Defendant's primary contention, the Claimant did not fully hear or understand the said warning,
      (i)   failing to seek clarification of the same and
      (ii)   indicating to the said Donna Kebab that he had heard and understood by nodding his head as aforesaid, thereby indicating to the said Donna Kebab that no repetition was necessary.

12. As to paragraph 8 of the Particulars of Claim:

(a)   No admissions are made as to the alleged or any personal injuries, loss or damage.

(b)   The causation alleged therein is denied.

13. It is denied that the Claimant is entitled to interest on any sum found due to him on the basis pleaded at paragraph 10 of the Particulars of Claim or at all.

[Signed.]

DATED etc.

A.24   PARTICULARS OF CLAIM IN ACTION BROUGHT BY NON-TENANT AGAINST LANDLORD; DEFECTIVE PREMISES ACT 1972, S 4; NEGLIGENCE

[Heading as before.]

1. At all material times the Defendant was the owner of premises known as and situate at 1 High Street, Blank ('the property').

2. By a lease made on 3 March 2000 between the Claimant and Mary Smith ('the tenant'), the Defendant let the property to the tenant.

3. Clause 4(a) of the said lease required the Defendant to repair and maintain the property.

4. At about 11 pm on 26 December 2008, while the Claimant was visiting the tenant at the property, the Claimant put his foot into a gap in the floorboards beneath the front window in the kitchen of the property, and tripped and fell.

5. The Claimant hereinafter refers to the said gap in the said floorboards as 'the defect'.

6. The Claimant was a person who might reasonably be expected to be affected by the defect.

7. The Defendant knew or ought in all the circumstances to have known of the defect.

(a)   The defect was created by the Defendant's servants or agents who, on 7 December 2003, took up the said floorboards in order to replace defective copper hot water piping, and thereafter failed to replace the same.

(b)   The tenant sent a letter to the Defendant's head office on Black Street, Blank, on or about 18 December 2008 notifying the Defendant of the existence of the said defect in the floorboards and asking that immediate corrective repairs be carried out.

8. The defect constituted a failure by the Defendant to carry out the obligation to the tenant to repair the property.

9. The said accident was caused by the Defendant's negligence and/or breach of statutory duty under section 4(1) of the Defective Premises Act 1972.

Particulars of Negligence/Breach of Statutory Duty

(a)   Failing to replace the said floorboards on or after 7 December 2008.

(b)   Failing to cover the gap created by the absence of the said floorboards with some other boarding or other material sufficient to make the defect safe.

(c)   Failing by provision of warning notices or otherwise, to provide any warning of the existence of the defect.

(d)   Failing to fence off or otherwise make safe the defect.

(e)   If the Defendant's servants or agents who carried out the said works on 7 December 2008 did not report the defect so as to enable the Defendant to take immediate steps to remedy the same, failing so to report/failing to ensure that they so reported.

(f)   Failing to take any or sufficient heed of the tenant's said letter of about 18 December 2008.

(g)   In the premises failing to take such care as in all the circumstances was reasonable to see that the Claimant was reasonably safe from personal injury.

10. By reason of the matters aforesaid the Claimant has sustained personal injuries, loss and damage.

[Continue as before.]

A.25 PARTICULARS OF CLAIM: BREACH OF A LANDLORD'S IMPLIED COVENANT TO REPAIR UNDER S 11 OF THE LANDLORD AND TENANT ACT 1985

[Heading as before.]

1. At all material times the Defendant was the owner of a dwelling house known as and situate at 123 The Road, Blank ('the property').

2. By a lease made on 13 April 2005 between the Claimant as tenant and the Defendant as landlord, the Defendant let the property to the Claimant for a term of 5 years commencing on 13 April 2005.

3. It was an implied covenant of the said lease (implied by operation of section 11A of the Landlord and Tenant Act 1985) that the Defendant would keep in repair the structure and exterior of the property.

4. On or about 4 August 2008 the Claimant notified the Defendant by telephone of the deteriorating condition of the steps leading to the front door of the property, and in particular told him:

(a)   that after frost and heavy rain large sections of the concrete filler which bound together the bricks making up the said steps would crumble away, leaving gaps between the said bricks where the filler had previously been and

(b)   that there were several such gaps present on or in the said pathway at the time of writing and

(c)   that the said steps were consequently dangerous and needed immediate repair.

5. The Defendant took no action pursuant to the said telephone conversation.

6. By 15 October 2008 a hole about 1 inch × 2 inches square in cross-sectional area and 3 inches deep had formed in the centre of the third of the said steps as a result of the crumbling away of concrete filler between the bricks making up the said steps.

7. At about 2.30 pm on 15 October 2008 the Claimant was returning to the property when the heel of her left shoe caught in the hole and she fell, injuring herself.

8. The said accident was caused by the breach by the Defendant of the implied covenant set out in paragraph 3 hereof.

Particulars of Breach of Covenant

(a)   Before the said telephone conversation on or about 4 August 2008, failing to repair or cause to be repaired properly the said step, and in particular:
   (i)   Failing, when concrete filler was last applied to the brick of the said steps (which the Claimant avers was in or about May 2002) to ensure that the concrete used was of good quality and was properly packed. Thin Stuff concrete was used and/or it was loosely packed in the gaps between the said bricks. The Defendant should have used or caused to be used Hot Stuff concrete, and should have ensured that it was tightly packed.
   (ii)   failing to take any heed of previous complaints and warnings about the state of the said steps which were given orally to the Defendant by the Claimant in about August 2008. On the said occasion the Claimant told the Defendant that the steps were 'crumbling and dangerous' but did not give any further particulars.

(b)   After the said telephone conversation, failing to take any steps whatever to effect repairs of the said steps. The Defendant should have:
   (i)   Repaired the said steps or caused them to be repaired within 24 hours of the said complaint/notification.
   (ii)   Ensured that the said hole was filled in as set out in (a)(i) above.

9. By reason of the matters aforesaid the Claimant, who was born on 15 July 1923, has sustained personal injuries, loss and damage.

[Set out particulars and continue as before.]

A.26 DEFENCE BY A LANDLORD TO AN ACTION BROUGHT AS A BREACH OF COVENANT UNDER SS.11 AND 11A OF THE LANDLORD AND TENANT ACT 1985 RELYING ON S 3A OF THE 1985 ACT

[Note that s 3A does not apply to a lease entered into before January 1989 or a lease entered into pursuant to a contract made before that date.

[Formal admissions as to identity and status and the nature of the lease and the implied covenants thereunder.]

(a)   The said dwelling house formed part only of the building known as Nelson Mandela House.

(b)   In order to comply with the said covenant the Defendant would have to, and at all material times would have had to, carry out works or repairs otherwise than in or to an installation in the said dwelling house, namely to the hot water pipes running through the east side of the said Nelson Mandela House.

(c)   The Defendant has no right whatsoever in the east side of the said Nelson Mandela House such as would enable him to carry out the said works or repairs.

(d)   The Defendant has used all reasonable endeavours to obtain, but was unable to obtain, such rights as would be adequate to enable him to carry out the said works or repairs.

(e)   In particular the Defendant wrote on 24 May 2008 and 3 June 2008 and 13 June 2008 to A Plc, the owners and occupiers of the east side of the said Nelson Mandela Building, seeking permission to enter there to perform the said works/repair, and by letters dated 26 May 2008 and 4 June 2008 and 14 June 2008 A Plc expressly refused to grant the Defendant such permission.

(f)   In the premises it is denied that the Defendant is liable to the Claimant as alleged or at all.

[Signed.]

DATED etc.

[STATEMENT OF TRUTH.]

APPENDIX B

CASE SUMMARIES

B.1   INTRODUCTION

The case summaries in this Appendix do not eliminate the need for further legal research. Where a case featured here is to be argued in court, the report for that case must be used. Not all authorities important in the huge field of tripping and slipping litigation are summarised here, as some of the most important are dealt with sufficiently in the text.

The summaries are meant to be used alongside the text. They are not definitive guides to the law in the areas covered. Readers are advised, therefore, not to refer only to these as a summary of all the relevant law.

B.2   HIGHWAYS ACT 1980, S 41

B.2.1   The duty in general

1.   *Goodes v East Sussex County Council [2000] 1 WLR 1356; [2000] 3 All ER 603; [2000] PIQR P148, (HL)*

Text references: **4.2.3**; **4.3.4**

Facts: The claimant was injured in a road traffic accident when his car skidded on an icy road. He contended that this was caused by the highway authority's breach of duty under HA 1980, s 41 in failing adequately to grit or salt the road.

Held: The duty to maintain was an absolute duty, subject only to the s 58 defence, but the 1980 Act had to be read in the light of the law which preceded it. The Act preserved the common law idea of what was meant by maintenance. The common law definition encompassed only maintenance of the fabric of the highway. Gritting and salting had nothing to do with the fabric. Accordingly s 41 did not require gritting or salting.

2.   *Bartlett v Department of Transport, The Times, January 8, 1985 (QBD, Boreham J)*

Text references: **4.2.3**

Facts: The claimant's husband was killed in a road traffic accident. The accident was caused, at least in part, by the icy road surface. The road had not been gritted because the defendant highway authority was in dispute with its employees, who were members of NUPE. The union had instructed the employees to do no work on the road. The claimant sued the defendant for breach of statutory duty.

Held: The defendant was not liable. The claimant could succeed only if the failure to maintain was related to want of repair or if an obstruction caused or contributed to want of repair. The claimant could not rely on any breach of the employees' duty to the defendant unless the defendant had itself induced or condoned that breach. That was clearly not the case here.

3.   *Sharpness New Docks and Gloucester and Birmingham Navigation Co v Att-Gen [1915] AC 654 (HL)*

Text references: **4.2.3**; **4.4.2.1**

Facts: An Act of 1791 empowered a canal company to make a canal. It provided that the canal should not pass across any highway until the company had, at its own expense, built bridges across the canal to carry the highway. These bridges had to be built to standards and specifications approved by the commissioners appointed under the Act. The Act further provided that such bridges should ' . . . from time to time be supported, maintained and kept in sufficient repair' by the company. A canal was completed in 1812. Several bridges carrying highways were built at the same time and approved by the commissioners. About 100 years later the Attorney General brought an action against the company seeking a declaration that the company was obliged to keep the bridges in repair so as to be sufficient to bear the traffic which might reasonably be expected to pass along the highway over the bridges, and the Attorney General contended that the requisite standard of maintenance and repair was the standard appropriate to the present character and nature of the road and the traffic then using it. The company contended that it was not obliged to do any more than satisfy the commissioners appointed under the 1791 Act. It had satisfied them when the bridges were built. It did not acquire a more onerous obligation as the volume of traffic using the bridges increased. It was obliged to maintain the bridges only to the standard which originally satisfied the commissioners.

Held: the company's submissions set out above succeeded in full.

4.   *Jones v Rhondda Cynon Taff County Borough Council [2008] EWCA Civ 1497*

Text references: **4.1.1**

Facts: While on duty, and in the course of putting out a small fire, a fireman stumbled and fell on a depression situated at the edge of a footpath. The local authority had known of the defect for 3 years, but had failed to repair it. The trial judge held that the footpath was used only on rare occasions, and that given the footpath's level of use, general state of repair and location (amongst other matters), there was no breach of s 41.

Held: The Claimant's appeal was dismissed. However, the Court of Appeal made a number of relevant comments in respect of the interplay between ss 41 and 58. Laws LJ said this, at paragraph 16:

> 'I do not consider that a finding here that there was no breach of s 41 in some way conflates the test or tests for s 41 and those for the s 58 defence. There is, on the authorities . . . no breach of s 41 if the highway is reasonably passable for ordinary traffic without danger. If that test is not met, then there will be a breach; but the local authority may show that they have taken reasonable care to avoid the danger, albeit on the particular facts they have not succeeded in doing so. The two sections both require regard to be had to the circumstances of the case but there is no need for conflation between the two. For s 41 the circumstances of the case are relevant to the ascertainment of a standard of repair that is required for s 58. They are relevant to an assessment of what a reasonable highway authority should put into effect by way of maintenance and repair.'

B.2.2   To whom the duty is owed

5.   *Haley v London Electricity Board [1965] AC 778 (HL)*

Text reference: **4.2.2**

Facts: The claimant was blind. He was injured when he tripped over an obstacle placed by the defendant in the course of statutory works it was executing.

Held: The defendant owed a duty of care to all persons whose use of the highway was reasonably likely and thus reasonably foreseeable. It was reasonably foreseeable that a blind person would use the pavement. No adequate protection or warning had been given. The claimant therefore succeeded in an action in negligence against the defendant. There would of course, and for the same reasons, have been liability under the statutory duty to maintain.

B.2.3   Dangerousness and foreseeability

6.   *Griffiths v Liverpool Corporation [1967] 1 QB 374 (CA)*

Text references: **4.3.1**; **4.4.1**; **4.5.2**

Facts: The claimant slipped and fell while walking on a flagstone which formed part of a pavement. This flagstone rocked on its centre. It also protruded half an inch above the adjacent flagstones. The judge at first instance made the following findings of fact:

(a)   The flagstone was dangerous. This finding was not contested on appeal.

(b)   A regular system of highway inspection was desirable.

(c)   Such a system could have been implemented.

(d)   If this particular defect had been discovered on such an inspection, it could have been made safe.

(e)   The highway authority did not have sufficient manpower to deal generally with the defects that could have been discovered on inspection.

(f)   It was not proved that, if regular inspections had been carried out, the danger from the flagstone would not have been discovered and prevented.

Held:

(a)   Of the trial judge's finding that a three-monthly inspection would be desirable, Sellers LJ said:

> 'There are many things in life which might be said to be desirable if they were attainable, but I do not understand desirability to be a principle underlying our common law. Such evidence does not establish a reasonable standard of routine inspection. Reasonableness must have some regard to cost and capacity.'

(b)   On the facts, a three-monthly inspection was, under the labour conditions then pertaining, wholly impracticable.

(c)   The finding that the half inch defect was dangerous was criticised. Sellers LJ said:

> 'We are all of us accustomed to walk on uneven and irregular surfaces and we can all of us trip on cobblestones, cat's eyes, studs marking pedestrian crossings, as well as other projections. If the finding that the half inch projection of a solitary flagstone in a wide pavement has to be accepted because of the technicalities of this case . . . I have perhaps said enough to indicate that it is a standard which in my view should not become a precedent or guide in ordinary circumstances.'

(d)   The requirements for a successful action in negligence and under the statutory predecessor to HA 1980, s 41 were compared. Diplock LJ said:

> 'To succeed in an action for negligence the plaintiff must prove *inter alia* (i) that the defendant had been guilty of lack of reasonable care and (ii) that such lack of reasonable care was the cause of the injury to him. In an action under the statute against a highway authority for injury sustained from a danger on a highway the plaintiff need prove neither of these things in order to succeed. Unless the highway authority proves that it did take reasonable care the statutory defence under sub-section 2 is not available to it at all. Nor is it a defence for the highway authority to show that even had it taken all reasonable care this might not have prevented the danger which caused the injury. It may be that if the highway authority could show that no amount of reasonable care on their part could have prevented the danger the common law defence of inevitable accident would be available to them: but that is not relied on in the present case and it is not necessary to express a final opinion on it . . . The duty which the highway authority must prove they have fulfilled is not a duty to secure a certain result but to "take care" to do so, and such a duty is fulfilled by the person on whom it is imposed if he has done all that it is reasonably practicable for him to do to secure that result even though, through circumstances which are beyond his control, he does not succeed in achieving it.'

7.   *Meggs v Liverpool Corporation [1968] 1 WLR 689 (CA);* *[1968] 1 All ER 1137*

Text reference: **4.3.1**

Facts: The claimant tripped on a flagstone which protruded either a quarter or three quarters of an inch above the surrounding flag-stones – the report contradicts itself. Local inhabitants knew of the defect but had not reported it to the defendant highway authority. Two members of the defendant authority passed the relevant stretch of pavement regularly. They had never considered that it needed to be repaired. The claimant sued the defendant for breach of its statutory duty to maintain the highway.

Held: The defendant was not liable. Lord Denning MR said, [1968] 1 All ER 1137 at 1139:

> '. . . at the onset . . . in order to make a prima facie case the plaintiff must show that the highway was not reasonably safe, i e that it was dangerous to traffic . . . it seems to me, using ordinary knowledge of pavements, that everyone must take account of the fact that there may be unevenness here and there. There may be a ridge of half an inch or three quarters of an inch occasionally, but that is not the sort of thing which makes it dangerous or not reasonably safe.'

8.   *Littler v Liverpool Corporation [1968] 2 All ER 343* *(Liverpool Assizes. Cumming-Bruce J)*

Text reference: **4.3.1**

Facts: The claimant, who was 19 years old and mentally defective, gave evidence that, when running along a pavement, he had caught the toe of his shoe in a triangular defect in a paving stone which was half an inch deep and had a hypotenuse of 3 inches. After the accident the defect was filled in by the defendant. The claimant sued the defendant highway authority for breach of their duty to maintain the highway.

Held: (applying the *Meggs* test) it was not reasonably foreseeable that the defect would be a danger, and therefore the claimant must fail. Cumming-Bruce J said, at 345:

> 'The test in relation to a length of pavement is reasonable foreseeability of danger. A length of pavement is only dangerous if, in the ordinary course of human affairs, danger may reasonably be anticipated from its continued use by the public who usually pass over it. It is a mistake to isolate and emphasise a particular difference in levels between flagstones unless that difference is such that a reasonable person who noticed and considered it would regard it as presenting a real source of danger. Uneven surfaces and differences in level between flagstones of about an inch may cause a pedestrian temporarily off balance to trip and stumble, but such characteristics have to be accepted. A highway is not to be criticised by the standards of a bowling green.'

He also expressed his hope that those sitting on legal aid committees would remember that not every trifling defect in a footway makes it dangerous.

9.   Pitman v Southern Electricity Board [1978] 3 All ER 901 (CA)

Text reference: **4.3.1**

Facts: The claimant was 78 years old. She was walking at dusk along a pavement in the village where she lived. She tripped over a metal sheet which the defendant had placed over a hole. The area was unlit. The sheet stood only one eighth of an inch proud of the pavement.

Held: The defendant was liable. The plate had introduced a new and unexpected hazard which was potentially dangerous. It was an unexpected hazard (*cp Littler* and *Meggs*) because it had been suddenly introduced, without any warning, into the environment familiar to the claimant. She had become familiar with the unevenness of the pavement itself, but the plate confronted her with a novel danger. The court made it clear that if the claimant had tripped over a flagstone with such a tiny difference in level from the surrounding stones, the defendant would probably have escaped liability.

10.   Ford v Liverpool Corporation (1972) 117 SI 167 (QBD, Liverpool, Watkins J)

Text references: **4.3.2**

Facts: The claimant tripped while getting into her car. In the roadway there was a grid, which was 5 feet from the pavement and 43 inches long by 1.5 feet wide. At the edge of the grid which was furthest from the pavement the surrounding tarmac stood proud of the grid, forming a fairly sharp ridge about 1 inch high. It was this ridge over which the claimant had tripped. When she tripped she was looking round for traffic and did not have her eyes on the ground. She sued the highway authority for breach of statutory duty and/or negligence, contending that the part of the road where she had fallen was dangerous for pedestrians using the road. She contended that the ridge was more dangerous in the road than on the pavement because pedestrians crossing the road were more likely than pedestrians on the pavement to be looking around for traffic.

Held: The highway authority was not liable. *Meggs v Liverpool Corporation* was applied. The general public must expect obstructions such as cobblestones, cat's-eyes, pedestrian crossing studs and such-like to appear in the highway. Such obstructions were ordinary hazards of life. The ridge over which the claimant tripped had existed without complaint for more than 3 years and was the sort of defect commonly found around grids. It was more important that the pavement should be free of such defects than that the carriageway should be. The defect was not dangerous. It could not be reasonably anticipated that personal injury would result from it. If the court had held otherwise, it would have found the claimant guilty of significant contributory negligence because the defect was obvious and should have been seen and avoided by her if she had used reasonable care to ensure her own safety.

11. *Rider v Rider [1973] QB 505 (CA)*

Text reference: **4.2.2**

Facts: The claimant was injured in a road traffic accident on a narrow, unclassified road which had become a 'secondary through route' between two centres of population. The road had no real foundation. Its edges were unsupported and with the passage of traffic had become broken and uneven. It was found as a fact that the wheels of the car in which the claimant had been a passenger had met an obstruction in the road and that consequently the car had lost control. The trial judge found that, because of its condition, the road was foreseeably dangerous and that the standard of repair adopted by the highway authority was inadequate. The driver of the car was one-third to blame; he drove too fast. The highway authority was two-thirds to blame. The highway authority appealed, arguing that a sufficiently careful driver would not have been put at risk by the road and that the duty of the highway authority extended to such careful users only.

Held: The appeal failed. The highway authority was liable. It had to take into account the traffic which was reasonably to be expected on a road, and that drivers were liable to make mistakes. Lawton LJ at 518, said:

> '... highway authorities when performing their statutory duty to maintain their roads should keep in mind the driver who may take a corner too fast or who may be slow to notice changes in road conditions. Such drivers form part of the traffic on our roads and it would be unrealistic for highway authorities when deciding what standard of maintenance is necessary to forget their existence and to provide only for those who always use reasonable care – if any such paragons of driving virtue are to be found.'

In every case it was a matter of fact and degree whether any particular state of disrepair posed a danger to traffic using the road in the way normally expected. The test was an objective test. Here there was abundant evidence justifying the judge's finding that the road was foreseeably dangerous to careful drivers. The court also held, obiter, that mere unevenness, undulations and minor potholes do not normally constitute a danger. The normal run of drivers does not include drunk or reckless drivers. The need to consider the individual circumstances of each case and the inadvisability of laying down general rules were emphasised by Lawton LJ He said, at 518:

> 'In most cases proof that there were bumps or small holes in a road, or slight unevenness in flagstones on a pavement, will not amount to proof of a danger for traffic through failure to maintain. It does not follow, however, that such conditions can never be a danger for traffic. A stretch of uneven paving outside a factory probably would not be a danger for traffic, but a similar stretch outside an old peoples' home, and much used by the inmates to the knowledge of the highway authority, might be.'

12. *Cenet v Wirral Metropolitan Borough Council [2008] EWHC 1407 (QB)*

Text reference: **4.2.2**; **4.3.2**

Facts: The claimant tripped on a depression in the carriageway whilst crossing the street where she lived. The local authority appealed the decision of the county court which held that it was liable under the Highways Act 1980. Principally, it was argued that the trial judge was wrong to hold that the carriageway was 'dangerous'. The test he had applied was too stringent, and he had been wrong to find that the carriageway was more akin to a pavement.

Held: Appeal allowed. The trial judge had erred in holding that the carriageway was more akin to a pavement. Less stringent standards apply to the standards expected of a carriageway when compared to the expected standards for a pavement. Applying those lower standards, the Court of Appeal held that the depression was not dangerous.

13. *Fiona Thompson v Hampshire County Council [2004] EWCA Civ 1016*

Text reference: **4.2.3**

Facts: The claimant was walking along the edge of a highway, on an earth-beaten path/track. She strayed briefly from the path, and fell into a ditch situated in close proximity, breaking her ankle.

Held: A highway authority was not responsible for a highway's layout under its statutory duty to maintain the highway. Whilst the path created certain dangers, those dangers could be overcome by taking appropriate precautions. The essence of the claimant's complaint was about layout as opposed to state of repair. A complaint about layout falls outside the scope of the s 41 duty.

B.3   THE DEFENCE UNDER S 58

B.3.1   Basic principles

14. *Pridham v Hemel Hempstead Corporation (1970) 69 LGR 523 (CA)*

Text reference: **4.4.2.4**

Facts: The claimant tripped by putting her foot into a hole in a pavement. The judge found that the hole developed within a very short time before the accident – possibly about a week before. The claimant sued the highway authority for breach of statutory duty. It was found that the highway authority had considered carefully, after appropriate consultation, just what their maintenance and inspection regime should be, and had appointed an inspector to inspect the roads in its area. The roads were divided into classes. Inspection was carried out regularly. The frequency of the inspection varied with the class of road. Residential roads (such as that on which the claimant tripped) were to be inspected quarterly. The inspector recorded defects on a register which was examined daily by the works manager, and the highway authority also maintained a complaints book in which complaints about highway defects were entered. The road where the claimant tripped had been inspected about two months before the accident. No defect had been observed. No complaint had been entered in the complaints book. No expert evidence was called by the highway authority to explain the choice of categories or why a quarterly inspection of residential roads was considered sufficient.

Held: The highway authority had made out the statutory defence. A highway authority must prove, in order to make out the defence, that they had exercised such care as was 'reasonably required' and not such care as was reasonably practicable in the particular situation. Because the highway authority had, after careful consideration, decided on a quarterly inspection of residential roads and had also kept the complaints book as an additional check, they were not liable.

15. *Bramwell v Shaw [1971] RTR 167 (QBD, Ackner J)*

Text reference: **4.4.2.1**

Facts: The claimant was working inside a wooden cage which was placed on the highway. A lorry approached the part of the road where the cage was. The wheels of the lorry entered a pothole in the road. The pothole was about three feet in diameter and up to six inches deep. The lorry's trailer tilted and a container which it was carrying hit a tree and broke loose, injuring the claimant. The claimant sued the driver of the lorry and the local highway authority. It was found as a fact that the road was old and likely to break up, and that it carried heavy traffic. The part of the road concerned had last been inspected by the highway authority 3 days before the accident.

Held: Because the road was old and likely to break up and heavily used, an extremely high standard of maintenance was required. It was reasonable to expect a good state of repair. A careful inspection 3 days previously would have revealed the defect, and it could easily have been filled in. Since the highway authority had not taken such care as in all the circumstances was reasonable, they had not made out the statutory defence. The driver of the lorry had also driven too fast. The driver was 60 per cent to blame and the highway authority 40 per cent to blame.

16. *Jacobs v Hampshire CC, The Times, May 28, 1984 (QBD, Skinner J)*

Text reference: **4.4.2.1**

Facts: The claimant was injured when the front wheel of his bicycle went into a hole at the edge of the road. The hole was caused by the penetration of water into the fabric of the road. The defendant highway authority relied on HA 1980, s 58. The road had been inspected at 6-monthly intervals. This inspection regime had been decided on after having regard to the likely extent and type of use of the road, and to the area in which the road was.

Held: The s 58 defence was not made out. To succeed in establishing this defence the highway authority would also have had to show that it took properly into account, in deciding the frequency of inspection, the design of the road. The tarmac of the road met cobblestones at the road edge. This made the road particularly vulnerable to water penetration, which could cause damage within 2 months.

B.3.2   Examples

17.   *Whiting v Hillingdon LBC (1970) 68 LGR 437 (QBD, James J)*

Text reference: **4.4.2.4**

Facts: In April 1966 the claimant was injured when she stepped to one side of a footpath to pass someone else and hit her leg on a tree stump which was hidden by undergrowth. She contended, inter alia, that the highway authority was in breach of its statutory duty to maintain the footpath. The highway authority had inspected the path in the summers of 1964 and 1965 and had repaired it in February 1966. The tree stump had not been noticed.

Held: The highway authority was not liable. Because the authority's officer could not remember seeing the stump in February 1966, the tree must have been cut down since that date. It would not be reasonable to expect another inspection between February and April 1966.

18.   *Papworth v Mayor of Battersea [1916] 1 KB 583 (CA)*

Text reference: **4.4.2.4**

Facts: In 1883 a local authority, exercising a statutory power, constructed a road and a gulley covered with a grating. It was found that all due care and skill had been exercised in the construction of the gulley and grating. The grating formed a considerable depression in the road. In 1912 the claimant was injured when her bicycle passed over the grating.

Held: It was found that the grating was dangerous to a careful cyclist, but that the local authority was not negligent in failing to discover the danger posed by the grating. The local authority was not therefore liable.

19.   *Morris v Thyssen (GB) Ltd, unreported, but see 1983 Halsbury's Abridgment, para 2418 (QBD, Booth J)*

Text reference: **4.4.2.5**

Facts: The claimant lost control of his van when it hit a pool of water which had collected in the road. He sued the highway authority. There had been heavy rain. The road was low-lying and susceptible to flooding. The highway authority had been told about the flood by the police and by its own employees. There was only one flood warning sign, which was in a nearby lay-by.

Held: The highway authority was two thirds liable. The flooding was a danger to road users, and it was a reasonably foreseeable danger. The one warning sign was inadequate.

20. Whitaker v West Yorkshire Metropolitan CC and Metropolitan Borough of Calderdale [1982] CLY 1435 (QBD) (H.H. Judge Bennett QC)

Text reference: **4.4.2.4**

Facts: The claimant fell on an icy patch on a roadway. She contended that the water which formed the ice had been negligently allowed to escape onto the roadway by an adjoining landowner and that the highway authority was in breach of its statutory duty and/or was negligent in failing to notice the escape and take steps to abate it. The highway authority admitted that street inspectors were not employed and that there were no regular street inspections. Its evidence was that it relied on reports of defects made by council staff and members of the public and on an annual street inspection made by the area engineer.

Held: (obiter, the court having held that the claimant had not proved that she had slipped on ice resulting from the escape of water from adjoining land), that in the absence of evidence as to the resources available to the highway authority and the practice adopted by other highway authorities, it did not amount to negligence or breach of statutory duty by the highway authority not to have a system of inspection for defects or to employ street inspectors.

21. Birmingham v East Ham Corporation (1961) 60 LGR 111 (CA)

Text reference: **4.4.2.4**

Facts: The claimant was injured when his foot went into a hole in the highway which was nine inches wide and six inches deep. He sued the highway authority, whose highway superintendent gave evidence that 4 days before the accident he had noticed a depression in the road at the place where the accident had occurred, and that he had immediately caused repairs to be done. The area beneath the depression had been cleared of loose earth and a firm base reached. The sides of the hole so formed were made firm. The hole was filled, topped with asphalt and levelled. There was also evidence that there was a rat run nearby, and this was suggested as the cause of the rapid further subsidence. The claimant suggested that the highway authority should have taken special precautions against the rats, for instance by mixing broken glass with the material used for filling the defect.

Held: The defendant was not liable. The fact that rapid subsidence had occurred was not in itself evidence that the repair work had not been properly carried out. The evidence about the ran run did provide an explanation for the subsidence. The defendant was not under a further duty to take the suggested or any further precautions against the rats.

22.   *Atkins v Ealing London Borough Council [2006] EWHC 2515*

Text reference: **4.4.1**

Facts: The claimant injured her ankle after stepping on a broken manhole cover, situated on a busy shopping street. The manhole cover tilted, causing her foot to fall into the manhole. The claimant was successful at first instance. On appeal, the defendant local authority argued that the trial judge had placed too high a burden on it in holding that a visual inspect of the manhole covers was insufficient for the purposes of establishing a s 58 defence.

Held: The defendant's appeal was dismissed. The trial judge had properly weighed up the private interests of the individual (subject to serious injury by reason of the defective manhole cover) against the public interest and burden associated with ensuring that the manhole cover was secure.

In any event, the defendant had brought no evidence in an attempt to discharge the burden of proof upon it (ie to prove that tilting manhole covers were so rare, that it did not justify an arduous system of inspection in respect of their safety).

B.4   EVIDENCE OF FAILURE TO MAINTAIN

B.4.1   Standing water on the highway

23.   *Burnside v Emerson [1968] 1 WLR 1490 (CA)*

Text reference: **4.2.7**; **4.6**

Facts: The first claimant was driving his car along a road for which the local highway authority was liable. It was and had been raining heavily. The car was being driven responsibly. The car ran into a pool of water which was half way across the road. This caused the car to swing across the road into the path of another vehicle. There was a collision. The first claimant sued the highway authority, contending that the presence of the pool of water itself indicated that there had been a failure to maintain. The first claimant succeeded at first instance. The highway authority appealed.

Held: The appeal was allowed. Although the road was a danger to traffic, the judge was wrong to say that the pool of water was in itself evidence of failure to maintain. Lord Denning MR said, [1968] 3 All ER 741 at 743:

> ' . . . I would say that an icy patch in winter or an occasional flooding at any time is not in itself evidence of a failure to maintain. We all know that in times of heavy rain our highways do from time to time get flooded. Leaves and debris and all sorts of things may be swept in and cause flooding for a time without any failure to repair at all.'

24. *Tarrant v Rowlands [1979] RTR 144 (QBD, Cantley J)*

Text reference: **4.4.2.4**

Facts: The claimant and the first defendant were both injured when the first defendant's vehicle ran into a pool of water on a road. The pool was about 30 feet long and, at the deepest, about 5 inches deep. It covered about half the width of the road. Water usually lay in this place on the road after heavy rain. The second defendant was the highway authority. Its supervising foreman gave evidence that there was a monthly inspection of the road. He had not been aware, until the accident, of any drainage problems affecting the relevant part of the road.

Held: *Burnside v Emerson* (above) was approved, but it was found that the fact that water frequently accumulated on that part of the road indicated that the highway authority could reasonably have been expected to know that the condition of the highway was likely to cause danger to highway users. The fact that they did not know indicated that the system of inspection was inadequate. Liability was apportioned between the highway authority and the first defendant.

25. *Mott MacDonald Limited v Department of Transport [2006] EWCA Civ 1089*

Text reference: **4.2.7**

Facts: In three separate cases (conjoined in this action), it was accepted that a road traffic accident had been caused by standing water on the highway. The issue arose as to whether the accidents were attributable to the highway authority'

Held: *Burnside v Emerson* [1968] 1 WLR 1490 remains good law. *Burnside* established that liability can arise from a failure to maintain drainage provided that the claimant can establish that:

(a)   the road was in a condition such that it was dangerous to traffic;

(b)   the danger was caused by the authority's failure to maintain. A distinction is to be drawn between a permanent danger due to the want of repair, and a transient danger due to the elements. Where there is a transient danger due to the elements, the existence of a danger for a short period is not evidence of a failure to maintain.

The Court of Appeal rejected the submission that *Burnside* was no longer good law. Section 41 dictates that the 'structure and fabric of the roadway@ should be maintained as a whole (*Mott MacDonald*, at para 40). The duty is not 'confined' to the surface of the road alone.

B.5   NON-DELEGABILITY OF THE STATUTORY DUTY

26.   *Hardaker v Idle DC [1896] 1 QB 335 (CA)*

Text references: **1.2.1.2; 4.4.3**

Facts: A district council had a statutory power to build a sewer. It employed a contractor to build the sewer for it. The contractor was negligent in the execution of the works. A gas main was broken and an explosion occurred. The claimants were injured and suffered other loss, and sued both the district council and the contractor.

Held: Although the district council had delegated the exercise of its statutory power to the contractor, it was still liable to the claimants for the breach of the duty which the council owed the claimants.

B.6   DEFAULT OF ANOTHER STATUTORY UNDERTAKER IS NO DEFENCE

B.6.1   27.   *McNair v Dunfermline Corporation (1954) 104 LJ 66*

Text reference: **1.2.1.2**

Facts: A highway authority tried to escape liability for a dangerous pavement by contending that the Gas Board, which had recently interfered with the pavement in exercise of its statutory powers, had failed to discharge its obligations to reinstate the pavement under s 7 of the Public Utilities Street Works Act 1950.

Held: The Gas Board's failure was irrelevant. The highway authority remained liable for the highway.

B.6.2   Apportioning responsibility between the highway authority and statutory undertakers

28.   *Nolan v Merseyside County Council and North West Water Authority, unreported. Judgment of July 15, 1982 (CA)*

Text references: **5.2.4**

Facts: On 30 May 1979 the claimant tripped in a hole which had been created when vandals removed a stopcock box from the pavement. The box was the property of the water authority. The box had been inspected by the water authority between 26 March and 2 April 1979 and found to be in order. The claimant sued both the water authority and the highway authority. The trial judge found against the water authority, dismissed the action against the highway authority, and ordered the water authority to pay the highway authority's costs. The water authority appealed. They contended first that the judgment be set aside entirely and entered for the claimant against the first defendant, and in the alternative that judgment be entered for the claimant against both defendants with liability apportioned between the defendants. The highway authority did not invoke the statutory defence.

Held: Per May LJ:

(a) 'On the facts of this case, in whatever way the stopcock box came to lose its lid, the [highway authority was] clearly in breach of [its duty to maintain under the Highways Act] . . .'

(b) 'Similarly . . . the [water authority was] clearly in breach of [its duty under the Water Act 1945 to carry out any necessary works of maintenance or repair] . . . and such breach was also clearly also a cause of the plaintiff's accident.'

(c) 'In these circumstances the plaintiff was in our opinion entitled to judgment against both defendants . . .'

(d) 'In some cases, where for instance a highway authority draws the attention of a water authority to the absence of a lid to a stopcock box which renders the highway unsafe and the water authority takes no steps to replace the lid and in consequence a user of the highway has an accident, the particular facts may give rise to causes of action in negligence and nuisance, in addition to the breaches of the basic statutory duties . . . This must depend on the evidence given in the particular case and the facts found by the trial judge. Such was not, however, the position in the present case where the only facts proved and found were that the lid to the [water authority's] stopcock box was missing, that the box was thus out of repair, and that as a result of this along the highway itself was also out of repair . . .'

(e) 'The position with regard to apportionment in this and similar cases is now governed by the provisions of sections 1(1) and 2(1) of the Civil Liability (Contribution) Act 1978. Taken together these two sub-sections provide that any person liable in respect of any damage suffered by a plaintiff may recover contribution from any other person liable in respect of the same damage and that the amount of such contribution "shall be such as may be found by the court to be just and equitable having regard to the extent of that person's responsibility for the damage in question" . . . The application of these provisions to the facts of any given case has given rise to difficulties. Broadly speaking, two principal criteria of "responsibility" present themselves: causation on the one hand and blameworthiness and culpability on the other and the decided cases suggest that courts should consider both . . . To attempt to adopt this bifurcated approach in a particular case may be difficult if not impossible . . . In the result we think that the question of apportionment is in every case a question of fact and for the exercise of a discretion by the trial judge. He has to assess the relative responsibilities of the two or more defendants for the damage in question in and on the facts of the case before him. He should have in mind the two criteria of culpability and causation and apply them to the extent that they do have relevance in that particular case. Once he has decided upon the proper apportionment . . . his decision will not be varied on appeal unless and until, on the usual principles, he can be shown to have exercised his discretion wrongly.

With all respect to the learned county court judge in the present case, however, we think that he did exercise his discretion wrongly. If one remembers that the plaintiff was entitled to succeed against each of the defendants in this case on the ground of a breach by each of them respectively of an absolute statutory duty without otherwise any moral or legal "fault" or turpitude on either side, then we do not see how one can differentiate in any way between their several responsibilities for the plaintiff's damage. We think that it was clearly wrong to attribute entire responsibility to the [water authority] and none to the [highway authority]. We accordingly allow this appeal, order that judgment be entered for the plaintiff against each of the defendants for £730 with costs, that there be mutual contribution to the extent of one-half of the plaintiff's damages and costs below between the two defendants, and that each of the defendants should bear their own costs of the county court proceedings.'

B.7   HIGHWAY OUT OF REPAIR

29.   *Hereford & Worcester CC v Newman [1975] 1 WLR 901 (CA)*

Text reference: **4.2.3**

Facts: The complainant sought an order requiring the highway authority to put certain footpaths into proper repair. The highway authority was liable to intervene if the footpaths were 'out of repair', and the case concerned the construction of these words. One footpath had a hedge 7 feet high growing in the middle of it. Another had a barbed wire fence and thick undergrowth across it. The junction of two other footpaths was crossed by a barbed wire fence. The justices held that these footpaths were out of repair. The highway authority appealed.

Held: A highway was out of repair only if its surface was defective or disturbed. If it was unusable only because of an obstruction it was not out of repair. Merely to remove an obstruction was not to repair. Thus the footpaths with the hedge and the undergrowth growing in their surfaces were out of repair. The footpaths obstructed merely by the barbed wire fences were not out of repair.

B.8   BOUNDARIES OF A HIGHWAY

30.   *Bishop v Green (1971) 69 LGR 579*

Text reference: **2.4.1**

Facts: A byelaw made pursuant to s 249 of the Local Government Act 1933 provided that it was an offence for a person to permit a dog to foul ' . . . the footway of any street or public place . . .'" An information was preferred against the defendant alleging that she had allowed her dog to foul a 3-feet wide grass verge between a 6-feet wide pavement and a kerb bordering the carriageway. The justices concluded that this was not part of the footway of the street and dismissed the information. The prosecutor appealed.

Held: The byelaw was intended to protect only the made-up ways which had been prepared with the intention of being used by pedestrians, and accordingly the grass verge adjacent to the made-up way was not part of the footway.

B.9   NEGLIGENCE AND THE STANDARD OF CARE

B.9.1   Railway platforms

31.   *Stowell v Railway Executive [1949] 2 KB 519 (KBD, Lynskey J)*

Text reference: **4.5.1**; **5.2.5**

Facts: The claimant was injured when he slipped on an oily patch on a railway platform belonging to the defendants. He claimed damages for negligence.

Held: Most of the ratio of this case is now irrelevant, but the judge found that the claimant was taking reasonable care to ensure his own safety, saying, [1949] 2 All ER 193 at 196:

> 'If one is walking along a dockside where one expects mooring ropes and other obstructions one must watch every step, but if one is walking down a railway platform provided for the purpose of those who use the trains one is entitled to expect that it will be free from obstruction. It would not be reasonable to require that those using the platforms should be looking down at the ground at every step they take.'

B.9.2   Shops/supermarkets

32.   *Turner v Arding & Hobbs Ltd [1949] 2 All ER 911 (KBD, Lord Goddard CJ)*

Text reference: **7.5**

Facts: The claimant slipped on some vegetable matter while shopping in the defendant's shop. She sued in negligence.

Held: The defendant was liable. Lord Goddard CJ said, at 912:

> 'Assistants cannot be expected to walk behind each customer to sweep up anything that he or she may drop, and if this accident had happened at a very busy time when the shop was crowded with people I can well understand that it would be difficult to say that the defendants were negligent because something had got on the floor which they may not have had the opportunity of sweeping up. Here, however, I think that there is a burden thrown on the defendants either of explaining how this thing got on the floor or giving me far more evidence than they have as to the state of the floor and the watch that was kept on it immediately before the accident. I do not mean that it was their duty to have somebody going around watching it, but, in a store of this sort, into which people are invited to come, there is a duty on the shopkeeper to see that his floors are kept reasonably safe.'

33.   *Ward v Tesco Stores Ltd [1976] 1 All ER 219 (CA)*

Text reference: **7.5**

This case is summarised in the text, and has to be regarded as the leading authority on slipping in shops. See the commentary in Chapter 7 and the other authorities cited there.

B.10   NEGLIGENCE OF A HIGHWAY AUTHORITY

B.10.1   Duty of care extending beyond the boundaries of the highway

34.   *Stovin v Wise [1996] AC 923 (HL)*

Text reference: **5.3.4.1**; **5.3.5**; **6.1**

Facts: A collision occurred as a result, inter alia, of restricted visibility. The restricted visibility was caused by the existence of a bank on land belonging to British Rail. The land in question did not form part of the highway. Before the accident occurred the highway authority had recognised that there was a visibility problem and had contacted British Rail to have part of the bank removed at the highway authority's expense. That work was never done. The highway authority was joined as a third party to proceedings arising out of the accident.

Held: The highway authority was not liable. The reasons are set out in the discussion at **5.3.4.1**.

35.   *Gorringe v Calderdale Metropolitan Borough Council [2004] UKHL 15 (HL)*

Text reference: **5.3.4.2**

Facts: The claimant was seriously injured in an accident on the crest of a road. No sign or road marking warned of the danger at the crest. A sign saying 'Slow' had previously been present, but was no longer visible. The highway authority surveyed a stretch of country road and as a result made a policy decision to mark lines on the road permitting overtaking if it was safe to do so. The claimant contended that the failure to provide adequate road signs constituted a failure to maintain under HA 1980, s 41, and that the highway authority had a common law duty to discharge its statutory duty under s 39 of the Road Traffic Act 1988 by providing adequate signs.

Held: There was no breach of the s 41 duty. The accident was not caused by a failure to maintain the road. Maintenance had to be construed as it was in *Goodes*. There was no common law duty to erect or place warning signs. Section 39 of the 1988 Act did not create such a duty. If a highway authority created a reasonable expectation about the state of a highway, it would be under a duty to ensure that it did not create a trap for a road user who drove in reliance on that expectation. But that was not this case. The fact that there had previously been a warning neither created such an expectation nor created a requirement that the warning sign should be maintained.

36. *Sandhar v Department of Transport, Environment and the Regions [2004] EWCA Civ 1440 (CA)*

Text reference: **4.2.3**; **4.3.4**; **5.3.4.1**

Facts: The deceased's car skidded on hoar frost on a road. The highway authority had a winter maintenance programme in place. It had not salted the relevant part of the road. If it had the accident would not have happened. It was contended that there was a common law duty to salt because there was a public expectation that, a winter maintenance regime having been adopted, it would be done properly.

Held: There was no duty of care. An assumption of responsibility sufficient to create a duty of care would normally require a particular relationship with individuals. Further, reliance was an essential element of a common law duty, and there was no evidence in this case that the deceased relied on the performance of the winter maintenance duties. The deceased was not entitled to assume that the road had been salted. The highway authority had not created a trap.

B.10.2   Street furniture

37. *Shine v Tower Hamlets LBC [2006] EWCA 852*

Text reference: **4.2.6**

Facts: The claimant (a child) attempted to leapfrog a bollard which was insecure. The bollard wobbled, causing the claimant to fall and sustain injury.

Held: The maintenance of street furniture did not fall within the ambit of the s 41 duty. However, the local authority was liable in negligence for the injuries that the claimant sustained. It was foreseeable that a child would leapfrog the bollard. It had been established that the bollard was insecure, and that the defendant was aware that it was insecure. In those circumstances, the defendant was negligent in failing to repair the bollard.

B.10.3   Negligence in the performance of statutory works

38. *Baxter v Stockton-on-Tees Corporation [1959] 1 QB 441 (CA)*

Text reference: **1.2.1.9**

Facts: The claimant's husband was killed when his motor cycle collided with the kerb of an island next to a roundabout. The claimant sued the highway authority alleging that it was negligent in failing to light or give warning of a concealed danger or trap.

Held: Much of the decision in this case has been overtaken by more recent law, but it is still authority for the proposition that a highway authority which exercises a statutory power to construct a road for public use owes a duty to the public to take reasonable care to construct the road properly.

39.   *Newsome v Darton UDC [1938] 3 All ER 93 (CA)*

Text reference: **5.3.2**

Facts: The defendant highway and sanitary authority had made a trench in a road to perform drainage works. The trench was filled in and the surface finished off without negligence. About 2 years later the surface subsided, forming a dangerous depression. The claimant cyclist was injured as a result of the defect. He sued the highway authority.

Held: The highway authority was liable in negligence. If a highway authority interferes with a road it is bound to restore it to its original condition, and the operation of so restoring it includes making good the inevitable subsidence which results from the work.

B.11   INDEPENDENT CONTRACTORS

40.   *Salsbury v Woodland [1970] 1 QB 324 (CA)*

Text reference: **1.2.1.2**

The general rule is that no one is liable for the torts of his independent contractor. There are two exceptions: (a) extra hazardous acts, and (b) dangers created in or on a highway. There was no additional class of exceptions relating to work done near a highway.

41.   *Penny v Wimbledon Urban District Council [1899] 2 QB 72 (CA)*

Text reference: **1.2.1.2**

Facts: A district council engaged a contractor to make up a highway. The highway was not repairable by the public at large, but was used by the public. The contractor left an unlit and unfenced heap of soil on the road. The claimant walked along the road after dark and fell over the heap. He sued both the contractor and the district council.

Held: The district council was liable. The negligence of the contractor arose from the nature of the works being done, and was not collateral to it.

B.12 STATUTORY UNDERTAKERS

B.12.1 Public Utilities Street Works Act 1950

42. *Keating v Elvan Reinforced Concrete Co Ltd [1968] 2 All ER 139 (CA)*

Text reference: **1.3.1.11**

The Public Utilities Street Works Act 1950, s 8 does not create a statutory duty which gives rise to civil liability to a member of the public injured by a breach of the section.

B.12.2 The dangerousness criterion applied to non-highway authorities

43. *Cohen v British Gas Corporation [1978] CLY 2053 (Judge Lymbery QC)*

Text reference: **5.2.4**

Facts: The defendant re-excavated a road pursuant to its statutory powers. The excavation was about 5 feet by 3 feet. The temporary filling had sunk, causing a depression of about one inch, over which the claimant tripped.

Held: The depression was not dangerous. The defendant was not liable. Roads are not to be judged by the standards of bowling greens.

B.12.3 The standard of care

44. *Wells v Metropolitan Water Board [1937] 4 All ER 639 (QBD, Humphreys J)*

Text reference: **5.2.4**

Facts: The claimant tripped over the opened cover-plate of a valve-box which belonged to the defendant. When closed, the cover was not at all dangerous, but when it was open it projected 3 or 4 nches above the road surface and was dangerous. It could be opened easily. On this occasion it had probably been opened by a child. It was not fitted with any locking device, but it would have been perfectly practicable for such a lock to be fitted.

Held: The defendant was negligent in failing to make the cover-plate safe by fitting such a lock.

45. *Manchester Corporation v Markland [1936] AC 360 (HL)*

Text reference: **5.2.4**

Facts: The defendant was the statutory authority supplying water. One of its pipes, which ran in a highway, burst. A pool of water formed in the highway and lay there for 3 days, not noticed by the defendant. On the third day the water froze. A car, driven responsibly, skidded on the ice and killed a man. It was only after this accident that the defendant knew that the water pipe had burst.

Held: The defendant was liable. It should have taken more prompt steps to deal with the escaping water. The escape made the road dangerous to traffic.

46. *Reid v British Telecommunications plc, The Times, June 27, 1987 (CA)*

Text references: **1.3.1.13; 5.2.4**

Facts: The claimant tripped over a manhole cover owned by the defendant. The cover protruded 12 millimetres above the level of the pavement. At first instance the claimant succeeded. On appeal, the defendant contended that it was not negligent because it had relied on the half-yearly inspections of the pavement which had been carried out by the local highway authority.

Held: The appeal was dismissed. It was not negligent for a statutory undertaker to rely on the inspections of a local highway authority. But if the undertaker did so rely, it would be assumed to have the knowledge of the condition of the manholes which it would have got or should have got from carrying out its own inspection.

B.12.4   The standard of knowledge required for liability

47. *Longhurst v Metropolitan Water Board [1948] 2 All ER 834 (HL)*

Text reference: **5.2.4**

Facts: The defendant water board owned a stopcock beneath a public highway. The stopcock developed a leak and the water which escaped from it dislodged the paving stones of the highway. The defendant took up as much of the highway as was necessary to effect the repair. It temporarily made good the surface. It gave no warning to the public of the dangerous condition of the displaced stones. The water board was statutorily entitled to break up the pavement to effect the repairs. It was obliged (by the statutory predecessor of s 8 of the Public Utilities Street Works Act 1950) to reinstate and make good the highway, to fence or guard any defect and to light up any works at night and when the highway has been made good to keep it in good repair for 3 months. About 10 am on the day after the defendant completed its repairs, the highway authority was notified by the defendant of the need to effect permanent repairs. Before the highway authority had time to do those repairs the claimant tripped over a defective paving stone and was injured. He sued the water board.

Held: The water board was not liable. There was no evidence, nor could it be inferred, that the board knew or ought to have known of the danger posed to road users by the additional damage done by the escaping water. Since there was no negligence, the claimant's only remaining cause of action was nuisance. Here too the claimant failed. A statutory undertaker performing works authorised by statute would be liable only if those works were done negligently. They were not. The Act required the undertaker to reinstate and repair only the part of the highway taken up by it. Where, however, the undertaker had actual or constructive knowledge of an emergency not known to the highway authority, the undertaker may (per Lord du Parcq) be under a duty to warn of that emergency.

B.12.5   No obligation to provide street lighting if the road is not dangerous

48.   *Sheppard v Glossop Corporation [1921] 3 KB 132 (CA)*

Text reference: **1.3.1.17**

Facts: A street was vested in an urban authority which had decided to exercise its power to provide street lighting. It had also resolved to extinguish the lights at 9 pm. The claimant wandered off the road at 11.30 pm and was injured. He sued the authority.

Held: The authority was not liable. It was under no obligation to light the road. Having begun to light it, the authority was under no obligation to continue to light the road, having done nothing to make the road dangerous.

B.12.6   Things constructed under statutory powers must be kept safe

49.   *Fisher v Ruislip-Northwood UDC and Middlesex CC [1945] KB 584 (CA)*

Text reference: **1.3.1.17**

Facts: The defendant local authority had erected a shelter in the highway pursuant to statutory powers under the Civil Defence Act 1939. Sometimes warning lights were displaying at each corner of the shelter. One night when the lights were off, the claimant, who was driving responsibly, collided with the shelter and was injured.

Held: The local authority was liable. When statutory undertakers exercised a power given to them by statute, they were obliged to take reasonable care to construct and maintain whatever they constructed using the power to ensure that they were safe. Here the shelter was not safe because it was not illuminated.

B.12.7   The duty to warn

50.   *Whiting v Middlesex CC and Harrow UDC [1948] 1 KB 162 (QBD, Croom-Johnson J)*

Text reference: **1.3.1.17**

Facts: The claimant motorcyclist collided at night with a shelter which protruded into the highway. The only lamp near the shelter had been put out of action, probably by vandals, on the night of the accident. It had been repeatedly vandalised, to the knowledge of the defendant.

Held: The defendant was liable. It had not taken reasonable steps to ensure that the shelter was not dangerous to highway users. The duty on it was not a duty to light but a duty to warn. If the only effective way of warning was to light, then the duty might be tantamount to a duty to light properly.

51.   *Lilley v British Insulated Callenders Construction Co Ltd (1968) 67 LGR 224 (CA)*

Text reference: **1.3.1.17**

Facts: At about 10.50 pm the claimant was injured when his car hit a highway obstruction left by the defendant. The claimant's evidence was that the obstruction was unfenced and unlit. The defendant's evidence was that at 8.30 pm the obstruction was fenced round with barriers and illuminated.

Held: The defendant was not liable. To hold otherwise would be to hold that it was unreasonable for the defendant not to have provided an inspector to inspect the lights and the barriers periodically throughout the night. The defendant was not obliged to do this; it had taken reasonable precautions.

52.   *Murray v Southwark BC (1966) 65 LGR 145 (QBD)*

Text reference: **1.3.1.17**

Facts: The claimant drove his car into a trench in a highway created by the defendant. The trench had been guarded by a barrier and marked by lamps, but these had been removed by vandals by the time the accident occurred.

Held: The defendant was liable. The accident occurred in an area known for vandalism. To enable highway users to be reasonably safe, the authority was bound to provide watchmen who would guard the excavated areas and check that the barriers and lights required to make the road safe remained in place.

B.13   THE OWNER OF LAND ADJOINING THE HIGHWAY

53.   *Caseley v Bristol Corporation [1944] 1 All ER 14 (CA)*

Text reference: **1.3.2.5**; **6.5.2**

Facts: The claimant wandered from the highway in dense fog. He fell into a dock basin, owned by the defendant, which was 47 feet from the highway. The dock basin was not separated from the highway by any fence.

Held: The defendant was not liable. There is a duty on an occupier of land adjacent to the highway to fence any dangerous excavation adjoining the highway, and this can include fencing off a danger which is close to the highway although not actually adjoining it. But there is no duty to fence unless the danger is so near the highway that a man taking a false step or temporarily giddy might fall into that danger.

B.14   NUISANCE IN GENERAL

B.14.1   The nature of the duty

54.   *Leakey v National Trust for Places of Historical Interest or Natural Beauty [1980] QB 485 (CA)*

Text reference: **6.4**

Facts: The claimants owned houses which stood at the foot of a large mound which was on the defendant's land. Because of natural weathering and the type of soil which composed the mount, soil and rubble had, over the course of many years, fallen from the mound onto the claimants' land. A crack opened in the mound above the claimants' houses. The claimants told the defendant about the danger which a large fall of soil presented. The defendant's reply was that they would not be responsible for damage caused by a natural movement of land. Shortly after the claimants' warning, some debris did fall onto the claimants' land. The claimants sued in nuisance. The defendant was held liable at first instance. It appealed.

Held: The appeal was dismissed. An occupier owed a general duty to a neighbouring occupier in relation to a hazard occurring on his land. This duty existed whether the hazard was natural or man-made. The duty was a duty to take such steps as in all the circumstances were reasonable to prevent or minimise any risk, of which the occupier knew or ought to have known, of injury or damage to the neighbour or his property. The circumstances to be considered in deciding what steps were reasonable included the occupier's knowledge of the nature and extent of the hazard, the risk involved, the practicability of preventing or minimising the risk (which included the time available to deal with it and the cost of dealing with it), and the relative financial and other resources of both parties to the action. In this case, since the defendant accepted that the cost and magnitude of the work required was not beyond it, and was not greater than the cost of curing the damage which had resulted to the claimants, the defendant was liable.

B.14.2   Foreseeability

55.   *The Wagon Mound (No 2) [1967] 1 AC 617 (PC)*

Text reference: **6.5.3.3; 6.5.3.4**

Facts: Inflammable oil was discharged by the defendants into Sydney harbour. It ignited. The claimant's ships were damaged by fire. The claimant sued in negligence and nuisance. The trial judge held that the damage was not reasonably foreseeable and so the defendants were not liable in negligence. They were, however, liable in nuisance, since in nuisance liability did not depend on foreseeability. The case came before the Privy Council on several points.

Held: To recover damages for nuisance the claimant must establish that the injury resulting from the nuisance was foreseeable.

B.15   HIGHWAY NUISANCE

B.15.2   The test of reasonable user

56.   *Harper v Haden & Sons Ltd [1933] Ch 298 (CA)*

Text reference: **6.3**

Facts: The defendant erected scaffolding in connection with building works. The claimant claimed that his business had been damaged by the presence of the scaffolding because, inter alia, the scaffolding constituted an obstruction, and therefore a nuisance, to the highway by which customers gained access to his shop. At first instance the trial judge held that although the scaffolding was reasonably necessary for the execution of the works, would not remain in situ for any longer than was necessary and was not more obstructive than necessary, the claimant was nonetheless entitled to recover damages. The defendant appealed.

Held: The appeal was allowed. Since the highway obstruction was reasonable in extent and duration the claimant had no remedy (per Lord Hanworth MR and Romer LJ). Since the defendant had complied with the relevant statutory provisions for the erection of scaffolding and with the conditions contained in the licence granted by the local authority, the scaffolding could not be a public nuisance (per Lawrence LJ).

57.   *Trevett v Lee [1955] 1 WLR 113*

Text reference: **6.3**

Facts: The defendant occupied a house which abutted a country lane, which was a highway. During times of drought they obtained water from a tank on the opposite side of the lane. The water flowed through a hosepipe about half an inch in diameter. The hosepipe crossed the highway. The claimant tripped over the hosepipe. He sued the defendants, contending that the hosepipe constituted a highway nuisance. The county court judge held that it was reasonable for the defendant to use the highway in this way and accordingly the defendants were not liable. The claimant appealed.

Held: In deciding whether the occupier of premises adjoining a highway, who uses the highway for purposes connected with his occupation of the premises, is or is not obstructing the highway so as to be liable in nuisance, the court must balance, applying the test of reasonableness, the rights of the occupier and the rights of the public. Here, the county court judge was entitled to conclude that the defendant's user was reasonable, and therefore the laying of the pipe across the highway did not constitute a public nuisance.

B.15.3 Dangerousness

58. *Dymond v Pearce [1972] 1 QB 496 (CA)*

Text references: **6.3** and **6.5.3.1**

Facts: A lorry was parked overnight on a well-lit road. It was plainly visible to road users. The claimant was the passenger on the back of a motor cycle which collided with the lorry. He alleged that the lorry constituted a nuisance since it was an obstruction to the highway and the driver had no right to park it where it was parked. The trial judge held that the sole cause of the accident was the motor cyclist's negligence, that the lorry did not constitute a nuisance and that even if it did, it did not cause the accident, and the damage suffered by the claimant was not a foreseeable result of it. The claimant appealed.

Held: The appeal was dismissed. Leaving a lorry on the highway for a considerable period could constitute a nuisance by obstruction, and such a nuisance would be actionable if it caused damage to a member of the public. But on the facts the trial judge was right to find that the sole cause of the claimant's injury was the motor cyclist's negligence and the lorry owner and/or driver was/were not liable. For a claimant to recover damages for personal injuries resulting from a collision with a highway obstruction amounting to a nuisance, that claimant must show that the obstruction was a danger. In this case, although the lorry was an obstruction and accordingly a public nuisance, it was not dangerous to members of the public using the highway in a reasonable way.

59. *Maitland v Raisbeck & R T & J Hewitt Ltd [1944] KB 689 (CA)*

Text reference: **6.5.3.3**

Facts: The claimant was injured when a bus in which he was travelling collided with a lorry which was moving slowly ahead of and in the same direction as the bus, but which had a non-functioning rear light. Neither the bus driver nor the lorry driver or owner was negligent. The claimant contended that the fact that the light on the lorry had gone out meant that the lorry became an obstruction to the highway and that he could therefore sustain an action in nuisance against the owners of the lorry. This argument was rejected at first instance. The claimant appealed.

Held: The appeal was dismissed. Lord Greene MR said, at 691–692, that:

> 'Every person who uses the highway must exercise due care, but he has a right to use the highway and, if something happens to him which, in fact, causes an obstruction of the highway, but is in no way referable to his fault, it is wrong to suppose that ipso facto and immediately a nuisance is created. A nuisance will obviously be created if he allows the obstruction to continue for an unreasonable time or in unreasonable circumstances, but the mere fact that an obstruction has come into existence cannot turn it into a nuisance. It must depend on the facts of each case whether or not a nuisance is created.'

B.15.4   A nuisance need not be an obstruction

60.   *Almeroth v Chivers [1948] 1 All ER 53 (CA)*

Text reference: **6.5.3.1**

Facts: The claimant crossed the road to serve a customer at his barrow. He tripped on a small pile of slates which lay in the gutter and did not reach above the level of the kerb. The defendants had left this pile of slates for collection. The claimant sued the defendants, alleging nuisance. The defendants alleged that the claimant was guilty of contributory negligence.

Held: Although the slates did not cause an obstruction in the sense of impeding the flow of traffic, they nonetheless amounted to a nuisance. A normally careful pedestrian may well overlook a pile of slates such as constituted the nuisance, and there was no finding of contributory negligence.

B.15.5   The requisite knowledge

61.   *British Road Services v Slater [1964] 1 WLR 498 (Staffordshire Assizes, Lord Parker CJ)*

Text references: **6.5.3.3** and **6.5.4**

Facts: The defendants were the owners of land upon which grew an oak tree. A branch of that oak tree had protruded out over the highway for many years, going back to the time of the defendant's predecessors in title. Neither the defendants nor the highway authority had considered the branch to constitute a danger to traffic. A lawfully high-loaded lorry belonging to the claimants came along the road and the branch knocked off part of the load. The load fell into the road. In trying to avoid it, another lorry belonging to the claimants swerved off the road and was damaged. The claimants sued the defendants in nuisance.

Held: The defendants were not liable. The branch certainly was a nuisance because it prevented the convenient use of the highway, but although an occupier of land would be liable for failing to remedy a nuisance which he inherited from a predecessor in title, he was not liable until he became aware or should have become aware of its being a nuisance. The court also said that if the tree had grown from the verge which formed part of the highway the highway authority would have had the power, and arguably a duty, to remove the obstruction which it created, but that this would not necessarily have absolved the defendant, who owned the tree, from liability.

B.15.6   Only highway users may sue

62.   *Bromley v Mercer [1922] 2 KB 126 (CA)*

Text reference: **6.5.4**

Facts: The defendants owned a house and yard which abutted on a highway and were separated from the highway by a wall. This wall was in a poor state of repair. It constituted a public nuisance in the highway. The claimant, who was a nine-year-old child, was playing in the yard. She was injured when a heavy stone from the yard fell on her. For technical reasons the claimant could recover against the defendants only if she could sustain a *highway nuisance* as a cause of action.

Held: Since the claimant was not actually using the highway at the time of her injury, she could not succeed, even though her injury resulted from something which was itself a highway nuisance.

63.   *Jacobs v LCC [1950] AC 361 (HL)*

Text reference: **6.5.5**

Facts: The claimant was injured when she stepped from the pavement onto a forecourt between a shop and the pavement and tripped over a defective stopcock which protruded from the forecourt. The forecourt was owned and occupied by the defendant local council. The paving of the forecourt was such that there was a demarcation between the pavement and the forecourt, but to a casual passer-by the highway (pavement) and the forecourt would be indistinguishable. The claimant sued the defendant inter alia in nuisance, alleging that the condition of the stopcock and the paving stones surrounding it constituted a nuisance adjoining the highway which had caused her to suffer injury.

Held: (per Lord Simonds at 374–378) that the forecourt did not constitute part of a highway. Accordingly, even if the stopcock did constitute a highway nuisance (which in fact it was found not to do), the claimant was not a highway user at the time she was injured and therefore, following *Bromley v Mercer* (above), must fail.

B.15.7   Duty on owners of premises adjoining a highway

64.   *Wringe v Cohen [1940] 1 KB 229 (CA)*

Text reference: **8.3**

Facts: The claimant owned a shop. The defendant owned and let out an adjoining shop. The premises adjoined a highway. The gable end of the defendant's shop collapsed during a storm and fell through the roof of the claimant's shop.

Held: The defendant was liable. If, because of want of repair, premises adjoining a highway become dangerous and constitute a nuisance, collapsing and injuring an adjoining owner or a highway user, the occupier of the premises which constitute the nuisance, if he has (as here) undertaken the obligation of repairing the premises, is liable, whether or not he knew or ought to have known of the danger.

65.   *Mint v Good [1951] 1 KB 517 (CA)*

Text references: **6.5.4**; **8.3**

Facts: The claimant was walking along the highway when a wall which separated the highway from a house owned by the defendant collapsed and injured him. The house was let on a weekly tenancy. The defendant had not expressly reserved a right to enter. The trial judge held that the wall was a nuisance and that the defect in it could with reasonable inspection have been discovered, but that the defendant was not liable for the claimant's injuries because he had not specifically reserved right to enter. The claimant appealed.

Held: The appeal was allowed. The defendant was liable. A right to enter must be implied in circumstances such as these where a highway nuisance is or may be created. *Wringe v Cohen* (above) was applied.

B.15.8   Maintenance of potential dangers adjoining highways

66.   *Tarry v Ashton (1876) 1 QBD 314 (Blackburn J)*

Text reference: **6.5.4**

Facts: The defendant rented and occupied a house. A lamp projected several feet from the house over the highway. In August the lamp had been serviced by a gas-fitter engaged by the defendant. In November the lamp fell on the claimant pedestrian and injured her. At the time of the accident another workman employed by the defendant was servicing the lamp. His ladder slipped and he clung to the lamp-iron to stop himself falling. The following facts were found:

(a)   The immediate cause of the fall of the lamp was the slipping of the ladder.

(b)   The bracket upon which the lamp hung was in poor condition and dangerous.

(c)   The workman employed in August had been negligent in failing to note and/or remedy the defective bracket.

(d)   If the bracket had been in good repair the slipping of the ladder would not have caused the lamp to fall.

(e)   The defendant had not been personally negligent; he did not know about the state of the lamp bracket.

Held: That the defendant was liable to the claimant. The lamp constituted a nuisance to the highway. If someone maintains something projecting over a highway it is his duty to maintain it so that it is not dangerous to highway users. If it causes injury through want of repair it is no answer to assert that a competent person has been employed to repair it. Where something potentially dangerous is maintained next to a highway, the duty is therefore to ensure that it is not dangerous, rather than to ensure that reasonable steps are taken to ensure that it is not dangerous.

APPENDIX C

HSE RISK ASSESSMENT MATERIALS

(1) PREVENTING SLIPS AND TRIPS AT WORK

Over a third of all major injuries reported each year are caused as a result of a slip or trip (the single most common cause of injuries at work). These cost employers over £512 million a year in lost production and other costs. Slips and trips also account for over half of all reported injuries to members of the public.

Recognising the importance of slips and trips, the Health and Safety Executive and local authorities have included this topic in their programmes of work designed to achieve national targets set to improve health and safety performance. These targets were published by the Government and the Health and Safety Commission in the Revitalising Health and Safety strategy statement of June 2000.

Legal actions brought as a result of an injury can be extremely damaging to business, especially where the public are involved. Insurance covers only a small proportion of the costs.

Anyone at work, but particularly employers, can help to reduce slip and trip hazards through good health and safety arrangements.

Effective solutions are often simple, cheap and lead to other benefits.

Managing health and safety

A good management system will help you to identify problem areas, decide what to do, act on decisions made and check that the steps taken have been effective.

A good system should involve:

Planning Identify key areas of risk and set goals for improvement. Employers can work with employees to identify areas on site that they think are a slipping and tripping risk (remember that there will be about 40 cases of a slip or stumble, resulting in no or minor injury for every major injury accident). Careful selection of materials, equipment and work practices can prevent or contain slip and trip hazards from liquids, fine powders and objects. For example fit splash guards and anti-slip floorings in areas that can't be kept dry and use cordless tools to avoid trailing cables across working areas. This all helps to remove or minimise risks.

Organisation Workers need to be involved and committed to reducing risks. Give people (eg supervisors) responsibilities to ensure that areas of the workplace are kept safe, eg getting spillages and objects cleaned up quickly, keeping access routes clear and ensuring lighting is maintained. Keep a record of who is responsible for which arrangements; take special care to include cleaning and other contractors. Make these details clear to everyone.

Control Check to ensure that working practices and processes are being carried out properly, eg smooth floors are not left wet, housekeeping is good, and any leaks from equipment and roof lights are repaired quickly. Keep a record of cleaning and maintenance work etc and encourage good health and safety.

Monitor and review Monitor accident investigation and inspection reports. Try to identify any deficiencies in your management arrangements. Do they show any improvement? Talk to any safety representatives about slip and trip risks – they can be a great help when identifying and solving problems. Employees should also be encouraged to be involved in reviewing existing control measures. They are often better placed to assess the effectiveness of the measures implemented to reduce the risks of slipping and tripping.

Examine slip and trip risks

All employers have to assess the risks to employees and others who may be affected by their work, eg visitors and members of the public. This helps to find out what needs to be done to control the risk. It is also needed to satisfy the law.

HSE recommend a five-step approach to risk assessment, and slip and trip risks should be among the risks examined.

Step 1 Look for slip and trip hazards around the workplace, such as uneven floors, trailing cables, areas that are sometimes slippery due to spillages. Include outdoor areas.

Step 2 Decide who might be harmed and how. Who comes into the workplace? Are they at risk? Do you have any control over them? Remember that older people and people with disabilities may be at particular risk.

Step 3 Consider the risks. Are the precautions already taken adequate to deal with the risks?

Step 4 Record your findings if you have five or more employees.

Step 5 Regularly review the assessment. If any significant changes take place, make sure existing precautions and management arrangements are still adequate to deal with the risks.

What the law says

The **Health and Safety at Work etc Act 1974** (HSWA) requires employers to ensure the health and safety of all employees and anyone who may be affected by their work. This includes taking steps to control slip and trip risks.

Employees must not endanger themselves or others and must use any safety equipment provided.

Manufacturers and suppliers have a duty to ensure that their products are safe. They must also provide adequate information about appropriate use.

The **Management of Health and Safety at Work Regulations 1999** build on HSWA and include duties on employers to assess risks (including slip and trip risks) and where necessary take action to safeguard health and safety.

The **Workplace (Health, Safety and Welfare) Regulations 1992** require floors to be suitable, in good condition and free from obstructions. People must be able to move around safely.

Good working practice

Get conditions right from the start – this will make dealing with slip and trip risks easier. Choose only suitable floor surfaces and particularly avoid very smooth floors in areas that will become wet/contaminated (such as kitchens and entrance halls). Ensure lighting levels are sufficient, properly plan pedestrian and traffic routes and avoid overcrowding.

Cleaning and maintenance

Train workers in the correct use of any safety and cleaning equipment provided.

Cleaning methods and equipment must be suitable for the type of surface being treated. You may need to get advice from the manufacturer or supplier. Take care not to create additional slip or trip hazards while cleaning and maintenance work is being done.

Carry out all necessary maintenance work promptly (you may need to get outside help or guidance). Include inspection, testing, adjustment and cleaning at suitable intervals. Keep records so that the system can be checked.

Lighting should enable people to see obstructions, potentially slippery areas etc, so they can work safely. Replace, repair or clean lights before levels become too low for safe work.

Floors need to be checked for loose finishes, holes and cracks, worn rugs and mats etc. Take care in the choice of floor if it is likely to become wet or dusty due to work processes. Seek specialist advice when choosing a floor for difficult conditions.

Obstructions and objects left lying around can easily go unnoticed and cause a trip. Try to keep work areas tidy and if obstructions can't be removed, warn people using signs or barriers. Cardboard should not be used to absorb spillages as this itself presents a tripping hazard.

Footwear can play an important part in preventing slips and trips. This is especially important where floors can't be kept dry. Your footwear supplier should be able to advise on shoes/boots with slip-resistant soles. Employers need to provide footwear, if it is necessary to protect the workers' safety.

There are many simple steps you can take to reduce risks. You will find a few examples below.

Hazard	Suggested Action
Spillage of wet and dry substances	Clean spills up immediately, if a liquid is greasy, make sure a suitable cleaning agent is used. After cleaning the floor can be wet for some time; dry it where possible. Use appropriate barriers to tell people the floor is still wet and arrange alternative bypass routes. If cleaning is done once a day, it may be possible to do it last thing at night, so it is dry for the start of the next shift.
Trailing cables	Position equipment to avoid cables crossing pedestrian routes, use cable covers to securely fix to surfaces, restrict access to prevent contact. Consider use of cordless tools. Remember that contractors will also need to be managed.
Miscellaneous rubbish, e g plastic bags	Keep areas clear, remove rubbish and do not allow it to build up.
Rugs/mats	Ensure mats are securely fixed and do not have curling edges.
Poor lighting	Improve lighting levels and placement of light fittings to ensure more even lighting of all floor areas.
Slippery surfaces	Assess the cause and treat accordingly, for example always keep them dry if wet causes the problem. In certain situations you may have to treat them chemically and use appropriate cleaning method etc.
Change from wet to dry floor surface	Provide suitable footwear, warn of risks by using signs, locate doormats where these changes are likely.
Changes of level	Try to avoid. If you can't, improve lighting, add high visible tread nosings (ie white/reflective edge to step).
Slopes	Improve visibility, provide hand rails, use floor markings.

Smoke/steam obscuring view	Eliminate or control by redirecting it away from risk areas; improve ventilation and warn of it.
Unsuitable footwear	Ensure workers choose suitable footwear, particularly with the correct type of sole. If the type of work requires special protective footwear, the employer is required by law to provide it free of charge.

Further advice

Further advice is available in the following HSE publications.

Slips and trips: Guidance for employers on identifying hazards and controlling risks HSG155 HSE Books 1996 ISBN 0 7176 1145 0

Slips and trips: Guidance for the food processing industry HSG156 HSE Books 1996 ISBN 0 7176 0832 8

Further information

HSE priced and free publications are available by mail order from HSE Books, PO Box 1999, Sudbury, Suffolk CO10 2WA Tel: 01787 881165 Fax: 01787 313995 Website: www.hsebooks.co.uk (HSE priced publications are also available from bookshops and free leaflets can be downloaded from HSE's website: www.hse.gov.uk.)

For information about health and safety ring HSE's Infoline Tel: 0845 345 0055 Fax: 0845 408 9566 Textphone: 0845 408 9577 e-mail: hse.infoline@natbrit.com or write to HSE Information Services, Caerphilly Business Park, Caerphilly CF83 3GG.

Information can also be found on the HSE slips and trips website: www.hse.gov.uk/slips/index.htm.

This leaflet contains notes on good practice which are not compulsory but which you may find helpful in considering what you need to do.

This leaflet is available in priced packs of 15 from HSE Books, ISBN 0 7176 2760 8. Single free copies are also available from HSE Books and a web version can be found at: www.hse.gov.uk/pubns/indg225.pdf.

(2) FIVE STEPS TO RISK ASSESSMENT

This leaflet aims to help you assess health and safety risks in the workplace

A risk assessment is an important step in protecting your workers and your business, as well as complying with the law. It helps you focus on the risks that really matter in your workplace – the ones with the potential to cause real harm. In many instances, straightforward measures can readily control risks, for example ensuring spillages are cleaned up promptly so people do not slip, or cupboard drawers are kept closed to ensure people do not trip. For most, that means simple, cheap and effective measures to ensure your most valuable asset – your workforce – is protected.

The law does not expect you to eliminate all risk, but you are required to protect people as far as 'reasonably practicable'. This guide tells you how to achieve that with a minimum of fuss.

This is not the only way to do a risk assessment, there are other methods that work well, particularly for more complex risks and circumstances. However, we believe this method is the most straightforward for most organisations.

What is risk assessment?

A risk assessment is simply a careful examination of what, in your work, could cause harm to people, so that you can weigh up whether you have taken enough precautions or should do more to prevent harm. Workers and others have a right to be protected from harm caused by a failure to take reasonable control measures.

Accidents and ill health can ruin lives and affect your business too if output is lost, machinery is damaged, insurance costs increase or you have to go to court. You are legally required to assess the risks in your workplace so that you put in place a plan to control the risks.

How to assess the risks in your workplace

Follow the five steps in this leaflet:

Step 1

Identify the hazards

Step 2

Decide who might be harmed and how

Step 3

Evaluate the risks and decide on precautions

Step 4

Record your findings and implement them

Step 5

Review your assessment and update if necessary

Don't overcomplicate the process. In many organisations, the risks are well known and the necessary control measures are easy to apply. You probably already know whether, for example, you have employees who move heavy loads and so could harm their backs, or where people are most likely to slip or trip. If so, check that you have taken reasonable precautions to avoid injury.

If you run a small organisation and you are confident you understand what's involved, you can do the assessment yourself. You don't have to be a health and safety expert.

If you work in a larger organisation, you could ask a health and safety advisor to help you. If you are not confident, get help from someone who is competent. In all cases, you should make sure that you involve your staff or their representatives in the process. They will have useful information about how the work is done that will make your assessment of the risk more thorough and effective. But remember, you are responsible for seeing that the assessment is carried out properly.

When thinking about your risk assessment, remember:

- a **hazard** is anything that may cause harm, such as chemicals, electricity, working from ladders, an open drawer etc;

- the **risk** is the chance, high or low, that somebody could be harmed by these and other hazards, together with an indication of how serious the harm could be.

Step 1

Identify the hazards

First you need to work out how people could be harmed. When you work in a place every day it is easy to overlook some hazards, so here are some tips to help you identify the ones that matter:

- **Walk around** your workplace and look at what could reasonably be expected to cause harm.

- **Ask your employees** or their representatives what they think. They may have noticed things that are not immediately obvious to you.

- **Visit the HSE website** (www.hse.gov.uk). HSE publishes practical guidance on where hazards occur and how to control them. There is much information here on the hazards that might affect your business.

- Alternatively, **call HSE Infoline** (Tel: 0845 345 0055), who will identify publications that can help you, or contact **Workplace Health Connect** (Tel: 0845 609 6006), a free service for managers and staff of small and medium-sized enterprises providing practical advice on workplace health and safety.

- If you are a member of a **trade association**, contact them. Many produce very helpful guidance.

- **Check manufacturers' instructions** or data sheets for chemicals and equipment as they can be very helpful in spelling out the hazards and putting them in their true perspective.

- Have a look back at your **accident and ill-health records** – these often help to identify the less obvious hazards.

- **Remember to think about long-term hazards to health** (e g high levels of noise or exposure to harmful substances) as well as safety hazards.

Step 2

Decide who might be harmed and how

For each hazard you need to be clear about who might be harmed; it will help you identify the best way of managing the risk. That doesn't mean listing everyone by name, but rather identifying groups of people (eg 'people working in the storeroom' or 'passers-by').

In each case, identify how they might be harmed, i e what type of injury or ill health might occur. For example, 'shelf stackers may suffer back injury from repeated lifting of boxes'.

Remember:

- some workers have particular requirements, e g new and young workers, new or expectant mothers and people with disabilities may be at particular risk. Extra thought will be needed for some hazards;

- cleaners, visitors, contractors, maintenance workers etc, who may not be in the workplace all the time;

- members of the public, if they could be hurt by your activities;

- if you share your workplace, you will need to think about how your work affects others present, as well as how their work affects your staff – talk to them; and

- ask your staff if they can think of anyone you may have missed.

Step 3

Evaluate the risks and decide on precautions

Having spotted the hazards, you then have to decide what to do about them. The law requires you to do everything 'reasonably practicable' to protect people from harm. You can work this out for yourself, but the easiest way is to compare what you are doing with good practice.

There are many sources of good practice – **HSE's website** (www.hse.gov.uk), **HSE Infoline** (Tel: 0845 345 0055) and **Workplace Health Connect** (Tel: 0845 609 6006) will all help.

So first, look at what you're already doing, think about what controls you have in place and how the work is organised. Then compare this with the good practice and see if there's more you should be doing to bring yourself up to standard. In asking yourself this, consider:

- Can I get rid of the hazard altogether?

- If not, how can I control the risks so that harm is unlikely?

When controlling risks, apply the principles below, if possible in the following order:

- try a less risky option (eg switch to using a less hazardous chemical);

- prevent access to the hazard (eg by guarding);

- organise work to reduce exposure to the hazard (eg put barriers between pedestrians and traffic);

- issue personal protective equipment (eg clothing, footwear, goggles etc); and

- provide welfare facilities (eg first aid and washing facilities for removal of contamination).

Improving health and safety need not cost a lot. For instance, placing a mirror on a dangerous blind corner to help prevent vehicle accidents is a low-cost precaution considering the risks. Failure to take simple precautions can cost you a lot more if an accident does happen.

Involve staff, so that you can be sure that what you propose to do will work in practice and won't introduce any new hazards.

Step 4

Record your findings and implement them

Putting the results of your risk assessment into practice will make a difference when looking after people and your business.

Writing down the results of your risk assessment, and sharing them with your staff, encourages you to do this. If you have fewer than five employees you do not have to write anything down, though it is useful so that you can review it at a later date if, for example, something changes.

When writing down your results, keep it simple, for example 'Tripping over rubbish: bins provided, staff instructed, weekly housekeeping checks', or 'Fume from welding: local exhaust ventilation used and regularly checked'.

We do not expect a risk assessment to be perfect, but it must be suitable and sufficient. You need to be able to show that:

- a proper check was made;

- you asked who might be affected;

- you dealt with all the significant hazards, taking into account the number of people who could be involved;

- the precautions are reasonable, and the remaining risk is low; and

- you involved your staff or their representatives in the process.

There is a template at the end of this leaflet that you can print off and use.

If, like many businesses, you find that there are quite a lot of improvements that you could make, big and small, don't try to do everything at once. Make a plan of action to deal with the most important things first. Health and safety inspectors acknowledge the efforts of businesses that are clearly trying to make improvements.

A good plan of action often includes a mixture of different things such as:

- a few cheap or easy improvements that can be done quickly, perhaps as a temporary solution until more reliable controls are in place;

- long-term solutions to those risks most likely to cause accidents or ill health;

- long-term solutions to those risks with the worst potential consequences;

- arrangements for training employees on the main risks that remain and how they are to be controlled;

- regular checks to make sure that the control measures stay in place; and

- clear responsibilities – who will lead on what action, and by when.

Remember, prioritise and tackle the most important things first. As you complete each action, tick it off your plan.

Step 5

Review your risk assessment and update if necessary

Few workplaces stay the same. Sooner or later, you will bring in new equipment, substances and procedures that could lead to new hazards. It makes sense, therefore, to review what you are doing on an ongoing basis. Every year or so formally review where you are, to make sure you are still improving, or at least not sliding back.

Look at your risk assessment again. Have there been any changes? Are there improvements you still need to make? Have your workers spotted a problem? Have you learnt anything from accidents or near misses? Make sure your risk assessment stays up to date.

When you are running a business it's all too easy to forget about reviewing your risk assessment – until something has gone wrong and it's too late. Why not set a review date for this risk assessment now? Write it down and note it in your diary as an annual event.

During the year, if there is a significant change, don't wait. Check your risk assessment and, where necessary, amend it. If possible, it is best to think about the risk assessment when you're planning your change – that way you leave yourself more flexibility.

Some frequently asked questions

What if the work I do tends to vary a lot, or I (or my employees) move from one site to another?

Identify the hazards you can reasonably expect and assess the risks from them. This general assessment should stand you in good stead for the majority of your work. Where you do take on work or a new site that is different, cover any new or different hazards with a specific assessment. You do not have to start from scratch each time.

What if I share a workplace?

Tell the other employers and self-employed people there about any risks your work could cause them, and what precautions you are taking. Also, think about the risks to your own workforce from those who share your workplace.

Do my employees have responsibilities?

Yes. Employees have legal responsibilities to co-operate with their employer's efforts to improve health and safety (eg they must wear protective equipment when it is provided), and to look out for each other.

What if one of my employee's circumstances change?

You'll need to look again at the risk assessment. You are required to carry out a specific risk assessment for new or expectant mothers, as some tasks (heavy lifting or work with chemicals for example) may not be appropriate. If an employee develops a disability then you are required to make reasonable adjustments. People returning to work following major surgery may also have particular requirements. If you put your mind to it, you can almost always find a way forward that works for you and your employees.

What if I have already assessed some of the risks?

If, for example, you use hazardous chemicals and you have already assessed the risks to health and the precautions you need to take under the Control of Substances Hazardous to Health Regulations (COSHH), you can consider them 'checked' and move on.

Getting help

If you get stuck, don't give up. There is a wealth of information available to help you. More information about legal requirements and standards can be found on our website at: www.hse.gov.uk, and in particular in our publications (available from HSE Books):

An introduction to health and safety: Health and safety in small businesses Leaflet INDG259(rev1) HSE Books 2003 (single copy free).

Essentials of health and safety at work (Fourth edition) HSE Books 2006 ISBN 0 7176 6179 2.

Help is also available from Workplace Health Connect, a free service for managers and staff of small and medium-sized enterprises that provides practical advice on workplace health and safety. Tel: 0845 609 6006.

Website: www.workplacehealthconnect.co.uk.

Further information

HSE priced and free publications are available by mail order from HSE Books, PO Box 1999, Sudbury, Suffolk CO10 2WA Tel: 01787 881165 Fax: 01787 313995 Website: www.hsebooks.co.uk (HSE priced publications are also available from bookshops and free leaflets can be downloaded from HSE's website: www.hse.gov.uk/pubns).

Company name: **Date of risk assessment:**

Step 1
What are the hazards?

Spot hazards by:

■ walking around your workplace;
■ asking your employees what they think;
■ visiting the *Your industry* areas of the HSE website or calling HSE Infoline;
■ calling the Workplace Health Connect Adviceline or visiting their website;
■ checking manufacturers' instructions;
■ contacting your trade association.

Don't forget long-term health hazards.

Step 2
Who might be harmed and how?

Identify groups of people. Remember:

■ some workers have particular needs;
■ people who may not be in the workplace all the time;
■ members of the public;
■ if you share your workplace think about how your work affects others present.

Say how the hazard could cause harm.

Step 3
What are you already doing?

List what is already in place to reduce the likelihood of harm or make any harm less serious.

Step 4
What further action is necessary?

You need to make sure that you have reduced risks 'so far as is reasonably practicable'. An easy way of doing this is to compare what you are already doing with good practice. If there is a difference, list what needs to be done.

Step 4
How will you put the assessment into action?

Remember to prioritise. Deal with those hazards that are high-risk and have serious consequences first.

Action   Action   Done
by whom   by when

Step 5 Review date:

■ Review your assessment to make sure you are still improving, or at least not sliding back.
■ If there is a significant change in your workplace, remember to check your risk assessment and, where necessary, amend it.

For information about health and safety ring HSE's Infoline Tel: 0845 345 0055 Fax: 0845 408 9566 Textphone: 0845 408 9577 e-mail: hse.infoline@natbrit.com or write to HSE Information Services, Caerphilly Business Park, Caerphilly CF83 3GG.

This leaflet contains notes on good practice which are not compulsory but which you may find helpful in considering what you need to do.

This leaflet is available in priced packs of 10 from HSE Books, ISBN 0 7176 6189 X. Single free copies are also available from HSE Books.

(3) ASSESSING THE SLIP RESISTANCE OF FLOORING

Introduction

This technical document considers a number of test methods for assessing floor slip resistance and describes those used by HSE/HSL in more detail. It is intended for organisations which need to perform accurate measurements of floor slipperiness, such as manufacturers and research and testing bodies. It will also help employers and other dutyholders with assessing slip risks in workplaces by helping them to interpret flooring manufacturers' test data. This should allow them to make an informed decision in choosing new floors. In the light of this information, manufacturers and suppliers of flooring are recommended to review the floor slip resistance information they provide when producing flooring data sheets for customers.

Background

Slips and trips consistently account for around 1 in 3 non-fatal major injuries, and for over 1 in 5 over-3-day injuries in workplace areas throughout Great Britain, a total of at least 35 000 injuries per annum (one serious slip accident every 3 minutes). HSE statistics suggest that most of these accidents are slips, most of which occur when floor surfaces are contaminated (water, talc, grease, etc).

Research by the Health and Safety Laboratory (HSL) on behalf of HSE has shown that a combination of factors can contribute to slip accidents. A slip potential model has been developed, in which the relative importance of the factors contributing to a slip are assessed and quantified (see Figure 1 [not reproduced]).

This document describes methods of assessing the slipperiness of floors, including profiled floors and stairs. It aims to give enough information to correctly select a method to test the slipperiness of the floor and interpret the results.

The assessment of slipperiness: The HSE approach

The law requires that floors must not be slippery so they put people's safety at risk (The Workplace (Health, Safety and Welfare) Regulations 1992).[1] It was thought that the characteristics of floor surface materials needed for satisfactory slip resistance were difficult to assess. However, research carried out by HSL, in conjunction with the UK Slip Resistance Group (UKSRG) and the British Standards Institution, has shown they are not. The slipperiness of flooring materials can be accurately assessed by using commercially available, portable scientific test instruments.

On behalf of HSE, HSL has developed a reliable and robust test method using these instruments to assess floor surface slipperiness in workplace and public areas. The method has been used as the basis of significant HSE and local authority action, from advice to improvement notices and prosecution.

The methodology is based on using two instruments:

- a pendulum coefficient of friction (CoF) test (HSE's preferred method of slipperiness assessment, see Figure 2 [not reproduced]);

- a surface microroughness meter (see Figure 3 [not reproduced]).

This methodology is ideally suited to both laboratory-based assessment, and for use on installed floors.

The data generated may be strengthened by considering additional test data where appropriate.

Pendulum

The pendulum CoF test (also known as the portable skid resistance tester, the British pendulum, and the TRRL pendulum, see Figure 2 [not reproduced]) is the subject of a British Standard, BS 7976: Parts 1-3, 2002.[2]

This instrument, although often used in its current form to assess the skid resistance of roads, was originally designed to simulate the action of a slipping foot. The method is based on a swinging, imitation heel (using a standardised rubber soling sample), which sweeps over a set area of flooring in a controlled manner. The slipperiness of the flooring has a direct and measurable effect on the pendulum test value (PTV) given (previously known as the Slip Resistance Value).

The preparation of the standard rubber sliders is detailed in BS 7976 and the UKSRG guidelines.[3] There is a small difference between the two methods of slider preparation, and in certain limited situations the two methods may give slightly different results. HSE and the UKSRG believe the changes in the latest version of the UKSRG guidelines (2005) are best practice.

Research has confirmed the pendulum to be a reliable and accurate test, leading to its adoption as the standard HSE test method for the assessment of floor slipperiness in dry and contaminated conditions. However, to use it reliably needs a suitably trained and competent person to operate it and to interpret the results.

Interpretation of pendulum results

Pendulum results should be interpreted using the information reproduced in Table 1 (from UKSRG, 2005).

Table 1 Slip potential classification, based on pendulum test values (PTV)

	PTV
High slip potential	0–24
Moderate slip potential	25–35
Low slip potential	36 +

Practical considerations

Information generated by the pendulum using Slider 96 rubber, also known as Four-S rubber (Standard Simulated Shoe Sole) is sufficient for assessing slipperiness in most circumstances. However, for assessing barefoot areas, unusually rough or profiled floors, the use of Slider 55 rubber, also known as TRRL rubber (a similar but softer, more malleable compound) may be advantageous.

Although using the pendulum on heavily profiled flooring materials, stair treads and nosings is possible, doing so can be difficult, and should only be undertaken by experienced operators.

The pendulum test equipment is large and heavy, so consider the manual handing of the equipment carefully for testing in the field.

Surface microroughness

An indication of slipperiness in water-contaminated conditions may be simply obtained by measuring the surface roughness of flooring materials. Roughness measurements may also be used to monitor changes in floor surface characteristics, such as wear. Research has shown that measurement of the Rz parameter allows slipperiness to be predicted for a range of common materials. Rz is a measure of total surface roughness, calculated as the mean of several peak-to-valley measurements.

Interpretation of surface roughness

When surface microroughness data is used to supplement pendulum test data, the roughness results should be interpreted using the information reproduced in Table 2 (from UKSRG, 2005). Where only roughness data is available, use it in conjunction with the Slips Assessment Tool (SAT) detailed below.

Table 2 Slip potential classification, based on Rz microroughness values (applicable for water-wet pedestrian areas)

Rz surface roughness	
Below 10 μm	High slip potential
10–20 μm	Moderate slip potential
20 + μm	Low slip potential

Practical considerations: Roughness meters

Research has shown that the Rz roughness parameter gives a good indication of floor slipperiness in water-contaminated conditions. The measurement of Rz using a hand-held meter is simple and quick. It is possible to measure other roughness parameters that give a more complete picture of floor surface slipperiness (this is the subject of ongoing research). Although the use of portable, commercially available roughness meters (see Figure 3 [not reproduced]) for assessing floor surface slipperiness is increasing, they are unsuitable for use on carpet, undulating or very rough floors.

The figures quoted in Table 2 relate to floor surface slipperiness in water-contaminated conditions. If there are other contaminants, differing levels of roughness will be needed to lower slip potential. As a general rule, a higher level of surface roughness is needed to maintain slip resistance with a more viscous (thicker) contaminant. Note that the figures in Table 3 are typical Rz surface microroughness levels at which floors are likely to result in a low slip potential, as a function of contaminant type and should not be used on their own for specifying floors.

Table 3 Typical Rz surface microroughness levels for a low slip potential, as a function of contaminant type

Minimum roughness (Rz)	Contaminant
20 μm	Clean water, coffee, soft drinks
45 μm	Soap solution, milk
60 μm	Cooking stock
70 μm	Motor oil, olive oil
above 70 μm	Gear oil, margarine

Where the size of the pendulum tester limits its use, such as on stairs, surface microroughness can be used to compare the surface with an area of the same surface that can be tested using the pendulum.

Slips assessment tool (SAT)

HSE and HSL have produced a PC-based software package to assess the slip potential presented by level pedestrian walkway surfaces. The SAT prompts the user to collect surface microroughness data from the test area, using a hand-held meter. The SAT supplements the surface microroughness data (Rz) with other relevant information from the pedestrian slip potential model. This includes the causes of floor surface contamination, the regimes used to clean the floor surface (both in terms of their effectiveness and frequency), the footwear types worn in the area, along with associated human factors and environmental factors. On completion, a slip risk classification is supplied to the user; this gives an indication of the potential for a slip. SAT is designed to assist in the decision-making process when considering the risk of slipping in a defined area, and can be used iteratively to show the influence of different control measures. However, it should not be relied upon when considering the performance of just the flooring; in this instance a suitable CoF test should be used. The SAT software can be downloaded free from www.hsesat.info.

The UKSRG ramp test

The UKSRG ramp test (Figure 4 [not reproduced]) is designed to simulate the conditions commonly encountered in typical workplace slip accidents. Clean water is used as the contaminant and footwear with a standardised soling material is used, although barefoot testing may also be undertaken. The test method involves using test subjects who walk forwards and backwards over a contaminated flooring sample. The inclination of the sample is increased gradually until the test subject slips. The average angle of inclination at which slip occurs is used to calculate the CoF of the flooring. The CoF measured relates to the flooring used on a level surface. It is possible to assess bespoke combinations of footwear, flooring and contamination relating to specific environments using this method; HSL also use the ramp to assess the slipperiness of footwear.

Other ramp tests

Many European flooring manufacturers use ramp-type tests to classify the slipperiness of their products before sale. Such tests are generally carried out using German National Standard test methods (DIN 51097:1992[4] and DIN 51130:2004[5]).

DIN 51097 involves the use of barefoot operators with a soap solution as the contaminant, and DIN 51130 uses heavily-cleated EN:ISO 20345 safety boots with motor oil contamination. HSE has reservations about these test methods, as neither uses contaminants that are representative of those commonly found in workplaces and the way the results are sometimes interpreted and applied (see below) is a cause for concern.

Floor surface materials are often classified on the basis of the DIN standards. The classification schemes outlined in DIN 51130 (Table 4) and DIN 51097 (Table 5) have led to some confusion, resulting in the wrong floor surfaces sometimes being installed.

Table 4 DIN 51130 R-Value slipperiness classification

Classifica-tion	R9	R10	R11	R12	R13
Slip angle (°)	6-10	10-19	19-27	27-35	> 35

Table 5 DIN 51097 slipperiness classification

Classification	A	B	C
Slip angle (°)	12-17	18-23	> 24

A common problem stems from the misconception that the 'R' scale runs from R1 to R13, where R1 is the most slippery, and R13 the least slippery. HSE have been involved in cases where R9 floors have been specified as specialist anti-slip surfaces. In reality, the R scale runs from R9 to R13, where R9 is the most slippery, and R13 the least slippery. Floor surfaces that are classified by the DIN 51130 standard as R9 (or in some instances R10) are likely to be unacceptably slippery when used in wet or greasy conditions. Further problems may arise from the wide range of CoF within a given classification, for example R10 covers a CoF range from 0.18 to 0.34, which represents a very wide range of slip potential. The same limitations apply to DIN 51097 for barefoot areas.

The EN13845:2005[6] standard for slip resistance of safety floors addresses some of the shortcomings of the DIN tests above, but one area of concern is the different thresholds set for shod (20° = CoF 0.36) and barefoot (15° = CoF 0.27) conditions. The level of friction needed by a person to walk without slipping is thought to be the same whether the person is barefoot or wearing shoes. Flooring reported to 'pass' this standard for barefoot use may actually present a moderate slip potential.

Roller-coaster tests

HSL have evaluated two new instruments for the assessment of floor slip resistance on a wide range of installed floor surfaces, in dry, wet and contaminated conditions.[7] The instruments have been dubbed 'rollercoaster tests' as both involve a trolley rolling down a ramp and skidding across the floor surface. The first was developed by SlipAlert LLP (and is commercially available), the second was a laboratory prototype. The results show good agreement with the pendulum, provided that Slider 96 is used as the test slider material. Roller-coaster tests are more portable than the pendulum and may be used by people with little or no experience of floor surface assessment. A large test area is required, however, which can limit their applicability in some situations. As the test slider can travel a significant distance over the floor surface, it measures the average slip resistance of the area tested. This may limit the ability of these tests to identify small areas of slippery flooring surrounded by more slip-resistant flooring; it may be important to identify such small areas during an investigation. However, if visual inspection reveals areas with differing visual appearance (due to wear or inconsistency), microroughness measurements may be taken to highlight these differences. Furthermore, although it may be difficult to demonstrate the effect of a liquid spill on the slip resistance of the floor using these test methods, the effects of such spills can be accurately measured.

Sled-type tests

The instruments that have been dubbed 'sled tests' involve a self-powered trolley that drags itself across the floor surface, measuring the CoF as it moves. Laboratory-based assessments have strongly suggested that several tests currently available (particularly those based on 'sled-type' principles) can produce misleading data in wet conditions. Information from such tests shows that some smooth flooring appears to be less slippery in wet conditions than when dry; this is clearly at odds with everyday experience. Such tests may give credible results in dry conditions, though it should be stressed that the vast majority of slipping accidents occur in wet, contaminated conditions.

Interpretation of manufacturers' data

Most slip resistance information provided by flooring manufacturers is produced from as-supplied products (ie ex-factory). The slipperiness of flooring materials can change significantly due to the installation process (due to grouting, burnishing, polishing), after short periods of use, due to inappropriate maintenance or longer-term wear. Furthermore, data quoted simply as CoF should be viewed with uncertainty, as the type of CoF test used can have a critical affect on the validity of the data.

The test data needed to characterise a floor should relate to the floor as finished for the intended use and with any contamination present in normal use.

References and further reading

References

[1] Workplace health, safety and welfare. Workplace (Health, Safety and Welfare) Regulations 1992. Approved Code of Practice L24 HSE Books 1992 ISBN 0 7176 0413 6

[2] BS 7976-1:2002 Pendulum testers. Specification British Standards Institution 2002 ISBN 0 580 40144 8

BS 7976-2:2002 Pendulum testers. Method of operation British Standards Institution 2002 ISBN 0 580 40145 6

BS 7976-3:2002 Pendulum testers. Method of calibration British Standards Institution 2002 ISBN 0 580 40146 4

[3] The assessment of floor slip resistance Issue 3 United Kingdom Slip Resistance Group, 2005

[4] DIN 51097: 1992 Testing of floor coverings; determination of the anti-slip properties; wet-loaded barefoot areas; walking method; ramp test German National Standard 1992

[5] DIN 51130: 2004 Testing of floor coverings; determination of the anti-slip properties; workrooms and fields of activities with slip danger; walking method; ramp test German National Standard 2004

[6] EN13845:2005 Resilient floor coverings: Polyvinyl chloride floor coverings with particle based enhanced slip resistance. Specification British Standards Institution 2005 ISBN 0 580 46677 9

[7] Evaluation of the Kirchberg Rolling Slider and SlipAlert Slip Resistance Meters Available at www.hse.gov.uk/research/hsl_pdf/2006/hsl0665.pdf

Further reading

Safer surfaces to walk on, reducing the risk of slipping CIRIA C652 2006

Slips and trips: Guidance for employers on identifying hazards and controlling risks HSG155 HSE Books 1996 ISBN 0 7176 1145 0

Slips and trips: Guidance for the food processing industry HSG156 HSE Books 1996 ISBN 0 7176 0832 8

More information about slips and trips can be found at www.hse.gov.uk/slips and at www.hsl.gov.uk/capabilities/pedestrian.htm.

Further information

HSE priced and free publications are available by mail order from HSE Books, PO Box 1999, Sudbury, Suffolk CO10 2WA Tel: 01787 881165 Fax: 01787 313995 Website: www.hsebooks.co.uk (HSE priced publications are also available from bookshops and free leaflets can be downloaded from HSE's website: www.hse.gov.uk.)

For information about health and safety ring HSE's Infoline Tel: 0845 345 0055 Fax: 0845 408 9566 Textphone: 0845 408 9577 e-mail: hse.infoline@natbrit.com or write to HSE Information Services, Caerphilly Business Park, Caerphilly CF83 3GG.

British Standards are available from BSI Customer Services, 389 Chiswick High Road, London W4 4AL Tel: 020 8996 9001 Fax: 020 8996 7001 e-mail: cservices@bsi-global.com Website: www.bsi-global.com.

This document contains notes on good practice which are not compulsory but which you may find helpful in considering what you need to do.

This document is available web only at: www.hse.gov.uk/pubns/web/slips01.pdf.

(4) SLIPS AND TRIPS: SUMMARY GUIDANCE FOR THE FOOD INDUSTRY

Food Sheet No 6

Why it is important to tackle slips and trips risks

Slips and trips risks are especially important in the food industry because:

- they occur four times more often than the average for industry, and are the main reason for the relatively high overall injury rate in the food industry;

- they are the largest cause of serious injury (32%) in the industry, there is a high rate in all sectors;

- the potential losses could be significant, including costs (estimated at £22 million annually to employers in food, drink and tobacco); loss of key staff; liability (compensation, legal costs, insurance premiums and enforcement action) and individual suffering and disability.

Positively managing the implementation of a comprehensive programme of measures is likely to be cost effective: successful initiatives have reduced injuries by upwards of 66%. Slips and trip injuries can be prevented in the food industry: they are not inevitable.

Understanding how slips and trips risks can be controlled

Slips account for about 86% of the total slips and trips injuries. In 90% of cases they happen because the floor is wet.

Table 1 shows how to keep floors dry. If it is not possible to do that, the floor has to be sufficiently rough, and the environment, task and footwear have to be suitable; individuals have to walk appropriately to the circumstances. High surface roughness is obtained from larger and sharper grains making up the floor surface.

Trips are caused in 75% of cases by obstructions and in 25% by uneven surfaces. Table 2 indicates how to control trip risks.

Managing the control of slips and trips risks

- What practical measures you take will vary for different situations.

- You will need to assess each situation, identify what factors cause slips and trips and match practical control measures to these factors.

- You will need management arrangements to identify and implement the necessary package of control measures for each situation. The four steps to achieve this are listed below.

- plan your overall arrangements to manage slips and trips risks. In most cases, the risks will justify setting these slips and trips arrangements out separately and specifically within the overall safety policy document. Assess the risks and identify what more you need to do by looking at the tables. Get the commitment and support of others, especially senior management;

- organise so that staff know what to do; establish systems for inspection, maintenance, training and consultation with safety representatives;

- control the risks by taking the measures you identify;

- monitor your achievements, eg from accident information, inspections, audits and reports from employees and review your plan regularly.

Legal requirements

Although previous legislation had always required measures against slips and trips risks, recent Regulations have re-emphasised the importance of such measures and shown how to take them.

The Management of Health and Safety at Work Regulations 1999 specify the four steps required for effective risk control arrangements as well as employee duties, training and consultation with safety representatives.

The Workplace (Health, Safety and Welfare) Regulations 1992 requirements for the construction of the floor surface to be suitable by not being 'slippery so as to expose any person to a risk to their safety' and for the floor to have 'effective drainage' are absolute. This duty can be met by preventing contamination rather than increasing the slip resistance to counteract it.

There are also duties on suppliers of equipment, floor surfaces, floor treatment substances and slip resistant shoes to ensure, so far as reasonably practicable, the inherent safety of their products and to provide information to users.

The Workplace Regulations also absolutely requires the floor construction to have 'no holes, or slope or be uneven so as to . . . expose a person to a risk'; and so far as reasonably practicable to keep floors 'free of obstructions and from any article . . . which may cause a person to . . . trip' and 'waste materials shall not be allowed to accumulate . . . except in suitable receptacles'.

Table 1 Slips risks controls

Causative factors	*Practical measures for slips risk control*
ENVIRONMENTAL FACTORS	
(a) Contamination of the floor	**(1) Eliminate contamination in the first place**
Eg from:	Eg maintain equipment to prevent leakage, enclose transfer systems, cover outside areas, use dry methods for cleaning floors

- spillages
- wet cleaning methods
- shoes
- water and grease laden vapour (poor ventilation)

If not reasonably practicable:

(2) Prevent contamination becoming deposited on to walking surfaces

Eg by lids on portable vessels, lips around tables, bunds around equipment, drip trays under taps, cleaning incoming footwear, using effective extraction ventilation of fumes and steam with grease filtration

- natural contamination such as wet, and/ or mud in outside areas
- dry contamination, e g polythene bags left on floors, product spillages or cardboard laid over spills

If not reasonably practicable:

(3) Limit the effects of contamination

- by immediate treatment of spillages
- by safe cleaning methods, minimising and drying wet floors
- by prompt repair of leaks
- by limiting the area of contamination, e g by the location of drainage channels

If there is still a risk:

(b) Inherent slip resistance of the floor not maintained adequately

Eg from incorrect or inadequate cleaning or maintenance or wear.

(4) Maximise the surface roughness and slip resistance of the existing floor surface

Eg follow an effective cleaning regime as indicated by the floor supplier. Find out from suppliers the correct cleaning regime to remove even thin layers of contamination and cleaning agent residue; and ensure the regime is repeated often enough and adhered to

- Train, supervise and equip those who clean floors to ensure effective and safe cleaning. Frequent spot cleaning can supplement whole-floor cleaning
- Maintain floors and drainage to maximise slip resistance

If this is not enough:

(c) The slip resistance of the floor is too low

(5) Increase the surface roughness of the existing floor

This is influenced by:

Eg stick-on anti-slip strips, matting, treatments and abrading that increase slip resistance

- surface roughness of floor

If this is still not enough:

- the friction between the floor and shoe

(6) Lay a more slip resistant floor with higher surface roughness

- the sharpness of the granular microsurface peaks

In a few cases a new floor may be needed:

- the shape and height of ridges in the floor surface if profiled

(1) Draw up a specification for the supplier to meet. Experience of how that floor performs in a similar situation will be the best guide

- the drainage capacity of the floor

(2) Select a floor with sufficient surface roughness. Floors with a rough surface, and, if appropriate, profiles to drain the wet away, are best for wet conditions

- the hardness of the floors

(3) Provide effective drainage – profiles, channels etc

- incorrect installation of the floor

(4) See the installation is correctly done

(5) Check to see the specification has been met

(Note: research has shown rough floors can be cleaned to the same level of cleanliness as smooth floors and should not conflict with food hygiene requirements but you should recognise that meeting both safety and hygiene requirements might require more cleaning effort and special equipment)

and:

(d) Steps and slopes: do they cause sudden changes in step or not offer adequate foot hold and/or hand hold?

(7) See steps and slopes give adequate foot and hand hold and have no sudden changes

Eg remove sudden changes in levels and see steps have clearly visible nosings, good hand holds etc.

and:

(e) Adverse conditions hiding the floor conditions and distracting attention

(8) See the prevailing conditions allow good visibility of and concentration on floor conditions

Eg

- low light levels

Eg provide adequate lighting, and see environmental demands do not distract attention from the floor condition

- shadows
- glare
- excess noise   and:
- extreme temperature
- bulky/awkward personal
  protective equipment

ORGANISATIONAL FACTORS

(f) The nature of the task

Eg

- the need to carry, lift, push, lower or pull loads
- the need to turn, to move quickly or take long strides

- distractions
- having no hands free to hold on to break a fall

(9) Analyse the tasks to see no more than careful walking is required in any slip risk area

Tasks should not compromise ability to walk safely. Tasks should be:

- mechanised to avoid the need for pushing, lifting, carrying, pulling etc while walking on a slippery floor
- moved to safer areas
- slowed so operators do not have to hurry

and:

(g) Placing vulnerable individuals

Eg

- poor knowledge of risks and measures
- poor health and agility
- poor eyesight
- fatigue

(10) Allocate tasks in slips risks areas only to those competent to follow slips precautions

and:

(h) Insufficient supervision

(i) Safety culture which is not supportive

(11) Supervise to monitor physical controls and to see safe practices are followed

and:

(12) Establish a positive attitude that slips risks can be controlled

and:

PERSONAL PROTECTIVE EQUIPMENT: SHOE FACTORS

(j) Shoes offer insufficient slip resistance in combination with the floor surface, because of

(13) Select suitable shoes for the floor, environment and the individual

Base this on experience. Microcellular urethane and rubber soles are the least slippery on level wet floors. Get employees to maintain the shoe soles in good repair and keep them free from contamination. Replace them before they have worn smooth

- type of shoe
- sole material
- contamination of shoes
- sole pattern
- wear

and:

- fit
- maintenance/renewal

INDIVIDUAL FACTORS

(k) Unsafe action from staff

(14) Train, inform and supervise employees

Eg from lack of:

Eg on the risk, the control arrangements and employees role(s), especially to:

- awareness of the risk
- knowledge of how slips occur
- information and training or
- distraction, carelessness

- clean as they go
- report contamination
- maintain footwear
- walk appropriately to circumstances

(15) Set procedures for visitors

Table 2 Trips risks controls

Causative factors

Practical measures for trips risks control

ENVIRONMENTAL FACTORS

(a) Uneven surfaces

(1) Eliminate holes, slopes or uneven surfaces which could cause trips risks

Eg gulleys, holes, steps

Eg inspect and maintain floors so they have a smooth finish and no holes to cause a tripping hazard. Highlight any changes in level and make slopes gradual and steps clearly visible, avoid open gulleys and channels

and:

(b) Obstructions

(2) Good housekeeping

Eg accumulation of articles such as work in progress or waste

(a) Eliminate materials likely to obstruct and cause trips

Eg analyse work flows and design process so waste and product does not accumulate

or if this is not reasonably practicable:

(b) Prevent material obstructing

Eg provide sufficient suitable receptacles for work in progress, correctly sited; mark out walkways, working areas and receptacle locations and make sure they are kept free of obstruction

(c) Adverse environment

and:

Eg inadequate illumination to see floor properly, or glare

(3) Provide suitable lighting to permit obstructions to be seen

and:

ORGANISATIONAL FACTORS

(d) The nature of the task creates obstructions

(4) Analyse the tasks and process flows to see if the work can be handled to eliminate or minimise obstructions

and:

(e) Safety culture which is not supportive

(5) Establish a positive attitude that trips can be prevented

INDIVIDUAL FACTORS

and:

(f) Safe practices not followed

(6) Train, inform and supervise employees

Further information

Further explanation about slips and trips is given in Slips and trips: Guidance for the food processing industry HSG156 HSE Books 1996 ISBN 0 7176 0832 8

HSE priced and free publications are available by mail order from HSE Books, PO Box 1999, Sudbury, Suffolk CO10 2WA Tel: 01787 881165 Fax: 01787 313995 Website: www.hsebooks.co.uk (HSE priced publications are also available from bookshops and free leaflets can be downloaded from HSE's website: www.hse.gov.uk.)

For information about health and safety ring HSE's Infoline Tel: 0845 345 0055 Fax: 0845 408 9566 Textphone: 0845 408 9577 e-mail: hse.infoline@natbrit.com or write to HSE Information Services, Caerphilly Business Park, Caerphilly CF83 3GG.

This guidance is issued by the Health and Safety Executive. Following the guidance is not compulsory and you are free to take other action. But if you do follow the guidance you will normally be doing enough to comply with the law. Health and safety inspectors seek to secure compliance with the law and may refer to this guidance as illustrating good practice.

This information sheet sets out what industry representatives agree is acceptable practice in the food industry.

APPENDIX D

CIVIL PROCEDURE RULES

(1) PRACTICE DIRECTION – PRE-ACTION CONDUCT

Section I – Introduction

Aims

1.1 The aims of this Practice Direction are to –

(1) enable parties to settle the issue between them without the need to start proceedings (that is, a court claim); and

(2) support the efficient management by the court and the parties of proceedings that cannot be avoided.

1.2 These aims are to be achieved by encouraging the parties to –

(1) exchange information about the issue, and

(2) consider using a form of Alternative Dispute Resolution ('ADR').

2 Scope

2.1 This Practice Direction describes the conduct the court will normally expect of the prospective parties prior to the start of proceedings.

2.2 There are some types of application where the principles in this Practice Direction clearly cannot or should not apply. These include, but are not limited to, for example –

(1) applications for an order where the parties have agreed between them the terms of the court order to be sought ('consent orders');

(2) applications for an order where there is no other party for the applicant to engage with;

(3) most applications for directions by a trustee or other fiduciary;

(4)   applications where telling the other potential party in advance would defeat the purpose of the application (for example, an application for an order to freeze assets).

2.3   Section II deals with the approach of the court in exercising its powers in relation to pre-action conduct. Subject to paragraph 2.2, it applies in relation to all types of proceedings including those governed by the pre-action protocols that have been approved by the Head of Civil Justice and which are listed in paragraph 5.2 of this Practice Direction.

2.4   Section III deals with principles governing the conduct of the parties in cases which are not subject to a pre-action protocol.

2.5   Section III of this Practice Direction is supplemented by two annexes aimed at different types of claimant.

(1)   Annex A sets out detailed guidance on a pre-action procedure that is likely to satisfy the court in most circumstances where no pre-action protocol or other formal pre-action procedure applies. It is intended as a guide for parties, particularly those without legal representation, in straightforward claims that are likely to be disputed. It is not intended to apply to debt claims where it is not disputed that the money is owed and where the claimant follows a statutory or other formal pre-action procedure.

(2)   Annex B sets out some specific requirements that apply where the claimant is a business and the defendant is an individual. The requirements may be complied with at any time between the claimant first intimating the possibility of court proceedings and the claimant's letter before claim.

2.6   Section IV contains requirements that apply to all cases including those subject to the pre-action protocols (unless a relevant pre-action protocol contains a different provision). It is supplemented by Annex C, which sets out guidance on instructing experts.

3 Definitions

3.1   In this Practice Direction together with the Annexes –

(1)   'proceedings' means any proceedings started under Part 7 or Part 8 of the Civil Procedure Rules 1998 ('CPR');

(2)   'claimant' and 'defendant' refer to the respective parties to potential proceedings;

(3)   'ADR' means alternative dispute resolution, and is the collective description of methods of resolving disputes otherwise than through the normal trial process; (see paragraph 8.2 for further information); and

(4) 'compliance' means acting in accordance with, as applicable, the principles set out in Section III of this Practice Direction, the requirements in Section IV and a relevant pre-action protocol. The words 'comply' and 'complied' should be construed accordingly.

Section II – The Approach of the Courts

4 Compliance

4.1 The CPR enable the court to take into account the extent of the parties' compliance with this Practice Direction or a relevant pre-action protocol (see paragraph 5.2) when giving directions for the management of claims (see CPR rules 3.1(4) and (5) and 3.9(1)(e)) and when making orders about who should pay costs (see CPR rule 44.3(5)(a)).

4.2 The court will expect the parties to have complied with this Practice Direction or any relevant pre-action protocol. The court may ask the parties to explain what steps were taken to comply prior to the start of the claim. Where there has been a failure of compliance by a party the court may ask that party to provide an explanation.

Assessment of compliance

4.3 When considering compliance the court will –

(1) be concerned about whether the parties have complied in substance with the relevant principles and requirements and is not likely to be concerned with minor or technical shortcomings;

(2) consider the proportionality of the steps taken compared to the size and importance of the matter;

(3) take account of the urgency of the matter. Where a matter is urgent (for example, an application for an injunction) the court will expect the parties to comply only to the extent that it is reasonable to do so. (Paragraph 9.5 and 9.6 of this Practice Direction concern urgency caused by limitation periods.)

Examples of non-compliance

4.4 The court may decide that there has been a failure of compliance by a party because, for example, that party has –

(1) not provided sufficient information to enable the other party to understand the issues;

(2) not acted within a time limit set out in a relevant pre-action protocol, or, where no specific time limit applies, within a reasonable period;

(3) unreasonably refused to consider ADR (paragraph 8 in Part III of this Practice Direction and the pre-action protocols all contain similar provisions about ADR); or

(4)   without good reason, not disclosed documents requested to be disclosed.

Sanctions for non-compliance

4.5   The court will look at the overall effect of non-compliance on the other party when deciding whether to impose sanctions.

4.6   If, in the opinion of the court, there has been non-compliance, the sanctions which the court may impose include –

(1)   staying (that is suspending) the proceedings until steps which ought to have been taken have been taken;

(2)   an order that the party at fault pays the costs, or part of the costs, of the other party or parties (this may include an order under rule 27.14(2)(g) in cases allocated to the small claims track);

(3)   an order that the party at fault pays those costs on an indemnity basis (rule 44.4(3) sets out the definition of the assessment of costs on an indemnity basis);

(4)   if the party at fault is the claimant in whose favour an order for the payment of a sum of money is subsequently made, an order that the claimant is deprived of interest on all or part of that sum, and/or that interest is awarded at a lower rate than would otherwise have been awarded;

(5)   if the party at fault is a defendant, and an order for the payment of a sum of money is subsequently made in favour of the claimant, an order that the defendant pay interest on all or part of that sum at a higher rate, not exceeding 10% above base rate, than would otherwise have been awarded.

(2) PRE-ACTION PROTOCOL FOR PERSONAL INJURY CLAIMS

Aims of the Protocol

The Pre-Action Protocol for Personal Injury Claims was produced as part of Lord Woolf's *Access to Justice* Report (1996). It was produced by a group representing both claimants and defendants, and was designed to achieve the following aims:

- more pre-action contact between the parties;

- better and earlier exchange of information;

- better pre-action investigation by both sides;

- to put the parties in a position where they may be able to settle cases fairly and early without litigation;

- to enable proceedings to run to the court's timetable and efficiently, if litigation does become necessary; and

- to promote the provision of medical or rehabilitation treatment (not just in high value cases) to address the needs of the claimant.

The Protocol has had a great impact on the way in which such claims have been conducted since their introduction. Many of the evils of the adversarial approach to conducting personal injury claims have been ameliorated. It has also been of the greatest assistance in ensuring that a case is managed as efficiently as possible.

The Government is discussing with stakeholders how the new claims process for road traffic accidents less than £10,000 will interact with the Protocol.

The Protocol was designed primarily for those cases which fall within the fast track (ie of a value of less than £15,000), but it was always intended by the Working Party that the spirit should be followed in higher value claims also:

> 'The spirit, if not the letter of the protocol, should still be followed for multi-track type claims. In accordance with the sense of the civil justice reforms, the court will expect to see the spirit of reasonable pre-action behaviour applied in all cases, regardless of the existence of a specific protocol. In particular with regard to personal injury cases worth more than £15,000, with a view to avoiding the necessity of proceedings parties are expected to comply with the protocol as far as possible e.g. in respect of letters before action, exchanging information and documents and agreeing experts.'

The timetable is not expected to be rigidly applied and the parties should be prepared to be flexible where this would be a reasonable approach, but an efficient solicitor will always comply with the timetable as far as possible and use this as a way of ensuring that the case is dealt with efficiently.

The main idea behind the Protocol was that in return for the insurers receiving more detailed information about the claim they, in turn, would carry out investigations promptly. The claimant would delay running up costs in investigating liability in detail to give the insurers an opportunity to admit liability.

However, it must be noted that nothing in the Protocol stops time running for the purpose of limitation, so if the case is close to limitation, the correct procedure is to serve a letter of claim at the same time as issuing proceedings. If necessary, the court should then be asked to stay the proceedings while the defendants complete their investigations.

The Protocol has changed the culture in the way in which personal injury claims are conducted. There is much more co-operation between the two sides. The claimant lawyer now has to do much more work at the beginning of the case (front-loading). It is no longer feasible for the claimant's solicitor to send a brief letter of claim and subsequently make inquiries into the case.

There is now an emphasis on considering other forms of resolution of the dispute rather than litigation and this is set out both in the Protocol itself and in the Practice Direction. The Protocol makes it clear that claims should not be issued prematurely when a settlement is still being actively explored.

Letter of claim

The Protocol provides for the claimant to write a detailed letter of claim to the defendant. This arose because insurers had complained that they had difficulty in investigating claims where the information provided on behalf of the injured person was inadequate.

A draft letter is helpfully provided at Annex A to the Protocol which should be followed as far as possible. The letter has to contain the following:

- Sufficient details of the accident to enable investigations to be carried out.
  These are not equivalent to a pleading, but nonetheless it is clear that if the description of the accident were to change drastically in the particulars of claim, there would need to be a proper explanation.

- Allegations of fault.
  These do not have to represent a pleaded case, but must be sufficiently detailed to enable the insurer to investigate properly. For example, if a claimant has slipped on a floor during his employment, there may be allegations of failure to clean/defective flooring/inadequate footwear. Setting these out gives the insurer the opportunity to investigate and respond properly to each allegation and will ultimately achieve the aim of narrowing the issues between the parties.

- Sufficient information to enable the insurers to put a broad value on the case.
  At this stage it is not envisaged that the claimant will have a medical report but the insurers need to know the kind of claim which they are dealing with

so the claimant's solicitor needs to set out the injury and the length of time the claimant has been absent from work with details of his average weekly earnings.

- Other potential defendants.
  Where claims are being made against other defendants, then this must be stated in the letter.

- Road traffic cases.
  In these cases, where the claimant has been treated at a hospital, details of this must be given. Where a police report has been obtained or is awaited (which will usually be relevant in a road traffic case), then the claimant's solicitor should offer to let the insurers have a copy upon payment of half the fee.

- Conditional fee agreements.
  The latest version of the Protocol sets out the necessity to give notice of a conditional fee agreement in the letter of claim, following the Protocol Practice Direction.

- Rehabilitation.
  Following the new focus on rehabilitation in the Protocol, provision is made in the draft letter of claim for an invitation to consider rehabilitation where the claimant is still suffering from the effects of the injury.

- Wage details – where the potential defendant is the employer, the draft letter provides for a request for earning details

- Documents – a standard list of documents which may in appropriate in different types of cases is set out at Annex B to the Protocol and in the draft letter the documents which are considered to be relevant to the action are set out.

The letter is addressed to the defendant but because of the concern expressed by insurers in the Working Party that they may not be passed the letter by their insured, the letter emphasises the importance of the letter being passed to the insurer.

> 'Please note that the insurers will need to see this letter as soon as possible and it may affect your insurance cover and/or the conduct of any subsequent legal proceedings if you do not send this letter to them.'

A further copy of the letter of claim should be supplied to be sent by the defendant to his insurers.

As can been seen, proper instructions should be taken from the claimant before the letter of claim can be written and the more care that is taken at this stage, the easier it will be to run the case.

Early notification

It is possible for the claimant to notify the defendant of the claim before the detailed letter of claim is written and if he chooses to do so, the timetable for response does not start to run. This is not a practice which has been widely used since the introduction of the Protocol.

Response

The defendant or his insurer has 21 days to acknowledge receipt of the letter of the claim and if he fails to do so, then the claimant can proceed to issue proceedings without penalty. The insurer is quite entitled to argue that there are significant omissions from the letter of claim and that therefore the timetable has not started to run, so the claimant's solicitor must be careful to ensure that the letter of claim is sufficiently detailed.

Once an insurer has responded, then the claimant's solicitor should supply the claimant's National Insurance number and date of birth. This information should no longer be given in the letter of claim.

The defendant has a further 3 months to investigate the claim and to provide a detailed response to the letter of claim.

Denial

If liability is denied, then the defendant or his insurer must set out his detailed reasons for the denial and if he disputes the version of events as set out in the letter of claim he should set out his version.

It was very common in the early days of the Protocol for insurers to give bare denials of the claim without going into detail, but as parties have become more accustomed to the Protocol, this kind of response is becoming rarer. Nonetheless, claimant's solicitors must remain vigilant and if a full response is not given, then this must be pursued.

In addition, the defendant must supply copies of documents which are likely to be material to the issues between the parties and as previously mentioned, standard lists are set out in Annex B to the Protocol. The copies should be supplied without charge. A survey commissioned jointly by the Law Society and the Civil Justice Council showed that the provision of documents was the part of the Protocol which was most poorly complied with. If documents are not supplied or the documents which are supplied are inadequate, then the claimant should request these from the insurer and in default should consider an application for pre-action discovery.

If primary liability is admitted, but an allegation of contributory negligence is made, then the defendant or insurer must give reasons for these allegations together with documents in support.

Admission

If the defendants intend to admit liability, this must be a clear admission. It is not sufficient for the defendant to say that it 'is prepared to negotiate'. Once liability has been admitted, then the parties deal with medical evidence.

An admission of liability is binding upon the defendant as long as the value of the case does not exceed £15,000. It seems illogical that claims should be treated differently depending upon the value of the claim but it remains the case that the claimant's solicitor has to be vigilant and review the issue of the admission as soon as the medical report is to hand. If it becomes clear that the value of the claim may exceed £15,000, then the claimant's solicitor should advise the insurer as soon as possible but must be prepared for a withdrawal of the admission. If the defendant fails to withdraw the admission, then the claimant's solicitors should invite it to confirm that it continues to admit liability. This may prove to be some protection if at a later date (eg in the defence), the defendants seek to resile from the admission.

An admission should be pleaded in the particulars of claim if the case is subsequently issued.

However, in the case of *Sowerby v Charlton*, the Court of Appeal made it clear that admissions made pre-action could be withdrawn particularly in multi-track cases. This immediately presented problems for the claimant solicitor in balancing how far he could reasonably rely upon an insurer's admission and cease enquiries into liability.

This has now been reversed by the introduction of Part 14.1A.

This makes it clear that a pre-action admission is binding if received once a letter of claim has been received or is made before a letter of claim is received but is stated to be made under Part 14. Such an admission cannot be withdrawn without the other party's consent.

The procedure then envisaged is that the claimant will apply for judgment on the pre-action admission and it may be that the defendant will seek to withdraw the pre-action admission as a cross-application. It is to be hoped that such a withdrawal will only be exceptionally allowed.

Medical reports

The process provided for by the Protocol is for the claimant to nominate one or more medical experts. The defendant may object to any of the experts named within 14 days. If the nomination is made in the letter of claim, then the 14 days does not run until the 21 days for the acknowledgement has expired. If the defendant (or insurer) does object then it must be prepared to justify this in due course.

If there is no objection to the choice of expert then the other party (usually the defendant) is not allowed to obtain its own report without consent or the leave of the court unless the report has been amended and the instructing party does not disclose the original report. (This is to deal with the situation where the report is amended for an innocuous reason, e g to correct a reference to the wrong limb.)

It is not clear what is an acceptable objection to a choice of doctor. Insurers frequently insist upon a CV of a proposed doctor before they will indicate their agreement. There is nothing in the Protocol to indicate that this is a reasonable request but it is suggested that unless the provision of such a CV is very difficult or likely to cause delay, then it is probably appropriate to co-operate with such a request. However, objections along the lines of questioning a doctor's expertise or possible bias should not be accepted without careful consideration.

In practice, in a fast track case, if the chosen doctor produces a sensible report, then it is unlikely that the insurer will raise any objection.

One of the great achievements of the Protocol has been the reduction in the use of doctors who were perceived to be biased on one side or the other. When it was first published it was envisaged that there would be considerable arguments about the choice of these doctors but this fear has not been borne out by experience.

It is rare in a fast track case for leave to be given for oral evidence from the doctors so the choice of the doctor must be informed by the ability of the doctor to be clear and lucid on paper. The Protocol provides standard instructions for the expert at Annex C.

Joint selection – not joint report

One of the problems which arose following the introduction of the Protocol was the selection of the medical expert. There was some confusion about whether this should be a joint report and insurers frequently insisted that this was the correct interpretation of the Protocol. The case of *Carlson v Townsend* clarified the position. In this case the Court of Appeal considered the operation of the Protocol in some detail. They held that the use of the Protocol was not limited to fast track cases. The spirit, if not the letter, of the Protocol was equally appropriate to some higher value claims. In accordance with the sense of the civil justice reforms, the court expected to see the spirit of reasonable pre-action behaviour applied in all cases, regardless of the existence of a specific protocol.

The Protocol plainly encouraged and contemplated the voluntary disclosure of a claimant's expert's report in the vast majority of cases, and certainly where the report had been obtained from an 'agreed expert'. That reflected the modern and highly desirable 'cards on the table' approach and best facilitated settlement of claims, ideally before but failing that after the issue of proceedings. However, that was not to say that the Protocol specifically required disclosure in every case and still less that its effect was to override the substantive law with regard to privilege.

The claimant's withholding of the expert's report did not constitute non-compliance with the Protocol although the instruction of a second consultant without first giving the other side an opportunity to object plainly did. However, if the claimant had gone on to instruct the other consultant orthopaedic surgeon to whom the defendant had not objected after instructing their first expert they would not have had to disclose the report.

The court cannot override a claimant's privilege. On a true understanding of the Protocol, the defendant's non-objection to a nominated expert did not transform the expert, once instructed, into a single joint expert whose report was accordingly available to both parties. That was not an argument that was acceptable either in principle or on the scheme or language of the Protocol.

This approach has been confirmed in the latest version of the Protocol.

The Protocol recognises that some solicitors use medical agencies and provides that this should be flagged up with the other side who can insist that the agency supply the name of the doctor before instruction.

Questions can be sent to the doctor by either party once the report has been disclosed and the doctor should give replies to both parties. Unlike the Civil Procedure Rules 1998 (CPR) Part 36, the cost of the doctor replying to these questions is borne by the party asking the questions.

Special damages

The claimant's solicitor should send a detailed schedule of special damages as soon as possible. In practice, this should be prepared once the medical expert has been instructed and quantum is being addressed.

Stocktake

It is envisaged that the parties will try to resolve issues before embarking upon litigation. Thus, the Protocol provides that where liability has been admitted and the medical report has been obtained, it should be sent to the defendants and proceedings delayed for at least 21 days. A similar provision applies to the schedule of special damages.

Parties are encouraged to make Part 36 offers at this stage. The competent claimant's solicitor will always seek to value the case as early as possible in order to be able to discuss the possibility of making a Part 36 offer with the claimant.

Rehabilitation

There is an emphasis on rehabilitation introduced in the latest version of the Protocol and parties are encouraged to consider this possibility as early as possible. Whilst use of the Rehabilitation Code is not mandatory, its use is encouraged and following the Code, it is clear that any medical report obtained for rehabilitation purposes shall not be used in the litigation.

Rehabilitation can not be used to avoid the time limits set out in the Protocol which remain unaffected unless the parties consent.

Non-compliance

The Pre-Action Protocol Practice Direction sets out the penalties attached for non-compliance. It gives some examples of failure to comply:

> A claimant may be found to have failed to '3.1 comply with a protocol by, for example:
> (a)   not having provided sufficient information to the defendant, or
> (b)   not having followed the procedure required by the protocol to be followed (e.g. not having followed the medical expert instruction procedure set out in the Personal Injury Protocol).
>
> A defendant may be found to have failed to 3.2 comply with a protocol by, for example:
> (a)   not making a preliminary response to the letter of claim within the time fixed for that purpose by the relevant protocol (21 days under the Personal Injury Protocol, 14 days under the Clinical Negligence Protocol),
> (b)   not making a full response within the time fixed for that purpose by the relevant protocol (3 months of the letter of claim under the Clinical Negligence Protocol, 3 months from the date of acknowledgement of the letter of claim under the Personal Injury Protocol),
> (c)   not disclosing documents required to be disclosed by the relevant protocol.'

The sanctions include costs (including costs on an indemnity basis) for the issuing of proceedings which would have been unnecessary if there had been compliance. There is also a penalty of extra interest for a claimant who ultimately recovers damages where the defendant is in default (up to 10% above base rate), or reduced interest on damages ultimately recovered where the claimant is at fault.

APPENDIX E

GUIDELINES

(1) EXTRACT FROM THE APPROVED CODE OF PRACTICE AND GUIDELINES TO THE MANAGEMENT OF HEALTH AND SAFETY AT WORK REGULATIONS 1999

Introduction

1. The original Management of Health and Safety at Work Regulations ('the Management Regulations') came into force in 1993[1] as the principal method of implementing the EC Framework Directive (89/391/EEC), adopted in 1989. The Regulations were supported by an Approved Code of Practice. The original Regulations have had to be amended four times since 1992 by the Management of Health and Safety at Work (Amendment) Regulations 1994,[2] which relates to new or expectant mothers, the Health and Safety (Young Persons) Regulations 1997,[3] the Fire Precautions (Workplace) Regulations 1997[4] and by the Management of Health and Safety at Work Regulations 1999.[5] Because the original Regulations have been so significantly amended, they have been revised and published with this new Approved Code of Practice.

2. The Fire Precautions (Workplace) Regulations 1997, as amended by the Fire Precautions (Workplace) (Amendment) Regulations 1999[6] ('the Fire Regulations'), introduced by the Home Office, amend the Management Regulations in several respects. The amendments made by the Fire Regulations make explicit the risk assessment requirement, in so far as it relates to fire safety. They directly require employers to take account of their general fire precautions requirements in Part II of the Fire Regulations (concerning fire-fighting, fire detection, emergency routes and exits and their maintenance) in their assessments. The amendments made by the Fire Regulations affect employers but not self-employed people who do not employ others. The Fire Regulations also introduce:

(a)   a requirement for competent assistance to deal with general fire safety risks;

(b)   a requirement to provide employees with information on fire provisions; and

---

[1]   SI 1992/2051.
[2]   SI 1994/2865.
[3]   SI 1997/135.
[4]   SI 1997/1840.
[5]   The Management of Health and Safety at Work Regulations 1999 introduced amendments proposed by the Health and Safety (Miscellaneous Modification) Regulations 1999.
[6]   SI 1999/1877.

(c)   a requirement on employers and self-employed people in a shared workplace
to co-operate and co-ordinate with others on fire provisions and to provide
outside employers with comprehensive information on fire provisions.

3. The duties of the Management Regulations overlap with other regulations
because of their wide-ranging general nature. Where duties overlap, compliance
with the more specific regulation will normally be sufficient to comply with the
corresponding duty in the Management Regulations. For example, the Control of
Substances Hazardous to Health Regulations (COSHH) require employers and
the self-employed to assess the risks from exposure to substances hazardous to
health. An assessment made for the purposes of COSHH will not need to be
repeated for the purposes of the Management Regulations. Other instances where
overlap may occur include the appointment of people to carry out specific tasks or
arrangements for emergencies. However, where the duties in the Management
Regulations go beyond those in the more specific regulations, additional measures
will be needed to comply fully with the Management of Health and Safety at
Work Regulations.

4. Although only the courts can give an authoritative interpretation of law, in
considering the application of these regulations and guidance to people working
under another's direction, the following should be considered.

5. If people working under the control and direction of others are treated as
self-employed for tax and national insurance purposes they may nevertheless be
treated as their employees for health and safety purposes. It may therefore be
necessary to take appropriate action to protect them. If any doubt exists about
who is responsible for the health and safety of a worker this could be clarified and
included in the terms of a contract. However, remember, a legal duty under
section 3 of the Health and Safety at Work etc Act 1974 (HSW Act)[7] cannot be
passed on by means of a contract and there will still be duties towards others
under section 3 of HSW Act. If such workers are employed on the basis that they
are responsible for their own health and safety, legal advice should be sought
before doing so.

6. Words or expressions which are defined in the Management Regulations or in
the HSW Act have the same meaning in this Code unless the context requires
otherwise.

Regulation 1 – Citation, commencement and interpretation

. . .

Regulation 2 – Disapplication of these Regulations

7. Regulation 2(1) excludes the master and crew of a sea-going ship, as similar
duties are placed on them by the Merchant Shipping and Fishing Vessels (Health
and Safety at Work) Regulations 1997.[8] However, when a ship is in a port in Great
Britain and shoreside workers and the ship's crew work together, e.g. in dock

---

[7]   1974 c 37.
[8]   SI 1997/2962.

operations, or in carrying out repairs to the ship, these Regulations may apply. Dock operations, ship construction, ship repair carried out in port with shoreside assistance, and work connected to construction or the offshore industry (other than navigation, pollution prevention and other aspects of the operation of the ship, which are subject to international shipping standards) are not considered as 'normal ship-board activities' and are therefore subject to these Regulations.

8. Regulation 2(2) clarifies that these Regulations do not apply to domestic services in a private household.

Regulation 3 – Risk assessment

. . .

General principles and purpose of risk assessment

9. This regulation requires all employers and self-employed people to assess the risks to workers and any others who may be affected by their work or business. This will enable them to identify the measures they need to take to comply with health and safety law. All employers should carry out a systematic general examination of the effect of their undertaking, their work activities and the condition of the premises. Those who employ five or more employees should record the significant findings of that risk assessment.

10. A risk assessment is carried out to identify the risks to health and safety to any person arising out of, or in connection with, work or the conduct of their undertaking. It should identify how the risks arise and how they impact on those affected. This information is needed to make decisions on how to manage those risks so that the decisions are made in an informed, rational and structured manner, and the action taken is proportionate.

11. A risk assessment should usually involve identifying the hazards present in any working environment or arising out of commercial activities and work activities, and evaluating the extent of the risks involved, taking into account existing precautions and their effectiveness. In this Approved Code of Practice:

(a) a hazard is something with the potential to cause harm (this can include articles, substances, plant or machines, methods of work, the working environment and other aspects of work organisation);

(b) a risk is the likelihood of potential harm from that hazard being realised. The extent of the risk will depend on:
   (i) the likelihood of that harm occurring;
        the potential severity of that harm, i.e. of any resultant injury or adverse health effect; and
   (iii) the population which might be affected by the hazard, i.e. the number of people who might be exposed.

12. The purpose of the risk assessment is to help the employer or self-employed person to determine what measures should be taken to comply with the employer's or self-employed person's duties under the 'relevant statutory provisions' and

Part II of the Fire Regulations. This covers the general duties in the HSW Act and the requirements of Part II of the Fire Regulations and the more specific duties in the various acts and regulations (including these Regulations) associated with the HSW Act. Once the measures have been determined in this way, the duty to put them into effect will be defined in the statutory provisions. For example a risk assessment on machinery would be undertaken under these Regulations, but the Provision and Use of Work Equipment Regulations (PUWER 1998)[9] determine what precautions must be carried out. A risk assessment carried out by a self-employed person in circumstances where he or she does not employ others does not have to take into account duties arising under Part II of the Fire Regulations.

Suitable and sufficient

13. A suitable and sufficient risk assessment should be made. 'Suitable and sufficient' is not defined in the Regulations. In practice it means the risk assessment should do the following:

(a) The risk assessment should identify the risks arising from or in connection with work. The level of detail in a risk assessment should be proportionate to the risk. Once the risks are assessed and taken into account, insignificant risks can usually be ignored, as can risks arising from routine activities associated with life in general, unless the work activity compounds or significantly alters those risks. The level of risk arising from the work activity should determine the degree of sophistication of the risk assessment.

    (i) For small businesses presenting few or simple hazards a suitable and sufficient risk assessment can be very straightforward process based on informed judgement and reference to appropriate guidance. Where the hazards and risks are obvious, they can be addressed directly. No complicated processes or skills will be required.

    (ii) In many intermediate cases the risk assessment will need to be more sophisticated. There may be some areas of the assessment for which specialist advice is required; for example risks which require specialist knowledge such as a particularly complex process or technique, or risks which need specialist analytical techniques such as being able to measure air quality and to assess its impact. Whenever specialist advisers are used, employers should ensure that the advisers have sufficient understanding of the particular work activity they are advising on, this will often require effective involvement of everyone concerned – employer, employees and specialist.

    (iii) Large and hazardous sites will require the most developed and sophisticated risk assessments, particularly where there are complex or novel processes. In the case of certain manufacturing sites who use or store bulk hazardous substances, large scale mineral extraction or nuclear plant, the risk assessment will be a significant part of the safety case or report which is legally required and may incorporate such techniques as quantified risk assessment. A number of other statutory requirements exist (e.g. the Control of Major Accident

---

9   SI 1998/2306.

Hazards (COMAH), and Nuclear Installations licensing arrangements) which include more specific and detailed arrangements for risk assessment.

(iv) Risk assessments must also consider all those who might be affected by the undertaking, whether they are workers or others such as members of the public. For example, the risk assessment produced by a railway company will *inter alia*, have to consider the hazards and risks which arise from the operation and maintenance of rail vehicles and train services and which might adversely affect workers (their own employees and others), passengers and any member of the public who could foreseeably be affected (e.g. level crossing users).

(b) Employers and the self-employed are expected to take reasonable steps to help themselves identify risks, e.g. by looking at appropriate sources of information, such as relevant legislation, appropriate guidance, supplier manuals and manufacturers' instructions and reading trade press, or seeking advice from competent sources. They should also look at and use relevant examples of good practice from within their industry. The risk assessment should include only what an employer or self-employed person could reasonably be expected to know; they would not be expected to anticipate risks that were not foreseeable;

(c) The risk assessment should be appropriate to the nature of the work and should identify the period of time for which it is likely to remain valid. This will enable management to recognise when short-term control measures need to be reviewed and modified, and to put in place medium and long-term controls where these are necessary.

14. For activities where the nature of the work may change fairly frequently or the workplace itself changes and develops (such as a construction site), or where workers move from site to site, the risk assessment might have to concentrate more on the broad range of risks that can be foreseen. When other less common risks arise, detailed planning and employee training will be needed to take account of those risks and enable them to be controlled.

Risk assessment in practice

15. There are no fixed rules about how a risk assessment should be carried out; indeed it will depend on the nature of the work or business and the types of hazards and risks. Paragraph 18 does, however, set out the general principles that should be followed. The risk assessment process needs to be practical and take account of the views of employees and their safety representatives who will have practical knowledge to contribute. It should involve management, whether or not advisers or consultants assist with the detail. Employers should ensure that those involved take all reasonable care in carrying out the risk assessment. For further guidance see HSE's publication *Five steps to risk assessment*.

16. Where employees of different employers work in the same workplace, their respective employers may have to co-operate to produce an overall risk assessment. Detailed requirements on co-operation and co-ordination are covered by Regulation 11.

17. In some cases employers may make a first rough assessment, to eliminate from consideration those risks on which no further action is needed. This should also show where a fuller assessment is needed, if appropriate, using more sophisticated techniques. Employers who control a number of similar workplaces containing similar activities may produce a 'model' risk assessment reflecting the core hazards and risks associated with these activities. 'Model' assessments may also be developed by trade associations, employers' bodies or other organisations concerned with a particular activity. Such 'model' assessments may be applied by employers or managers at each workplace, but only if they:

(a)   satisfy themselves that the 'model' assessment is appropriate to their type of work; and

(b)   adapt the 'model' to the detail of their own actual work situations, including any extension necessary to cover hazards and risks not referred to in the 'model'.

18. A risk assessment should:

(a)   ensure the significant risks and hazards are addressed;

(b)   ensure all aspects of the work activity are reviewed, including routine and non-routine activities. The assessment should cover all parts of the work activity, including those that are not under the immediate supervision of the employer, such as employees working off site as contractors, workers from one organisation temporarily working for another organisation, self-employed people, homeworkers and mobile employees. Details of where to find additional guidance on homeworkers and volunteers is given in the References and further reading section. Where workers visit members of the public in the home, e.g. nurses, employers should consider any risks arising from potential dangers;

(c)   take account of the non-routine operations, e.g. maintenance, cleaning operations, loading and unloading of vehicles, changes in production cycles, emergency response arrangements;

(d)   take account of the management of incidents such as interruptions to the work activity, which frequently cause accidents, and consider what procedures should be followed to mitigate the effects of the incident;

(e)   be systematic in identifying hazards and looking at risks, whether one risk assessment covers the whole activity or the assessment is divided up. For example, it may be necessary to look at activities in groups such as machinery, transport, substances, electrical etc, or to divide the work site on a geographical basis. In other cases, an operation by operation approach may be needed, dealing with materials in production, dispatch, offices etc. The employer or self-employed person should always adopt a structured approach to risk assessment to ensure all significant risks or hazards are addressed. Whichever method is chosen, it should reflect the skills and abilities of the individuals carrying out that aspect of the assessment;

(f)   take account of the way in which work is organised, and the effects this can have on health;

(g)   take account of risks to the public;

(h)   take account of the need to cover fire risks. The guide *Fire safety: An employer's guide* tells you how to comply with the law relating to fire issues and how to carry out a fire risk assessment (see References and further reading at the back of this document).

Identifying the hazards

19. First, identify what the hazards are.

20. If there are specific acts or regulations to be complied with, these may help to identify the hazards. Some regulations require the assessment of particular risks or types of risks. If these particular risks are present, they must all be addressed in a risk assessment process for the purpose of these Regulations.

Identifying who might be harmed and how

21. Identify people who might be harmed by the hazard, including employees, other workers in the workplace and members of the public. Do not forget office staff, night cleaners, maintenance staff, security guards, visitors and members of the public. You should identify groups of workers who might be particularly at risk, such as young or inexperienced workers, new and expectant mothers, night workers, homeworkers, those who work alone and disabled staff.

Evaluating the risks from the identified hazards

22. You need to evaluate the risks from the identified hazards. Of course, if there are no hazards, there are no risks. Where risks are already controlled in some way, the effectiveness of those controls needs to be considered when assessing the extent of risk which remains. You also need to:

(a)   observe the actual practice; this may differ from the works manual, and the employees concerned or their safety representatives should be consulted;

(b)   address what actually happens in the workplace or during the work activity; and

(c)   take account of existing preventive or precautionary measures; if existing measures are not adequate, ask yourself what more should be done to reduce risk sufficiently.

Recording

23. All employers and self-employed people are required to make a risk assessment. The regulation also provides that employers with five or more employees must record the significant findings of their risk assessment. This

record should represent an effective statement of hazards and risks which then leads management to take the relevant actions to protect health and safety. The record should be retrievable for use by management in reviews and for safety representatives or other employee representatives and visiting inspectors. Where appropriate, it should be linked to other health and safety records or documents such as the record of health and safety arrangements required by regulation 5 and the written health and safety policy statement required by section 2(3) of the HSW Act. It may be possible to combine these documents into one health and safety management document.

24. This record may be in writing or recorded by other means (e.g. electronically) as long as it is retrievable and remains retrievable even when, for example, the technology of electronic recording changes. The record will often refer to other documents and records describing procedures and safeguards.

25. The significant findings should include:

(a)   a record of the preventive and protective measures in place to control the risks;

(b)   what further action, if any, needs to be taken to reduce risk sufficiently;

(c)   proof that a suitable and sufficient assessment has been made. In many cases, employers (and the self-employed) will also need to record sufficient detail of the assessment itself, so that they can demonstrate (e.g. to an inspector or to safety representatives or other employee representatives) that they have carried out a suitable and sufficient assessment. This record of the significant findings will also form a basis for a revision of the assessment.

Review and revision

26. The regulation requires employers and the self-employed to review and, if necessary, modify their risk assessments, since assessment should not be a once-and-for-all activity. HSE's guide *Successful health and safety management* (see References and further reading section) provides sound guidance on good practice. The following sub-paragraphs identify particular examples of review and revision.

(a)   As the nature of work changes, the appreciation of hazards and risks may develop. Monitoring under the arrangements required by regulation 5 may reveal near misses or defects in plant or equipment. The risk assessment may no longer be valid because of, for example, the results of health surveillance, or a confirmed case of occupationally induced disease. Adverse events such as an accident, ill health or dangerous occurrences may take place even if a suitable and sufficient risk assessment has been made and appropriate preventive and protective measures taken. Such events should be a trigger for reviewing the original assessment.

(b)   The employer or self-employed person needs to review the risk assessment if developments suggest that it may no longer be valid (or can be improved). In most cases, it is prudent to plan to review risk assessments at regular intervals. The time between reviews is dependent on the nature of the risks and the degree of change likely in the work activity. Such reviews should form part of standard management practice.

Assessment under other regulations

27. Other regulations also contain requirements for risk assessment specific to the hazards and risks they cover. Where an employer is assessing a work situation or activity for the first time, an assessment is particularly useful to identify where a more detailed risk assessment is needed to fulfil the requirements of other regulations.

28. An assessment made for the purpose of other regulations will partly cover the obligation to make assessments under these regulations. Where employers have already carried out assessments under other regulations, they need not repeat those assessments as long as they remain valid; but they do need to ensure that they cover all significant risks.

Regulation 4 – Principles of prevention to be applied

29. Employers and the self-employed need to introduce preventive and protective measures to control the risks identified by the risk assessment in order to comply with the relevant legislation. A set of principles to be followed in identifying the appropriate measures are set out in Schedule 1 to the Regulations and are described below. Employers and the self-employed should use these to direct their approach to identifying and implementing the necessary measures.

30. In deciding which preventive and protective measures to take, employers and self-employed people should apply the following principles of prevention:

(a) if possible avoid a risk altogether, e.g. do the work in a different way, taking care not to introduce new hazards;

(b) evaluate risks that cannot be avoided by carrying out a risk assessment;

(c) combat risks at source, rather than taking palliative measures. So, if the steps are slippery, treating or replacing them is better than displaying a warning sign;

(d) adapt work to the requirements of the individual (consulting those who will be affected when designing workplaces, selecting work and personal protective equipment and drawing up working and safety procedures and methods of production). Aim to alleviate monotonous work and paced working at a predetermined rate, and increase the control individuals have over work they are responsible for;

(e) take advantage of technological and technical progress, which often offers opportunities for improving working methods and making them safer;

(f) implement risk prevention measures to form part of a coherent policy and approach. This will progressively reduce those risks that cannot be prevented or avoided altogether, and will take account of the way work is organised, the working conditions, the environment and any relevant social factors. Health and safety policy statements required under section 2(3) of the HSW Act should be prepared and applied by reference to these principles;

(g)   give priority to those measures which protect the whole workplace and everyone who works there, and so give the greatest benefit (i.e. give collective protective measures priority over individual measures);

(h)   ensure that workers, whether employees or self-employed, understand what they must do;

(i)   the existence of a positive health and safety culture should exist within an organisation. That means the avoidance, prevention and reduction of risks at work must be accepted as part of the organisation's approach and attitude to all its activities. It should be recognised at all levels of the organisation, from junior to senior management.

31. There are general principles rather than individual prescriptive requirements. They should, however, be applied wherever it is reasonable to do so. Experience suggests that, in the majority of cases, adopting good practice will be enough to ensure risks are reduced sufficiently. Authoritative sources of good practice are prescriptive legislation, Approved Codes of Practice and guidance produced by Government and HSE inspectors. Other sources include standards produced by standard-making organisations and guidance agreed by a body representing an industrial or occupational sector, provided the guidance has gained general acceptance. Where established industry practices result in high levels of health and safety, risk assessment should not be used to justify reducing current control measures.

Regulation 5 – Health and safety arrangements

32. This regulation requires employers to have arrangements in place to cover health and safety. Effective management of health and safety will depend, amongst other things, on a suitable and sufficient risk assessment being carried out and the findings being used effectively. The health and safety arrangements can be integrated into the management system for all other aspects of the organisation's activities. The management system adopted will need to reflect the complexity of the organisation's activities and working environment. Where the work process is straightforward and the risks generated are relatively simple to control, then very straightforward management systems may be appropriate. For large complicated organisations more complex systems may be appropriate. Although the principles of the management arrangements are the same irrespective of the size of an organisation. The key elements of such effective systems can be found in *Successful health and safety management* (see References and further reading section) or the British Standard for health and safety management systems BS8800. A successful health and safety management system will include all the following elements.

Planning

33. Employers should set up an effective health and safety management system to implement their health and safety policy which is proportionate to the hazards and risks. Adequate planning includes:

(a) adopting a systematic approach to the completion of a risk assessment. Risk assessment methods should be used to decide on priorities and to set objectives for eliminating hazards and reducing risks. This should include a programme, with deadlines for the completion of the risk assessment process, together with suitable deadlines for the design and implementation of the preventive and protective measures which are necessary;

(b) selecting appropriate methods of risk control to minimise risks;

(c) establishing priorities and developing performance standards both for the completion of the risk assessment(s) and the implementation of preventive and protective measures, which at each stage minimises the risk of harm to people. Wherever possible, risks are eliminated through selection and design of facilities, equipment and processes.

Organisation

34. This includes:

(a) involving employees and their representatives in carrying out risk assessments, deciding on preventive and protective measures and implementing those requirements in the workplace. This may be achieved by the use of formal health and safety committees where they exist, and by the use of teamworking, where employees are involved in deciding on the appropriate preventive and protective measures and written procedures etc;

(b) establishing effective means of communication and consultation in which a positive approach to health and safety is visible and clear. The employer should have adequate health and safety information and make sure it is communicated to employees and their representatives, so informed decisions can be made about the choice of preventive and protective measures. Effective communication will ensure that employees are provided with sufficient information so that control measures can be implemented effectively;

(c) securing competence by the provision of adequate information, instruction and training and its evaluation, particularly for those who carry out risk assessments and make decisions about preventive and protective measures. Where necessary this will need to be supported by the provision of adequate health and safety assistance or advice.

Control

35. Establishing control includes:

(a)   clarifying health and safety responsibilities and ensuring that the activities of everyone are well co-ordinated;

(b)   ensuring everyone with responsibilities understands clearly what they have to do to discharge their responsibilities, and ensure they have the time and resources to discharge them effectively;

(c)   setting standards to judge the performance of those with responsibilities and ensure they meet them. It is important to reward good performance as well as to take action to improve poor performance; and

(d)   ensuring adequate and appropriate supervision, particularly for those who are learning and who are new to a job.

Monitoring

36. Employers should measure what they are doing to implement their health and safety policy, to assess how effectively they are controlling risks, and how well they are developing a positive health and safety culture. Monitoring includes:

(a)   having a plan and making adequate routine inspections and checks to ensure that preventive and protective measures are in place and effective. Active monitoring reveals how effectively the health and safety management system is functioning;

(b)   adequately investigating the immediate and underlying causes of incidents and accidents to ensure that remedial action is taken, lessons are learnt and longer term objectives are introduced.

37. In both cases it may be appropriate to record and analyse the results of monitoring activity, to identify any underlying themes or trends which may not be apparent from looking at events in isolation.

Review

38. Review involves:

(a)   establishing priorities for necessary remedial action that were discovered as a result of monitoring to ensure that suitable action is taken in good time and is completed;

(b)   periodically reviewing the whole of the health and safety management system including the elements of planning, organisation, control and monitoring to ensure that the whole system remains effective.

39. Consulting employees or their representatives about matters to do with their health and safety is good management practice, as well as being a requirement

under health and safety law. Employees are a valuable source of information and can provide feedback about the effectiveness of health and safety management arrangements and control measures. Where safety representatives exist, they can act as an effective channel for employees' views.

40. Safety representatives' experience of workplace conditions and their commitment to health and safety means they often identify potential problems, allowing the employer to take prompt action. They can also have an important part to play in explaining safety measures to the workforce and gaining commitment.

Regulation 6 – Health surveillance

41. The risk assessment will identify circumstances in which health surveillance is required by specific health and safety regulations e.g. COSHH. Health surveillance should also be introduced where the assessment shows the following criteria to apply:

(a)   there is an identifiable disease or adverse health condition related to the work concerned; and

(b)   valid techniques are available to detect indications of the disease or condition; and

(c)   there is a reasonable likelihood that the disease or condition may occur under the particular conditions of work; and

(d)   surveillance is likely to further the protection of the health and safety of the employees to be covered.

42. Those employees concerned and their safety or other representatives should be given an explanation of, and opportunity to comment on, the nature and proposed frequency of such health surveillance procedures and should have access to an appropriately qualified practitioner for advice on surveillance.

43. The appropriate level, frequency and procedure of health surveillance should be determined by a competent person acting within the limits of their training and experience. This could be determined on the basis of suitable general guidance (e.g. regarding skin inspection for dermal effects) but in certain circumstances this may require the assistance of a qualified medical practitioner. The minimum requirement for health surveillance is keeping a health record. Once it is decided that health surveillance is appropriate, it should be maintained throughout an employee's employment unless the risk to which the worker is exposed and associated health effects are rare and short term.

44. Where appropriate, health surveillance may also involve one or more health surveillance procedures depending on suitability in the circumstances (a non-exhaustive list of examples of diseases is included in the footnote for guidance).[10] Such procedures can include:

---

[10]   If the worker is exposed to noise or hand-arm vibrations, health surveillance may be needed under these regulations. If the worker is exposed to hazardous substances such as chemicals, solvents,

(a)   inspection of readily detectable conditions by a responsible person acting within the limits of their training and experience;

(b)   enquiries about symptoms, inspection and examination by a qualified person such as an Occupational Health Nurse;

(c)   medical surveillance, which may include clinical examination and measurement of physiological or psychological effects by an appropriately qualified person;

(d)   biological effect monitoring, i.e. the measurement and assessment of early biological effects such as diminished lung function in exposed workers; and

(e)   biological monitoring, i.e. the measurement and assessment of workplace agents or their metabolites either in tissues, secreta, excreta, expired air or any combination of these in exposed workers.

45. The primary benefit, and therefore objective of health surveillance should be to detect adverse health effects at an early stage, thereby enabling further harm to be prevented. The results of health surveillance can provide a means of:

(a)   checking the effectiveness of control measures;

(b)   providing feedback on the accuracy of the risk assessment; and

(c)   identifying and protecting individuals at increased risk because of the nature of their work.

Regulation 7 – Health and safety assistance

. . .

46. Employers are solely responsible for ensuring that those they appoint to assist them with health and safety measures are competent to carry out the tasks they are assigned and are given adequate information and support. In making decision on who to appoint, employers themselves need to know and understand the work involved, the principles of risk assessment and prevention, and current legislation and health and safety standards. Employers should ensure that anyone they appoint is capable of applying the above to whatever task they are assigned.

47. Employers must have access to competent help in applying the provisions of health and safety law, including these Regulations. In particular they need competent help in devising and applying protective measures, unless they are competent to undertake the measures without assistance. Appointment of competent people for this purpose should be included among the health and safety arrangements recorded under regulation 5(2). Employers are required by

---

fumes, dusts, gases and vapours, aerosols, biological agents (micro-organisms), health surveillance may be needed under COSHH. If the worker is exposed to asbestos, lead, work in compressed air, medical examinations may be needed under specific regulations.

the Safety Representatives and Safety Committees Regulations 1977 to consult safety representatives in good time on arrangements for the appointment of competent assistance.

48. When seeking competent assistance employers should look to appoint one or more of their employees, with the necessary means, or themselves, to provide the health and safety assistance required. If there is no relevant competent worker in the organisation or the level of competence is insufficient to assist the employer in complying with health and safety law, the employer should enlist an external service or person. In some circumstances a combination of internal and external competence might be appropriate, recognising the limitations of the internal competence. Some regulations contain specific requirements for obtaining advice from competent people to assist in complying with legal duties. For example the Ionising Radiation Regulations requires the appointment of a radiation protection adviser in many circumstances, where work involves ionising radiations.

49. Employers who appoint doctors, nurses or other health professionals to advise them of the effect of work on employee health, or to carry out certain procedures, for example health surveillance, should first check that such providers can offer evidence of a sufficient level of expertise or training in occupational health. Registers of competent practitioners are maintained by several professional bodies, and are often valuable.

50. The appointment of such health and safety assistants or advisers does not absolve the employer from responsibilities for health and safety under the HSW Act and other relevant statutory provisions and under Part II of the Fire Regulations. It can only give added assurance that these responsibilities will be discharged adequately. Where external services are employed, they will usually be appointed in an advisory capacity only.

51. Competence in the sense it is used in these Regulations does not necessarily depend on the possession of particular skills or qualifications. Simple situations may require only the following:

(a)   an understanding of relevant current best practice;

(b)   an awareness of the limitations of one's own experience and knowledge; and

(c)   the willingness and ability to supplement existing experience and knowledge, when necessary to obtaining external help and advice.

52. More complicated situations will require the competent assistant to have a higher level of knowledge and experience. More complex or highly technical situations will call for specific applied knowledge and skills which can be offered by appropriately qualified specialists. Employers are advised to check the appropriate health and safety qualifications (some of which may be competence-based and/or industry specific), or membership of a professional body or similar organisation (at an appropriate level and in an appropriate part of health and safety) to satisfy themselves that the assistant they appoint has a sufficiently high level of competence. Competence-based qualifications accredited by the Qualifications and Curriculum Authority and the Scottish Qualifications Authority may also provide a guide.

Regulation 8 – Procedures for serious and imminent danger and for danger areas

. . .

Regulation 9 – Contacts with external services

53. Employers should establish procedures for any worker to follow if situations presenting serious and imminent danger were to arise, e.g. a fire, or for the police and emergency services an outbreak of public disorder. The procedures should set out:

(a) the nature of the risk (e.g. a fire in certain parts of a building where substances might be involved), and how to respond to it;

(b) additional procedures needed to cover risks beyond those posed by fire and bombs. These procedures should be geared, as far as is practicable, to the nature of the serious and imminent danger that those risks might pose;

(c) the additional responsibilities of any employees, or groups of employees, who may have specific tasks to perform in the event of emergencies (e.g. to shut down a plant that might otherwise compound the danger); or who have had training so that they can seek to bring an emergency event under control. Police officers, fire-fighters and other emergency service workers, for example, may sometimes need to work in circumstances of serious or imminent danger in order to fulfill their commitment to the public service. The procedures should reflect these responsibilities, and the time delay before such workers can move to a place of safety. Appropriate preventive and protective measures should be in place for these employees;

(d) the role, responsibilities and authority of the competent people nominated to implement the detailed actions. The procedures should also ensure that employees know who the relevant competent people are and understand their role;

(e) any requirements laid on employers by health and safety regulations which cover some specific emergency situations;

(f) details of when and how the procedures are to be activated so that employees can proceed in good time to a place of safety. Procedures should cater for the fact that emergency events can occur and develop rapidly, thus requiring employees to act without waiting for further guidance. It may be necessary to commence evacuation while attempts to control an emergency (e.g. a process in danger of running out of control) are still under way, in case those attempts fail.

54. Emergency procedures should normally be written down as required by regulation 5(2), clearly setting out the limits of actions to be taken by employees. Information on the procedures should be made available to all employees (under regulation 10), to any external health and safety personnel appointed under regulation 7(1), and where necessary to other workers and/or their employers

under regulation 12. Induction training, carried out under regulation 13, should cover emergency procedures and should familiarise employees with those procedures.

55. Work should not be resumed after an emergency if a serious danger remains. If there are any doubts, expert assistance should be sought, e.g. from the emergency services and others. There may, for certain groups of workers, be exceptional circumstances when re-entry to areas of serious danger may be deemed necessary, e.g. police officers, fire-fighters and other emergency service workers, where, for example, human life is at risk. When such exceptional circumstances can be anticipated, the procedures should set out the special protective measures to be taken (and the pre-training required) and the steps to be taken for authorisation of such actions.

56. The procedure for any worker to follow in serious and imminent danger, has to be clearly explained by the employer. Employees and others at work need to know when they should stop work and how they should move to a place of safety. In some cases this will require full evacuation of the workplace; in others it might mean some or all of the workforce moving to a safer part of the workplace.

57. The risk assessment should identify the foreseeable events that need to be covered by these procedures. For some employers, fire (and possibly bomb) risks will be the only ones that need to be covered. For others, additional risks will be identified.

58. Where different employers (or self-employed people) share a workplace, their separate emergency procedures will need to take account of everyone in the workplace, and as far as is appropriate the procedures should be co-ordinated. Detailed requirements on co-operation and co-ordination are covered by regulation 11.

Danger areas

59. A danger area is a work environment which must be entered by an employee where the level of risk is unacceptable without taking special precaution. Such areas are not necessarily static in that minor alterations or an emergency may convert a normal working environment into a danger area. The hazard involved need not occupy the whole area, as in the case of a toxic gas, but can be localised, e.g. where there is a risk of an employee coming into contact with bare live electrical conductors. The area must be restricted to prevent inadvertent access.

60. This regulation does not specify the precautions to take to ensure safe working in the danger area – this is covered by other legislation. However, once the employer has established suitable precautions the relevant employees must receive adequate instruction and training in those precautions before entering any such danger area.

Contacts with external services

61. The employer should ensure that appropriate external contacts are in place to make sure there are effective provisions for first aid, emergency medical care and

rescue work, for incidents and accidents which may require urgent action, and/or medical attention beyond the capabilities of on-site personnel. This may only mean making sure that employees know the necessary telephone numbers and, where there is a significant risk, that they are able to contact any help they need. This requirement does not in any way reduce employers' duty to prevent accidents as the first priority.

62. Where a number of employers share a workplace and their employees face the same risks, it would be possible for one employer to arrange contacts on behalf of themselves and the other employers. In these circumstances it would be for the other employers to ensure that the contacts had been made. In hazardous or complex workplaces, employers should designate appropriate staff to routinely contact the emergency services to give them sufficient knowledge of the risks they need to take appropriate action in emergencies, including those likely to happen outside normal working hours. This will help these services in planning for providing first aid, emergency medical care and rescue work, and to take account of risks to everyone involved, including rescuers. Contacts and arrangements with external services should be recorded, and should be reviewed and revised as necessary, in the light of changes to staff, processes and plant, and revisions to health and safety procedures.

Regulation 10 – Information for employees

63. The risk assessment will help identify information which has to be provided to employees under specific regulations, as well as any further information relevant to risks to employees' health and safety. Relevant information on risks and on preventive and protective measures will be limited to what employees need to know to ensure their own health and safety and not to put others at risk. This regulation also requires information to be provided on the emergency arrangements established under regulation 8, including the identity of staff nominated to help if there is an evacuation.

64. The information provided should be pitched appropriately, given the level of training, knowledge and experience of the employee. It should be provided in a form which takes account of any language difficulties or disabilities. Information can be provided in whatever form is most suitable in the circumstances, as long as it can be understood by everyone. For employees with little or no understanding of English, or who cannot read English, employers may need to make special arrangements. These could include providing translation, using interpreters, or replacing written notices with clearly understood symbols or diagrams.

65. This regulation applies to all employees, including trainees and those on fixed-duration contracts. Additional information for employees on fixed-duration contracts is contained in regulation 15. Specific requirements relate to the provision of information to safety representatives, and enabling full and effective consultation of employees.[11]

66. While a child (below minimum school leaving age) is at work, the requirements to provide information are the same as for other employees. There is, however, an

---

[11]	Safety Representatives and Safety Committees Regulations 1977, SI 1977/500 and Health and Safety (Consultation with Employees) Regulations 1996, SI 1996/1513.

extra requirement on the employer to provide the parents or guardians of children at work (including those on work experience) with information on the key findings of the risk assessment and the control measures taken, before the child starts work. This information can be provided in any appropriate form, including verbally or directly to the parents or guardians, or in the case of work experience, via an organisation such as the school, the work experience agency, or, if agreed with the parents, via the child him or herself, as long as this is considered a reliable method.

Regulation 11 – Co-operation and co-ordination

67. To meet the requirements of these Regulations, such as carrying out a risk assessment under regulation 3 and establishing procedures to follow serious and dangerous situations under regulation 8, it is necessary to cover the whole workplace to be fully effective. When the workplace is occupied by more than one employer, this will require some degree of co-ordination and co-operation. All employers and self-employed people involved should satisfy themselves that the arrangements adopted are adequate. Employers should ensure that all their employees, but especially the competent people appointed under regulations 7 and 8, are aware of and take full part in the arrangements. Specific co-ordination arrangements may be required by other regulations.

68. Where a particular employer controls the workplace, others should assist the controlling employer in assessing the shared risks and co-ordinating any necessary measures. In many situations providing information may be sufficient. A controlling employer who has established site-wide arrangements will have to inform new employers or self-employed people of those arrangements so that they can integrate themselves into the co-operation and co-ordination procedures.

69. Where the activities of different employers and self-employed people interact, for example where they share premises or workplaces, they may need to co-operate with each other to make sure their respective obligations are met. This regulation does not extend to the relationship between a host employer and a contractor, which will be covered by regulation 12.

70. The duties to co-operate and co-ordinate measures relate to all statutory duties, except for Part II of the Fire Regulations, in the case of people who are self-employed and are not employers. Therefore, they concern all people who may be at risk, both on and off site, and not just where employers and self-employed people share workplaces all the time. They also include situations where an employer may not be physically present at the workplace.

Appointment of health and safety co-ordinator

71. Where there is no controlling employer, the employers and self-employed people present will need to agree any joint arrangements needed to meet the requirements of the Regulations, such as appointing a health and safety co-ordinator. This will be particularly useful in workplaces where management control is fragmented and employment is largely casual or short term (e.g. in

construction). The Construction (Design and Management) Regulations 1994[12] require principal contractors to ensure co-operation between all contractors. In workplaces which are complex or contain significant hazards, the controlling employer or health and safety co-ordinator (on behalf of the employers etc present) may need to seek competent advice in making or assisting with the risk assessment and determining appropriate measures. Employers do not absolve themselves of their legal responsibilities by appointing such co-ordinators who provide competent advice.

Person in control

72. The person in control of a multi-occupancy workplace may not always be an employer of the people working in that workplace or be self-employed, but will still need to co-operate with those occupying the workplace under their control. For example, procedures for authorising or carrying out repairs and modifications will have to take account of the need for co-operation and exchanges of information. Co-operation is needed to effectively carry out the general duties placed on those people under section 4 of the HSW Act, as well as more specific duties under other Regulations (e.g. in offshore health and safety legislation or in relation to welfare facilities provided under the Workplace (Health, Safety and Welfare) Regulations 1992).[13]

73. People who control the premises and make arrangements to co-ordinate health and safety activities, particularly for emergencies, may help employers and self-employed people who participate in those arrangements to comply with regulation 11(1)(b).

74. This regulation does not apply to multi-occupancy buildings or sites, where each unit under the control of an individual tenant employer or self-employed person is regarded as a separate workplace. In some cases, however, the common parts of such multi-occupancy sites may be shared workplaces (e.g. a common reception area in an office building) or may be under the control of a person to whom section 4 of the HSW Act applies and suitable arrangements may need to be put in place for these areas.

Regulation 12 – Persons working in host employers' or self-employed persons' undertakings

75. The risk assessment carried out under regulation 3 will identify risks to people other than the host employers' employees. This will include other employers' employees and self-employed people working in that business. Employers and self-employed people need to ensure that comprehensive information on those risks, and the measures taken to control them is given to other employers and self-employed people. Further guidance can be found under regulation 10.

76. Host employers and self-employed people must ensure that people carrying out work on their premises receive relevant information. This may be done by either providing them with information directly or by ensuring that their

---

[12]   SI 1994/3140.
[13]   SI 1992/3004.

employers provide them with the relevant information. If you rely on their employers to provide information to the visiting employees, then adequate checks should be carried out to ensure that the information is passed on. The information should be sufficient to allow the employer of the visiting employee to comply with their statutory duties, and should include the identity of people nominated by the host employer to help with an emergency evacuation under regulation 8.

77. Information may be provided through a written permit-to-work system. Where the visiting employees are specialists, brought in to do specialist tasks, the host employer's instructions need to be concerned with those risks which are peculiar to the activity and premises. The visiting employee may also introduce risks to the permanent workforce (e.g. from equipment or substances they may bring with them). Their employers have a general duty under section 3 of the HSW Act to inform the host employer of such risks and to co-operate and co-ordinate with the host employer to the extent needed to control those risks.

78. The guidance on information for employees under regulation 10 applies equally to information provided under regulation 12.

79. This regulation applies where employees or self-employed people carry out work for an employer other than their own or of another self-employed person. This will include contractors' employees carrying out cleaning, repair, or maintenance work under a service contract; and employees in temporary employment businesses, hired to work under a host employer's control (additional requirements for information to employment businesses are under regulation 15). Safety representatives and other employee representatives are often used to ensure information is supplied to everyone who comes on site.

Regulation 13 – Capabilities and training

80. When allocating work to employees, employers should ensure that the demands of the job do not exceed the employees' ability to carry out the work without risk to themselves or others. Employers should take account of the employees' capabilities and the level of their training, knowledge and experience. Managers should be aware of relevant legislation and should be competent to manage health and safety effectively. Employers should review their employees' capabilities to carry out their work, as necessary. If additional training, including refresher training, is needed, it should be provided.

81. Health and safety training should take place during working hours. If it is necessary to arrange training outside an employee's normal hours, this should be treated as an extension of time at work. Employees are not required to pay for their own training. Section 9 of the HSW Act prohibits employers from charging employees for anything they have to do or are required to do in respect of carrying out specific requirements of the relevant statutory provisions. The requirement to provide health and safety training is such a provision.

82. The risk assessment and subsequent reviews of the risk assessment will help determine the level of training and competence needed for each type of work. Competence is the ability to do the work required to the necessary standard. All employees, including senior management, should receive relevant training. This

may need to include basic skills training, specific on-the-job training and training in health and safety or emergency procedures. There may be a need for further training e.g. about specific risks, required by other legislation. For those working towards National and Scottish Vocational Qualifications, the Employment National Training Organisation has designed stand-alone training units in health, safety and the environment. These vocational units are for people at work who are not health and safety professionals/specialists.

83. Training needs are likely to be greatest for new employees on recruitment. They should receive basic induction training on health and safety, including arrangements for first-aid, fire and evacuation. Particular attention should be given to the needs of young workers. The risk assessment should identify further specific training needs. In some cases, training may be required even though an employee already holds formal qualifications (e.g. for an update on new technology). Training and competence needs will have to be reviewed if the work activity a person is involved in or the working environment changes. This may include a change of department or the introduction of new equipment, processes or tasks.

84. An employee's competence will decline if skills are not used regularly (e.g. in emergency procedures, operating a particular item of equipment or carrying out a task). Training therefore needs to be repeated periodically to ensure continued competence. This will be particularly important for employees who occasionally deputise for others, home workers and mobile employees. Information from personal performance monitoring, health and safety checks, accident investigations and near-miss incidents can help to establish a suitable period for re-training. Employers are required by the Safety Representatives and Safety Committees Regulations 1997 to consult safety representatives in good time about the planning and organisation of health and safety training required for the employees they represent.

Regulation 14 – Employees' duties

85. Employees' duties under section 7 of the HSW Act include co-operating with their employer to enable the employer to comply with statutory duties for health and safety. Under these Regulations, employers or those they appoint (e.g. under regulation 7) to assist them with health and safety matters need to be informed without delay of any work situation which might present a serious and imminent danger. Employees should also notify any shortcomings in the health and safety arrangements, even when no immediate danger exists, so that employers can take remedial action if needed.

86. The duties placed on employees do not reduce the responsibility of the employer to comply with duties under these Regulations and the other relevant statutory provisions. In particular, employers need to ensure that employees receive adequate instruction and training to enable them to comply with their duties.

87. Employees have a duty under section 7 of the HSW Act to take reasonable care for their own health and safety and that of others who may be affected by their actions or omissions at work. Therefore, employees must use all work items

provided by their employer correctly, in accordance with their training and the instructions they received to use them safely.

Regulation 15 – Temporary workers

88. This regulation supplements previous regulations requiring the provision of information with additional requirements on temporary workers (i.e. those employed on fixed-duration contracts and those employed in employment businesses, but working for a user company). The use of temporary workers needs to be notified to health and safety staff under regulation 7(4)(b), as necessary.

Fixed-duration contracts

89. Regulation 10 deals with the provision of information by employers to their employees. This includes those on fixed-duration contracts. Under regulation 15(1), employees on fixed-duration contracts also have to be informed of any special occupational qualifications or skills required to carry out the work safely and whether the job is subject to statutory health surveillance (the latter being a protective measure covered in general by regulation 10(1)(b)).

Employment businesses

90. Regulation 12(4) deals with the provision of information by a first employer to a second employer, whose employees are working on the premises. This includes employees of people who have an employment business. Under regulation 15(3), an employment business has to be informed of any special occupational qualifications or skills required to carry out the work safely and the specific features of the job which might affect health and safety (e.g. work at heights).

91. The person who has an employment business and the user employer both have duties to provide information to the employee. The person with the employment business has a duty under regulation 10 (as an employer) and a duty under regulation 15(3) to ensure that the information provided by the user employer is given to the employee. The user employer has a duty under regulation 12(4) to check that information provided to an employer (including someone carrying on an employment business) is received by the employee. In addition, regulations 15(1) and (2) require that information on qualifications, skills and health surveillance are given directly to employees in an employment business.

92. These duties overlap to make sure the information needs of those working for, but not employed by, user employers are not overlooked. User employers and people carrying on employment businesses should therefore make suitable arrangements to satisfy themselves that information is provided. In most cases, it may be enough for user employers to provide information directly to employees. Those carrying on employment businesses will need to satisfy themselves that arrangements for this are adequate. However, basic information on job demands and risks should be supplied to the employment business at an early stage to help select those most suitable to carry out the work (in accordance with regulation 15(3)).

Self-employed

93. Self-employed people have similar duties under regulations 11(2), 12, 15(2) and 15(3) to inform employment businesses and the employees of employment businesses who carry out work on their premises. They may also need to agree arrangements with the employment businesses concerned. Self-employed workers hired through employment businesses are entitled to receive health and safety information from the employers or self-employed people for whom they carry out work under regulation 12(2). There is a full definition of how these Regulations apply to self-employed workers in paragraphs 4 and 5. It explains how people working under the control and direction of others but are treated as self-employed for other reasons such as tax and national insurance, are nevertheless treated as their employees for health and safety purposes.

Regulation 16 – Risk assessment in respect of new or expectant mothers

. . .

Regulation 17 – Certificate from registered medical practitioner in respect of new or expectant mothers

. . .

Regulation 18 – Notification by new or expectant mothers

94. Where the risk assessment identifies risks to new and expectant mothers and these risks cannot be avoided by the preventative and protective measures taken by an employer, the employer will need to:

(a) alter her working conditions or hours of work if it is reasonable to do so and would avoid the risks or, if these conditions cannot be met;

(b) identify and offer her suitable alternative work that is available, and if that is not feasible;

(c) suspend her from work. The Employment Rights Act 1996 (which is the responsibility of the Department of Trade and Industry) requires that this suspension should be on full pay. Employment rights are enforced through the employment tribunals.

95. All employers should take account of women of child-bearing age when carrying out the risk assessment and identify the preventive and protective measures that are required in Regulation 3. The additional steps of altering working conditions or hours of work, offering suitable alternative work or suspension as outlined above may be taken once an employee has given her employer notice in writing that she is pregnant, has given birth within the last six months or is breastfeeding. If the employee continues to breastfeed for more than six months after the birth she should ensure the employer is informed of this, so that the appropriate measures can continue to be taken. Employers need to ensure

that those workers who are breastfeeding are not exposed to risks that could damage their health and safety as long as they breastfeed. If the employee informs her employer that she is pregnant for the purpose of any other statutory requirements, such as statutory maternity pay, this will be sufficient for the purpose of these Regulations.

96. Once an employer has been informed in writing that an employee is a new or expectant mother, the employer needs to immediately put into place the steps described in paragraph 94 and 95. The employer may request confirmation of the pregnancy by means of a certificate from a registered medical practitioner or a registered midwife in writing. If this certificate has not been produced within a reasonable period of time, the employer is not bound to maintain changes to working hours or conditions or to maintain paid leave. A reasonable period of time will allow for all necessary medical examinations and tests to be completed.

97. Further guidance on new and expectant mothers is contained in *New and expectant mothers at work: A guide for employers* (see References and further reading section). The table of hazards identified in the EC Directive on Pregnant Workers (92/85/EEC) is given in this publication, along with the risks and ways to avoid them. The DTI booklet *PL705 Suspension from work on medical or maternity grounds* and *PL958 Maternity rights*, both of which cover the maternity suspension provisions, are available from DTI.

Regulation 19 – Protection of young persons

98. The employer needs to carry out the risk assessment before young workers start work and to see where risk remains, taking account of control measures in place, as described in regulation 3. For young workers, the risk assessment needs to pay attention to areas of risk described in regulation 19(2). For several of these areas the employer will need to assess the risks with the control measures in place under other statutory requirements.

99. When control measures have been taken against these risks and if a significant risk still remains, no child (young worker under the compulsory school age) can be employed to do this work. A young worker, above the minimum school leaving age, cannot do this work unless:

(a)   it is necessary for his or her training; and

(b)   she or he is supervised by a competent person; and

(c)   the risk will be reduced to the lowest level reasonably practicable.

100. Further guidance on young workers is contained in *Young people at work: A guide for employers* (see References and further reading section). The table on hazards, risks and ways of avoiding them from the EC Directive on the protection of Young People at Work (94/33/EEC) is given in this publication.

Regulation 20 – Exemption certificates

. . .

Regulation 21 – Provisions as to liability

Employers' liability

101. An employer is not to be afforded a defence for any contravention of his health and safety obligations by reason of any act or default caused by an employee or by a person appointed to give competent advice. It does not affect employees' duties to take reasonable care of their own health and safety and that of others affected by their work activity.

102. In practice enforcers will take account of the circumstances of each case before deciding on the appropriateness of any enforcement action, and who this should be taken against. Where the employer has taken reasonable steps to satisfy him or herself of the competency of the employee or person appointed to provide competent advice or services, this will be taken into account.

Regulation 22 – Exclusion of civil liability

. . .

Regulation 23 – Extension outside Great Britain

103. The 1989 Order has been replaced by the Health and Safety at Work etc Act 1974 (Application outside Great Britain) Order 1995. This Order applies the Act to offshore installations, wells, pipelines and pipeline works, and to connected activities within the territorial waters of Great Britain or in designated areas of the United Kingdom Continental Shelf, plus certain other activities within territorial waters. Regulation 23(1) applies the Management of Health and Safety at Work Regulations to these places and activities. Regulation 23(2) ensures that workers are protected even while on duty offshore.

Regulation 24 – Amendment of the Health and Safety (First-Aid) Regulations 1981

104. Regulation 24 revokes the Health and Safety Executive's powers to grant exemptions from the Health and Safety (First-Aid) Regulations 1981.

Regulation 25 – Amendment of the Offshore Installations and Pipeline Works (First-Aid) Regulations 1989

105. Regulation 25 limits the scope of the exemptions that can be granted by the Health and Safety Executive to those specified in regulations 5(1)(b)(c) and (2)(a) of the Offshore Installations and Pipeline Works (First Aid) Regulations 1989. It also requires that where an exemption is granted the person provided under regulation 5(1)(a) shall have undergone adequate training.

Regulation 26 – Amendment of the Mines Miscellaneous Health and Safety Provisions Regulations 1995

106. Regulation 26 introduces a new paragraph into regulation 4 of the Mines Miscellaneous Health and Safety Provisions Regulations 1995. This requires that a fire protection plan be included in all cases in the health and safety document required by these Regulations. In all parts of the mine other than buildings on the surface, the mine owner is required to designate in the document those who are to implement the plan and include the arrangements for the necessary contacts with external services, especially rescue work and fire-fighting.

Regulation 27 – Amendment of the Construction (Health, Safety and Welfare) Regulations 1996

107. This regulation amends regulation 20 of the Construction (Health, Safety and Welfare) Regulations 1996, so that arrangements for dealing with foreseeable emergencies on construction sites include designating people to implement the arrangements and arranging necessary contacts with external services, especially rescue work and fire-fighting.

Regulation 28 – Regulations to have effect as health and safety regulations

. . .

Regulation 29 – Revocations and consequential amendments

. . .

Regulation 30 – Transitional provision

. . .

(2) PERSONAL PROTECTIVE EQUIPMENT AT WORK (SECOND EDITION)

Personal Protective Equipment at Work Regulations 1992 (as amended)

Guidance on Regulations (extract)

© Crown copyright 2005

First published 1992

Second edition 2005

ISBN 0 7176 6139 3

Foot protection

Types of protection

91 Footwear is available in a range of styles, for example shoe, low ankle boot, high ankle boot, knee boot, thigh boot and even chest-high waders. The different types of protective footwear include the following:

(a) **Safety boots or shoes** – These are the most common type of safety footwear. They normally have protective toe-caps and may also have other safety features including slip-resistant soles, penetration-resistant mid-soles and insulation against extremes of heat and cold.

(b) **Wellington boots** – These are usually made of rubber and used for working in wet conditions. They are also useful in jobs where the footwear needs to be washed and disinfected for hygiene reasons, eg in the food industry and the chemical industry.

(c) **Clogs** – These may also be used as safety footwear. They are traditionally made from beech wood and may be fitted with steel toe-caps and thin rubber soles for quieter tread.

(d) **Footwear for specific tasks** – These protect against hazards in these areas, for example foundry boots and chainsaw boots.

Examples of hazards which may require foot protection

92 The main hazards which may need foot protection are:

(a) Objects falling on and crushing the foot/toes – this will include jobs requiring manual handling, such as construction workers or removal people.

(b) Treading on pointed or sharp objects (eg nails) on the ground piercing the shoe, injuring the sole of the foot and resulting in cuts and wounds.

(c) Slips, trips and falls resulting in injuries such as sprained ankles. Although there is no such thing as non-slip footwear there are slip-resistant 'anti-slip' soles which can reduce the likelihood of slipping on certain floors.

(d) Working in cold or hot conditions. Working in the cold requires footwear with thermal insulation. Work in hot conditions requires footwear with heat-resistant and insulating soles. For protection against molten metal splash, footwear must have quick-release fastenings.

(e) Electrical hazards (see paragraph 85(c) for further information).

(f) Working in potentially explosive atmospheres or for the handling of sensitive materials (eg detonators). Footwear must be anti-static.

(g) Working with and handling hazardous chemicals. Footwear should be impermeable and resistant to that chemical.

(h) Wet work, for example using water sprays when cleaning. Water-resistant or waterproof material should be used. Wellington boot style footwear should be used for very wet work.

Key points

93 Key points to note about protective footwear are:

(a) Consider the comfort factors for the wearer. Generally footwear should be flexible, wet-resistant and absorb perspiration. Cushioned soles make standing more comfortable.

(b) Inspect for wear and tear and loose seams before use. Replace broken laces and remove materials lodged in the tread of the sole.

APPENDIX F

SAFETY AT STREET WORKS AND ROAD WORKS
EXTRACT FROM THE CODE OF PRACTICE

A Code of Practice issued by the Secretary of State for Transport, Local Government and the Regions, The Scottish Executive and the National Assembly for Wales under sections 65 and 124 of the New Roads and Street Works Act 1991, and by the Department for Regional Development (Northern Ireland) under article 25 of the Street Works (Northern Ireland) Order 1995.

Foreword

Today's roads are full of fast, heavy traffic. Drivers have to keep a constant look-out for changing road conditions. Whilst this code is primarily directed at you the operative, supervisors and managers have an important responsibility to make sure that all street and road works and operatives are safe. Road users should not be put at risk, and should be informed well in advance about the size and nature of any obstruction. This applies to vulnerable users – including pedestrians, cyclists, motorcyclists and horse riders – as well as drivers.

You must also pay particular attention to the needs of blind and disabled people, children, elderly people and people with prams.

This Code of Practice will help you to safely carry out signing, lighting and guarding of street works and road works on most roads.

With effect from 1st January 2002 this code has statutory backing for street works in England, Wales and Northern Ireland, and for road works in Scotland, as a Code of Practice under the New Roads and Street Works Act 1991 and the Street Works (Northern Ireland) Order 1995. Failure to comply may lead to criminal prosecution in addition to any civil proceedings.

Department for Transport, Local Government and the Regions

The Scottish Executive

The National Assembly for Wales

Department for Regional Development (Northern Ireland)

Key Question

Ask yourself this question:

> '*Will someone coming along the road or footway from any direction understand exactly what is happening in front of them?*'

Safe works – Basic principles

Who does what

It is your responsibility to sign, guard, light and maintain your works safely. Take time to plan how you will do this and to decide on what equipment you will need. There will be some pre-planned works where procedures will already have been decided for you.

Using this code

This Code shows the principles to follow when signing, guarding and lighting works on all highways and roads except motorways and dual carriageways with hard shoulders. It is impossible to illustrate every situation but some of the common ones are shown. Passages in blue ink indicate matters which are the responsibility of supervisors or managers.

Further advice about traffic safety measures for road works is given in Chapter 8 of the Traffic Signs Manual, including for dual carriageways with hard shoulders and motorways. Always consult your supervisor if you are in any doubt about correct procedures or if you are concerned about safety. It is management's responsibility to provide the signs and guarding equipment. It is your responsibility to use them in the right way.

Your supervisor needs to be aware if work is restricted to certain times of the day and whether other conditions may apply.

On-site risk assessment

To comply with Health and Safety legislation you must carry out an on-site risk assessment to ensure that a safe system of working in respect of signing, lighting and guarding is in place at all times.

Be seen

Whether on site or visiting, all personnel must wear a high visibility jacket or waistcoat, as appropriate. You may also need other protective clothing or equipment for your personal safety.

Fix signs properly

Signs, lights and guarding equipment must be secured against being blown over or out of position by the wind or by passing traffic. Use sacks at low level containing fine granular material. Alternatively, use equipment having ballasting as part of its construction. Do not use barrels, kerbstones or similar objects for this purpose – they could be dangerous if hit by traffic. Do not use road pins under any circumstances.

Place the first sign far enough from the works to give adequate warning of the hazard (see table inside back cover). Where signs have to be placed on a footway, they should be positioned so as to minimise inconvenience or hazard to pedestrians.

Check regularly that signs have not been moved or damaged or become dirty, including when the site is left unattended for a period of time. Consult your supervisor if the works will make it impossible for drivers to follow a permanent traffic sign. If it needs to be covered, your supervisor will need to notify the highway authority.

Don't forget the visibility of signs

Signs must be reflectorised unless otherwise indicated. Consult your supervisor at times of poor visibility or bad weather conditions as you may need to provide additional signs or to suspend the work. Keep signs clean.

Traffic on two-way roads

On a two-way road, signs should be set out for traffic approaching from both directions.

Traffic at junctions

Signs should be set out for traffic approaching from all directions.

Site layout

You must include the works area, working space and safety zone in the area to be marked off with cones, and lamps placed where necessary. Never use a safety zone as a work area or for storing plant or materials. See inside back cover for the minimum dimensions for the safety zone.

Additional areas to be signed

If there are any temporary footways in the carriage, or obstructions such as spoil or plant, which are not already within the working space, sign and guard them separately to the same standard.

Additional requirements

Sometimes you may have to duplicate the warning signs on both sides of the road. An example of this would be where signs on the left hand side become obscured by heavy traffic. On dual carriageway roads, the warning signs need to be duplicated on the central reservation.

The road width and volume of traffic at the works site may make traffic control necessary. See page 52 for details of which type of control is appropriate.

Drivers visiting the works must switch on their roof-mounted amber beacons, if they have them, before signalling to enter the works. This will help to make sure that other drivers will not be misled into entering the coned-off area as well. Hazard warning lights confuse other road users so don't use them when entering or leaving a site.

Maintenance of site

Always keep the site safe with signs, cones, lights and barriers clean and correctly placed. When no one is on site, make sure that the site is regularly inspected. Damaged or displaced equipment must be replaced promptly. Emergencies should be dealt with without delay.

Changing traffic conditions

Where site or traffic conditions change, appropriate adjustments should be made to signing, lighting and guarding.

Clearing up

On completion of the works, ensure that all plant, equipment and surplus materials are removed promptly from the site. All signs, lighting or guarding equipment should be removed immediately.

Site layout

What is the works area?

The works area is the excavation, chamber opening, etc, at which you will be working.

What is the working space?

The working space is the space around the works area where you will need to store tools, excavated material, equipment and plant, etc. It is also the space that you need to move around in to do the job.

You must leave enough working space to make sure that the movement and operation of the plant (e.g. swinging of jibs and excavator arms) is clear of passing traffic and is not encroaching into the safety zone, or adjacent footway or cycle track.

What is the safety zone?

The safety zone is the zone provided to protect you from traffic and to protect the traffic from you. **You must not enter the safety zone in the normal course of work.** Materials and equipment must not be placed in the zone. **You will need to enter the zone only to maintain cones and other road signs.**

The Safety Zone is made up of:

–   **The length of the lead-in taper of the cones (T)**
    This will vary with the speed limit and the width of the works.

–   **The longways clearance (L)**
    This is the length between the end of the lead-in taper of cones (T) and the working space. It will vary with the speed limit.

–   **The sideways clearance (S)**
    This is the width between the working space and moving traffic. The sideways clearance is measured from the outside edge of the working space to the bottom of the conical sections of the cones on the side nearest to the traffic (see page 8). It will vary with the speed limit.

–   **The exit taper**
    This is always at 45° to the kerbline or road edge.

You must provide working space and safety zones when personnel are present, but when no personnel are on site the width of the zone can be reduced to make it less of an obstruction to traffic. Dimensions L and S can be reduced (or these spaces omitted altogether) and T adjusted to match the reduced width. L, A and T should be restored to the appropriate dimensions when work on site restarts.

Always aim to provide full safety zone clearances consistent with the speed limit in force. To help achieve this, the unobstructed width of road available for traffic may be reduced to the desirable minimum or absolute minimum for the type of situation, but remember to leave enough room for the swept path of large vehicles at junctions and bends, bearing in mind that at widths of 3 metres or less, the wing mirrors of commercial vehicles could easily overhang the footway.

If pedestrians are diverted into the carriageway, you must provide a safety zone at all times between the outer pedestrian barrier and the traffic.

The recommended lead-in taper is given in the table on the inside back cover. This should be used wherever possible. Sometimes it may be impracticable to provide the full taper. If this happens on congested roads with speed limits of 30mph or less, it is permissible to reduce the lead-in taper to an angle of not more than 45° to the kerb, particularly if the parking of vehicles is usual.

The existing speed limit or temporary speed limit approved by the highway authority should be used to determine the appropriate clearances. If traffic consistently exceeds the speed limit, this should be taken into consideration when reviewing the width of the safety zone. If you feel at risk from vehicles exceeding the speed limit, your supervisor should be requested to contact the police.

Where the carriage width is so restricted as to prohibit the provision of the appropriate sideways clearance detailed above and diversion of traffic would be impracticable, traffic speeds must be reduced to less than 10 mph and an agreed safe method of working imposed on the site.

What you will need

It doesn't matter whether the works are small or large, on the ground or overhead, all street works require warning and information. In emergencies as much warning must be given as the circumstances permit, and full signing must be provided as quickly as possible.

High visibility clothing

You will have been provided with High Visibility Clothing conforming to BS EN471:1994, Table 1, Class 2 or 3, which must be worn at all times. It will comply with the requirements of Clause 4.2.3(b) in all cases.

Jackets with sleeves in accordance with Clause 4.2.4 and to Class 3 must be worn on dual carriageway roads with a speed limit of 50 mph or above, unless operatives stay within the working space at all times. The colour of the background material should normally be fluorescent yellow from table 2 of BS EN471:1994, and the retroreflective material should comply with Table 5. High Visibility Clothing to BS6629:1985 may continue in use until 30th September 2002.

Advance signs

These should be placed where they will be clearly seen, and cause minimum inconvenience to drivers, cyclists, pedestrians and other road users alike, and where there is a minimum risk of their being hit or knocked over by traffic. Where there is a grass verge the signs should normally be placed there; the placing of signs in the footway is permitted but in no circumstances must the footway width be reduced below 1 metre.

If there are already vehicles parked in the carriageway, place the advance signs so that they are not obscured.

The 'Road Works Ahead' sign is the first sign to be seen by the driver, so place it well before the works. Its size, the minimum distance from the start of the lead-in taper, and clear visibility distance will vary according to the type of road and its speed limit – see table on inside of back cover. The range of distances is given to allow the sign to be placed in the most convenient position bearing in mind available space and visibility for drivers. Do not simply choose the minimum distance – assess each site carefully.

A '**Road Narrows Ahead**' signs warns the driver which side of the carriageway is obstructed. Place it midway between the Road Works Ahead sign and the beginning of the lead-in taper.

On roads with speed limits of 50 mph or more, all advance signs should have plates giving the distance to the works in yards or miles (not in metres).

Keep right and keep left signs

Place '**Keep Right**', or as appropriate, '**Keep Left**' signs at the beginning and end of the lead-in taper of cones. These signs must be the same size as the Road Works Ahead sign. MAKE SURE THAT THE SIGNS POINT IN THE CORRECT DIRECTION. Do not turn the sign frame on its side to make it point in the correct direction. These signs must NOT be used for directing pedestrians.

Cones and lamps

Place a line of Traffic Cones to guide traffic past the works and add Road Danger Lamps in poor daytime visibility and bad weather. Where the traffic is faster the length of taper must be longer. Look at the table inside the back cover for details of positioning of cones and lamps.

Road Danger Lamps must be used at night on roads with a speed limit of 40 mph or above. On roads with a lower speed limit, judgment may be used as to whether Road Danger Lamps are needed, depending on the standard of street lighting.

Road Danger Lamps must not be higher than 1.5 metres above the road (or 1.2 metres where the speed limit is more than 40 mph).

The type of lamp to be used is as follows:

Type of Road Danger Lamp	*Conditions of use*
Flashing lamp (55 to 150 flashes per minute)	Only when ALL of the following conditions apply:
	– the speed limit is 40 mph or less
	– the Road Danger Lamp is within 50 metres of a street lamp, and
	– the street lamp is illuminated.
Steady lamp	On any road with or without street lighting.

Barriers

Barriers may comprise separate portable post and plank systems, 'gate frames' linked together, or semi-permanent constructions built to enclose the site.

There are several different requirements for the barrier planks associated with post and plank systems. The following explains the requirements and how they may be met using barrier planks which are red and white and manufactured in fully retroreflective materials. (Note: 'Retroreflective' means that at night the material reflects light back to the light source).

Barrier planks are required to carry out three functions:

1. As a **TRAFFIC BARRIER**. When a traffic lane is closed for works to take place, the regulations require this to be done with a retroreflective red and white barrier plank placed across the lane. This is illustrated on page 12 as a Traffic Barrier ('Lane Closed' sign).

2. As a **PEDESTRIAN BARRIER**. Pedestrians must be separated from the works by barriers which are conspicuous and mounted as part of a portable fencing system. Pedestrian barrier planks may be of several different contrasting colours; yellow, white or orange colours are best detected by partially sighted people, but red and white is one of the acceptable combinations.

3. As a **TAPPING RAIL** for blind and partially sighted people. Tapping rails are placed as the bottom rail in a pedestrian fencing system. A red and white barrier plank may be used.

All barriers facing vehicular traffic should be of the fully retroreflective red and white form. Red and white barrier planks do not have to be used for pedestrian barriers or tapping rails but, if they are, they must be retroreflective. Other planks used for these purposes do not need to be retroreflective.

There are other points to note about the use of barrier planks in portable fencing systems:

a) The TRAFFIC BARRIER ('Lane Closed' sign) is not needed if the works are protected by a conspicuous vehicle.

b) Pedestrian barrier systems must be rigid enough to guard pedestrians from traffic, excavations, plant or materials. They must be placed with sufficient clearance to prevent pedestrians falling into the excavation and, when placed to create a temporary footway in the carriageway parallel to the traffic stream, must be protected by a row of traffic cones between the barrier and the traffic stream. Consult your supervisor if the excavation is deep, or positioned close to pedestrians, as stronger barriers may be needed and/or other safety measures may be required e.g. covering or temporarily refilling the excavation.

c)   Where a work site may be approached by pedestrians crossing the road from the opposite side, you should place barriers, including tapping rails, all around the excavation, even when pedestrians are not diverted into the carriageway.

d)   Where long excavations are sited in situations where pedestrians are not expected to cross from the opposite side, barriers on the traffic stream side of the works area do not need the tapping rail. In these circumstances, on an unrestricted road, the barrier on the traffic stream side can be replaced with an additional row of cones. These cones should be linked with a suitably supported traffic tape to attract attention to the boundary of the safety zone.

Use pedestrian barriers to mark out any temporary footway. You must always use a rigid barrier to protect pedestrians from traffic, excavations, plant or materials. Place road danger lamps at the ends of the barriers at night so that they may be clearly seen by pedestrians.

PORTABLE PEDESTRIAN BARRIERS, which may include mesh, should be reasonably rigid, designed to resist being blown over by the wind or passing traffic, and have:

–   a handrail fixed at between 1 metre and 1.2 metres above ground level, which should be reasonably smooth and rigid to guide pedestrians and give them some measure of support; and a visibility panel of at least 150mm deep which may be integral with the handrail or, if separate, must be fixed so that its upper edge is a minimum of 0.9 metres above ground level.

–   a tapping rail (or equivalent reasonably rigid area if the barrier is a vertically continuous one) of minimum depth of 150mm with a lower edge at ground level or set at up to 200 mm above ground level.

Information board

An information board must be displayed at every site, except for mobile works and minor works which do not include excavation, involving use of a vehicle. This board should be placed so that it does not obstruct footways or carriageways but can be read mainly by pedestrians, and possibly by drivers who have stopped. (The boards are too detailed to be read easily by passing traffic.)

The board must give the name of the organisation for which the works are being carried out, and a telephone number which can be contacted in emergencies. It may also contain further information that will be helpful in explaining to the public why the work is being done, who is doing it and how long it will take. Such additional information is to be encouraged where practical and could include some or all of the following: a brief description of the works, the name of the contractor and a message apologising for inconvenience or delays. A completion date should normally be included if the works are expected to continue for more than a month.

End sign

The 'End' sign indicates not only the end of the works but also the end of any temporary restrictions, including temporary speed limits, associated with the works.

If the permanent speed limit changes within the length of the road covered by a temporary speed restriction, signs indicating the new speed limit must be provided on each side of the carriageway at the end of the works, in addition to the 'End' sign.

You must place an 'End' sign beyond works that are 50 metres or more in length (measured between the end of the lead-in taper and the beginning of the exit taper) and beyond two or more adjacent sites.

But an 'End' sign is not necessary on a road where ALL of the following conditions are met:

—   there are no temporary speed limits or other traffic restrictions

—   the speed limit is 30 mph or under

—   there is a total two-way traffic flow of less than 20 vehicles counted over 3 minutes (400 veh/hr)

—   less than 20 heavy goods vehicles pass the works site per hour.

Works on footways – look after pedestrians

Pedestrian safety

It is your responsibility to make sure that pedestrians are safe during the works. This means protecting them from both the works and passing traffic.

You **must** take into account the needs of children, elderly people and people with disabilities, having particular regard for visually impaired people. In order to do this you must provide a suitable barrier system which safely separates pedestrians from hazards and provides sufficient access for people using wheelchairs and those with prams or pushchairs.

Safe routes for pedestrians

If you have to close a footway or part of a footway, you must provide a safe route for pedestrians which should include access to adjacent buildings, properties and public areas.

Safe routes should always provide a minimum unobstructed width of 1 metre, increased wherever possible to 1.5 metres or more.

However, a balanced assessment must be made to provide pedestrians with the safest option. For example, a route of 1 metre unobstructed width which uses the existing footway is potentially safer than a wider temporary route placed in the carriageway.

When temporary pedestrian routes have to be placed in the carriageway, make sure the signing and guarding barriers are put into place before the footway is blocked. Make sure the sideways clearance (S) of the safety zone is on the traffic side of the barriers. Where necessary, provide ramps, or a raised footway or boards which are fit for the purpose.

The use of the other footway may be acceptable in some quiet roads, but if you select this option you must ensure that the alternative route is safe to use, and you must take account of the needs of children and people with disabilities.

Pedestrian crossings and pedestrianised areas

If the works are on or near pedestrian crossings turn to page 42 for advice. In pedestrianised areas the working space, including vehicles, plant or materials, must be enclosed with pedestrian barriers.

Safety zone for operatives

When working in a footway remember you must provide a safety zone in the carriageway if the working space is closer to the edge of the carriageway than the width of the sideways clearance (S). If cones are placed in the road, signing and guarding of the safety zone must be carried out.

These same principles apply when working in a verge adjacent to the carriageway.

Scaffolding

Any scaffolding erected in the highways must be licensed by the highway authority.

Footway ramps, footway boards and road plates

Footway ramps

When pedestrians are diverted to temporary footways in the carriageway, suitable ramps must be provided to enable people using wheelchairs or pushchairs to negotiate kerbs safely.

Ramps should cover the full width of the temporary footway (minimum of 1 metre), and should be constructed from materials strong enough to support pedestrians, preferably with edging to prevent wheelchairs slipping over the edge. They may be made on site, e.g. from wood or bitumastic materials, or prefabricated. Ramps should slope gently enough to enable wheelchair users and pushchairs to reach the kerb without undue difficulty. Ideally, the layout should include a platform at kerb level which would allow wheelchair users to turn through 90° before descending the ramp in a line that is parallel to the kerb. Ramps must be fixed in position, allow for rain water to run along the gutter, and should have a slip resistant surface.

Footway boards

Footway Boards should only be used on footways to maintain foot and light vehicle access to premises during excavation works.

Footway Boards used for bridging excavations must provide at least 1 metre width for pedestrians, but preferably 1.5 metres, must be strong enough to support pedestrians, and must be made from material which is unlikely to become distorted. Where used for light vehicles the boards must be capable of supporting the added load and, where used on a vehicle crossover the whole width of the crossover must be boarded.

The edges of footway boards must be chamfered to prevent tripping and should have a slip resistant surface. The sides of the excavation should be stable or suitably supported under the board, and the board should be rigidly fixed with sufficient length beyond the excavation to provide the necessary support. The edges of the footway boards adjacent to the excavation should be fenced to prevent falls.

Road plates

Road Plates may be required to bridge excavations in order to open the carriageway to traffic, e.g. during traffic sensitive periods, at night or at weekends. Their use must always be authorised by your supervisor who will decide on the size and thickness of the plate to be used. The thickness will depend on the width of excavation to be spanned and the type of traffic expected to use them.

Road Plates must be made of suitable material with an appropriate skid resistant surface. Their installation must not present a hazard to cyclists or motorcyclists.

The sides of the excavations must be suitably supported beneath the road plates, and they must be rigidly secured to the road surface. Road Plates must be either sunk into the surface or suitable bitumastic material used to provide a ramp to the plate level. Where ramps are used, appropriate Ramp Warning signs should be used when there is a significant change in the road level.

The edges of the Road Plates adjacent to the excavation should be fenced to prevent falls.

Works at pedestrian and cycle crossings

Before any work takes place at or near a pedestrian or cycle crossing you must consult your supervisor. Only the highway authority can authorise a crossing to be taken out of service. Where appropriate, alternative signed routes should be agreed with the highway authority.

If due to works the pedestrian or cycle crossing has to be closed, you should:

– ensure the closure has been authorised by the highway authority

– erect 'Crossing not in use' signs

– cover zebra crossing globes or signal heads/buttons, and any other signal operating device

– cover (or arrange with the highway authority to remove) tactile indicators so that visually impaired and deaf people are not misled, especially where tactile paving has been laid

– at signal-controlled crossings, erect 'Traffic signals not in use' signs and cover the signal heads

– if the limits of the crossing are obstructed, or the visibility between drivers and pedestrians/cyclists is reduced to an unacceptable degree, erect barriers across the accesses to the crossing.

Close both crossings if the works spread into one or both sides of a double crossing which has a central refuge.

Works at road junctions

Keep the two-way traffic flowing past the works if possible. If you can't, traffic control or a diversion may be required.

Put up 'Road Works Ahead' signs with arrow plates on the main route if the works are in a side road. Turn to page 45 for details.

Works on or near the far side of a junction. At works like these, take the taper of cones up to the approach side of the junction. Make sure that any cones near the junction help drivers turn left smoothly.

Works at road junctions controlled by permanent traffic signals

Approaches to junctions

A works site on the approach to a traffic signalled junction can cause significant disruption to the traffic flow at the junction. An adjustment of the traffic signals may be required, so consult your supervisor, who will then consult the highway authority.

At junctions

If traffic signals are not working, put up 'Traffic signals ahead not in use' signs on all approaches. Permanent traffic signals are often replaced by temporary or portable traffic signals for the duration of the works. Both will need approval by the highway authority.

If pedestrian lights at a junction are affected by the works, they should be treated in a similar manner to pedestrian crossings (see page 42). This must be discussed with the highway authority.

Consult your supervisor where the road has a speed limit of 40 mph or above.

Works at roundabouts

Works at the entrance to or exit from a roundabout

Use advance signs to warn traffic on all approaches that there are works at or near the roundabout. Use 'Keep Right/Left' signs to guide traffic around the coned-off works site.

Try to keep two-way traffic flowing if possible, but remember the width restrictions. However, if the works site makes the roads too narrow to allow two-way traffic to pass, restrict the road to 'Exit only' from the roundabout. **The traffic usually entering the roundabout on this road will then need to be diverted.** This requires permission of the highway authority and needs to be pre-planned as adequate notice has to be given. Consult your supervisor.

Extra cones will be needed to restrict traffic to one lane going towards this exit and additional advance warning using 'Road Narrows' signs provided on all approaches. Use 'Keep Right/Left' signs to guide traffic past coned areas.

Works in the circulatory area of a roundabout

Movement of traffic should be maintained if possible. Guard and cone the works and provide advance 'Road Narrows' signs on all approaches. Use 'Keep Right/Left' signs to guide the traffic past the works site.

Where works will completely obstruct the circulatory area of a roundabout, consult your supervisor who will then consult the highway authority.

Varying the number of lanes on the circulatory section of a roundabout can distract drivers, therefore consideration should be given to coning down to the same number of lanes unless the traffic pattern dictates otherwise. Lane dedication signs may be needed. Vehicle turning paths need to be carefully considered to ensure the rear wheels of long vehicles do not hit the cones and to ensure adequate width on the restricted approach.

Cycle lanes and cycle tracks

Where cycle lanes, cycle tracks and cycle routes are affected by street works and road works you should use your best endeavours to ensure the safety of cyclists passing or crossing by the works.

Cycle lanes marked with a solid white line have been created by means of Traffic Regulation Orders. Where one of these is affected by planned works, your supervisor will need to discuss the situation with the highway authority well before the work starts. It may be necessary to obtain a Temporary Notice or Traffic Regulation Order to suspend the cycle lane. Temporary Notices and Temporary Traffic Regulation Orders are not required for emergency works.

Cyclists may have to use the remainder of the carriageway, use an alternative route or, if an alternative route is not available, will have to dismount while passing the works. Your supervisor may need to discuss these alternatives with the highway authority.

When portable traffic signals are used, bear in mind when adjusting the timings that cyclists take longer to clear the controlled section than motor vehicles.

Where the carriageway is closed off but the footway remains open, cyclists should be advised to dismount by using a 'Cyclists Dismount and Use Footway' white on red temporary sign.

Wherever possible, a minimum lane width of 3.25 metres should be provided to allow a car to overtake a cyclist, more where lorries or buses will be present (see page 52).

Work near tramways

Special safety precautions must be taken when works are to be carried out near a tramway. A summary of the main safety points is given below. Detailed advice must be obtained by your supervisor from the relevant track or transport authority prior to starting work and given to those carrying out the works.

Risk of collision with the tramcar

Unlike other traffic a tramcar cannot swerve to avoid a person or obstruction. Tramcars are wider than the tracks on which they run. The path of a tramcar which must be left unobstructed is known as the 'swept path'. In some cases this is indicated by a line of yellow discs, a painted line or a raised kerb.

It is essential that signing and guarding equipment, operatives, vehicles and pedestrians are kept out of the swept path. Where the works cause the footway to be diverted into the carriageway, the barrier between the pedestrians and the tramway must be kept at least 0.5 metres away from the edge of the swept path.

Where the safety zone sideways clearance would intrude on the swept path, your supervisor should consult the transport authority. The safety zone may be reduced to 300mm and the transport authority may impose a speed restriction on tramcars, and/or provide a lookout.

Risk of electrocution

Tramway electrical cables consist of overhead lines and underground cables that may be placed outside the swept path.

Your supervisor should liaise with the track or transport authority before working close to overhead lines.

No equipment, plant, vehicles, etc. should be brought within 2 metres of the overhead lines.

Underground cables should be dealt with using standard safe digging practices.

Tramway crossings

Where a tramway runs on a reserved track but crosses the road at certain places, such crossings should be treated as railway level crossings. See page 70.

Reminder

Before you start – general

Is high visibility clothing being worn by everyone on site?

Are all signs, barriers, cones and lighting correctly placed?

Are signs obscured by bends, hills or dips in the road?

Are advance signs needed?

Will the site be safe at night or in wind, fog, snow or rain?

Are parked vehicles, trees, street furniture obscuring signs?

Is there enough road width remaining for two-way traffic?

Is traffic control with shuttle lane working required?

Are there any site specific risks requiring special guarding?

Has allowance been made for delivery and removal of materials?

Is the contact number displayed on the information board?

Before you start – pedestrians

Are pedestrians given protected routes which are wide enough?

Are pedestrian routes clearly indicated?

If the footway is closed, is there an alternative route? If so, is it clearly marked?

Are there any special hazards for disabled pedestrians? If so, how can they be made safe?

If a temporary footway in the road is to be used, are ramps to the kerb provided where necessary?

Before you start – traffic

Is type of traffic control right for work, traffic and speed?

Have any misleading permanent signs and road markings been covered?

Is there safe access to adjacent premises?

Have you a copy of portable traffic signals site approval?

Have you considered the needs of cyclists and horse riders?

When work is in progress

Does signing and guarding meet changing conditions?

Are signs, cones and lamps being kept clean?

Can traffic control arrangements be improved to reduce traffic delays as conditions change?

Are the carriageway and footway being kept clear of mud and surplus equipment?

Are materials that are left on verges or lay-bys being properly guarded and lit?

When work is suspended

Will checks be made on signing, lighting and guarding?

Has the arrangement been changed to reflect conditions?

When work is finished

Have all signs, cones, barriers, and lamps been removed?

Have any covered permanent signs been restored?

Have the authorities been told the work is completed?

APPENDIX G

PHOTOGRAPHS

Photo 1

Typical pavement tripping hazard. But is it dangerous?

Photo 2

It is often easy to establish liability where there is an obstruction like this. Reasonable pedestrians do not expect an iron bar to protrude from the pavement.

Photo 3

Clearly a dangerous hole. But has it been uncovered long enough to make the s 58 defence impossible?

Photo 4

There should be little difficulty in establishing liability here. The locus is a pavement. The defect is objectively dangerous and has plainly been present for a long time.

Photo 5

Typical weather and traffic erosion of a carriageway. Damage like this can often happen very fast in frosty weather, and the s 58 defence is often successful. Remember too that the law does not expect the same standards of a carriageway as of a pavement.

Photo 6

It is a good idea to show on photographs exactly how the trip occurred.

Photo 7

Indicate by the photo the direction of the claimant's fall.

Photo 8

Icy pavement, resulting from a defective drain. As in this photo, indicate as accurately as possible how the claimant landed.

Photo 9

Wider photographs, showing the broader context, are often useful.

APPENDIX H

ADDRESSES

The Automobile Association,
Contact Centre,
Lambert House,
Stockport Road,
Cheadle,
SK8 2DY
Tel: 0161 488 7544
www.theaa.com

Health and Safety Executive,
Bootle Knowledge Centre,
Redgrave Court,
Merton Road,
Bootle,
L20 3QZ
Tel: 0151 951 4000
www.hse.gov.uk

Institute of Highway Incorporated Engineers,
De Morgan House,
58 Russell Square.
London WC1B 4HS
Tel: 0207 436 7487
www.ihie.org.uk

Institute of Road Transport Engineers,
22 Greencoat Place,
London SW1P 1DX
Tel: 0207 630 1111
www.soe.org.uk

Institution of Civil Engineers,
One Great George Street,
London SW1P 3AA
Tel: 0207 222 7722
www.ice.org.uk

Institution of Structural Engineers,
11 Upper Belgrave Street,
London SW1X 8BH
Tel: 0207 235 4535
www.istructe.org

Local Government Association,
Local Government House,
Smith Square,
London SW1P 3HZ
Tel: 0207 664 3131
Fax: 0207 664 3030
www.lga.gov.uk

Meteorological Office,
Fitzroy Road,
Exeter,
Devon EX1 3PB
Tel: 0870 900 0100
www.metoffice.gov.uk

Royal Meteorological Society,
104 Oxford Road,
Reading,
Berkshire RG1 7LL
Tel: 0118 956 8500
www.rmets.org

APPENDIX I

METRIC AND IMPERIAL UNITS OF LENGTH

1 inch	=	2.54 centimetres
1 foot	=	0.3048 metres
1 yard	=	0.9144 metres
1 mile	=	1.6093 kilometres
1 millimetre	=	0.03937 inches
1 centimetre	=	0.3937 inches
1 metre	=	1.0936 yards
1 kilometre	=	0.6213 miles

INDEX

References are to paragraph numbers.